William Jennings Bryan:

Selections

THE AMERICAN HERITAGE SERIES

THE

American Heritage

Series

UNDER THE GENERAL EDITORSHIP OF

LEONARD W. LEVY AND ALFRED YOUNG

William Jennings Bryan:
Selections

EDITED BY

RAY GINGER

Brandeis University

THE BOBBS-MERRILL COMPANY, INC.

A Subsidiary of Howard W. Sams & Co., Inc.

PUBLISHERS • INDIANAPOLIS • NEW YORK • KANSAS CITY

Foreword

It was said of William Jennings Bryan, a three-time loser, that he would rather be wrong than be President. Yet he was probably right as often as any political leader of his time. Theodore Roosevelt, no less, acknowledged in his *Autobiography* that Bryan had championed many sorely needed reforms in the interest of the plain people. He backed tariff reform, woman suffrage, a federal income tax, direct election of Senators, railroad regulation, the initiative and referendum, and a Department of Labor. Not without reason, Bryan is traditionally regarded as a leader of Liberalism, a nexus between Jefferson and Franklin Roosevelt. But it is one of the fascinations of this provocative, always illuminating, sometimes exasperating book by Ray Ginger that Bryan's reputation as a Liberal is seriously drawn into question. If nothing else, Professor Ginger short-circuits an old query that has troubled historians for some time: What is the explanation of the great transformation that took place in Bryan's thinking from the beginning of his career, when he was the very model of the Liberal in politics, to its ending when he was an apologist for the Klan and Scopes's prosecutor? Professor Ginger contends, with the documentary evidence made available to the reader, that the young Bryan and the old Bryan were substantially the same man: The transformation need not be explained, because it never occurred.

Bryan's early ambitions were to become a Baptist minister or a pumpkin farmer. In a manner of speaking he succeeded. He claimed that he was more interested in religion than in politics, and that political questions in the final analysis were

moral questions. His statesmanship reflected that claim. No political leader was more aptly nicknamed than Bryan, the Great
Commoner; the reasons for the appropriateness may have less
to do with his leadership than his qualities of mind and personality. He was in many ways simple-minded and simple-hearted,
a man whose mind, as Professor Ginger says in his Introduction
to this collection, "was not much above the level of his listen-
ers." He was the apostle of the common man because he was
his apotheosis; he could not have talked over the heads of the
people if he had tried, as William Allen White sharply noted.
Although Bryan was a power in American politics for more
than a generation, he gave expression rather than leadership
to popular aspirations, anxieties, and axioms. In the Congressional election of 1892, for example, he admitted that he knew
nothing about free silver but was for it because the people of
Nebraska were for it; "I will look up the arguments later," he
said.

Professor Ginger, in his Introduction, headnotes, and documentary selections, seeks the roots and character of Bryan's
beliefs, personality, and leadership. No other collection has
made available to readers so extensive and representative a
sample of Bryan's thought. Here are significant speeches, articles from *The Commoner,* magazine essays, a generous display
of letters and other documents drawn from the unpublished
Bryan Papers in the Library of Congress, and a miscellany
from Bryan's career. Many of the papers in the volume are
enlightening; some will dismay Bryan champions. Henceforth,
simple generalizations about Bryan will be accountable to the
evidence that students and scholars may now judge for themselves, thanks to Professor Ginger's editing.

This book is one of a series created to provide the essential primary sources of the American experience, especially of
American thought. The series, when completed, will constitute
a documentary library of American history, filling a need long
felt among scholars, students, libraries, and general readers for

authoritative collections of original materials. Some volumes will illuminate the thought of significant individuals, such as James Madison or Louis Brandeis; some will deal with movements, such as the Antifederalists or the Populists; others will be organized around special themes, such as Puritan political thought, or American Catholic thought on social questions. Many volumes will take up the large number of subjects traditionally studied in American history for which surprisingly there are no documentary anthologies; others will pioneer in introducing new subjects of increasing importance to scholars and to the contemporary world. The series aspires to maintain the high standards demanded of contemporary editing, providing authentic texts, intelligently and unobtrusively edited. It will also have the distinction of presenting pieces of substantial length which give the full character and flavor of the original. The series will be the most comprehensive and authoritative of its kind.

Leonard W. Levy
Alfred Young

Contents

Introduction

The career of William Jennings Bryan forcefully testifies to a dilemma of modern republicanism. For thirty years a foremost spokesman of the Democratic party, he was three times its Presidential candidate. Yet in desires and in intelligence he was undistinguished. His indifference to facts was matched by his ignorance of them. He was meagerly equipped to cope with the nation's problems, but hordes of voters wanted to entrust them to him. So little deserving the public's confidence, he possessed it so much. The state of mind of millions of Americans can be inferred from Bryan's words, which would hold far less significance did they not register strong winds blowing in the country. As we watch our nation dangle over the chasm between this man's high position and his modest abilities, we are driven back to questions that repeatedly slip from consciousness, even though they were formulated at the first foundation of government in America. Where are, and where should be, the sources of political leadership in a republic? What are the relations of an elected officer to his constituents?

For the Puritan founders, John Winthrop was explicit. The responsibilities of a public official are not analogous to those of a workman. When a carpenter builds a house, he is paid both for his skill and for his faithfulness, and perforce he contracts for his competence as well as for his pure intentions. But when the citizens summon a man to serve as magistrate, he has his authority from God. The covenant between ruled and ruler demands that he should govern by the laws of God and the commonwealth, according to his own "best skill." Suppose the magistrate to hear a case in which both the evi-

xiii

dence and the rule of law are "clear to common apprehension"; "if he transgress here, the error is not in the skill, but in the evil of the will: it must be required of him." In such instances the magistrate exercises not "authority, but a distemper thereof." But so long as he keeps the covenant and rules according to his best ability, the citizens must obey, for he (unlike the carpenter) has never guaranteed that he is especially qualified to govern well. "I entreat you to consider, that when you choose magistrates, you take them from among yourselves, men subject to like passions as you are."[1]

From a similar premise, William Jennings Bryan would later conclude that the will of the majority should govern at all times. In contrast, Winthrop argued that "if the case be doubtful, or the rule doubtful, to men of such understanding and parts as your magistrates are, if your magistrates should err here, yourselves must bear it." Nor was Bryan's viewpoint held by the Founding Fathers. When Alexander Hamilton in the Seventy-First Federalist came to describe the duties of the president, he wrote that over an extended period a majority of the electorate must rule, because it has the power, and should rule, because "the people commonly *intend* the Public Good."[2] But they will often go wrong in choosing the means to that end. Hamilton sharply distinguished what a nation needs from what it wants. When the voters are seized by passions or whimsies, the magistrate must fend off the "very fatal consequences of their own mistakes . . ."

In addition to his responsibility to cast vetoes against folly, the president must constantly educate the people, not by sermons or by lectures but by inspiring and guiding their actions.

---

[1] John Winthrop, Speech to the General Court, July 3, 1645, in *Winthrop's Journal: "History of New England," 1630–1649*, ed. James Kendall Hosmer (New York: Charles Scribner's Sons, 1908), pp. 237–239.

[2] Alexander Hamilton, James Madison, and John Jay, *The Federalist: A Commentary on the Constitution of the United States*, ed. Paul Leicester Ford (New York: Henry Holt and Company, 1898), pp. 476–477.

Thus wrote Jane Addams in trying to decipher the lineaments of Lincoln's greatness as Chief Executive. By steering the behavior of many, he had reinforced the people in those habits that expressed their better selves. He had moved slowly, made compromises that were often "sickening" in his insistence upon carrying the people with him; but time after time he had managed to " 'provide the channels in which the growing moral force of their lives shall flow.' "[3]

If this achievement made a president great, what lesser things would make one acceptable? The formula inferred by Jane Addams' idealism can be tempered by the empiricism of John Peter Altgeld. When called upon to explain in 1899 why he thought Bryan should again be his party's nominee for president, Altgeld stated his sense of practical politics:[4]

. . . In order to carry an election, you must have a man upon whom enough voters who differ somewhat in individual views will unite in order to give him the majority. . . . Let me further suggest that if Mr. Bryan was to come out and play the role of an educator or an adjutator, he would simply be in a field that is already tolerably well filled . . . The moment Mr. Bryan would enter this field, he would cease to be an available candidate for the presidency. . . . Therefore, instead of coming out squarely on a radical platform, I think that it is his duty to leave those things to some of the rest of us. Should we get control of the government, there will be no trouble in carrying out any reform for which the people are ripe, and any attempt to carry out a great reform before the people are ripe for it, must prove a failure. I would remind you that Mr. Lincoln never was an abolitionist, and that even after he was elected President, he was opposed to interfering with slavery in the Southern states, yet he became the "great liberator." What we want is to get into the White House a man who is not necessarily radical to begin with, but whose sym-

---

[3] Jane Addams, "A Modern Lear," in *American Social Thought,* ed. Ray Ginger (New York: Hill and Wang, 1961), pp. 202–203.
[4] John Peter Altgeld to Henry Demarest Lloyd, August 2, 1899. Lloyd Papers, Wisconsin Historical Society.

pathies are with the great toiling masses, who will not be controlled by concentrated wealth, and who will be ready to carry out any great reform just as soon as the country is ready for it.

No brief for Bryan would remain accurate if it were stated more strongly than Altgeld's prescriptions. But by them, it was not for Bryan to create channels in which moral energies might flow. Rather, he was pictured as an inert conduit to carry the will of the people into the Statutes at Large. If the image seems harsh, it is not so passive as Bryan's own view of the role of public servants (see Document 23). While conceding that each person in his individual capacity was entitled to freedom of thought and speech (with, as will be seen, strait bounds), Bryan added: "The moment one takes on a representative character, he becomes obligated to represent faithfully and loyally those who have commissioned him to represent them."[5] Legislators should pass whatever laws the voters want, and "teachers in public schools must teach what the taxpayers desire taught."[6]

When he said, "Let the People Rule," he meant that the majority should always have its way. When he said, "The Bible is the Revealed Word of God," he meant that each passage had to be accepted at its literal meaning. These two dogmas, the most important ones of all to Bryan, were unusual in their precision. His shibboleths often were baffling in their intangibility. But he won the support of millions of citizens.

II

Even those who do not adhere to any school of psychoanalysis can agree that the emotional set with which an adult confronts his world has substantial roots in his early years. Therefore,

---

[5] William Jennings Bryan, *Seven Questions in Dispute* (New York: Fleming H. Revell Company, 1924), pp. 152–153.

[6] *Ibid.*, p. 154.

special interest attaches to certain facets of the childhood and youth of William Jennings Bryan.

He was born and reared in Salem, in a predominantly rural area in central downstate Illinois. During his first five years, the region was stripped of many of its men who were fighting the Civil War. In 1860, the year in which Bryan was born on March 19, his father, Silas Lillard Bryan, was elected judge of a spacious circuit. Serving on the bench until 1872, he spent much time holding court in each of five counties. The chief parental force in William's home was his mother. He grew up in a female-dominated society. For women in the region, virtually the only source of intellectual fodder was the Bible, and their thin social life revolved about the church. William's mother often sang to him, chiefly hymns or such wartime ballads as "Farewell, Mother, you may never press me to your heart again."

This song title calls forth an echo from *The Adventures of Huckleberry Finn*. In describing the crayon drawings made by 15-year-old Emmeline Grangerford, which featured death and sentimentality, Mark Twain wrote of one of "a young lady with her hair all combed up straight to the top of her head, and knotted there in front of a comb like a chair-back, and she was crying into a handkerchief and had a dead bird laying on its back in her other hand with its heels up, and underneath the picture it said 'I Shall Never Hear Thy Sweet Chirrup More Alas.'"[7] Mockery of such mawkishness is a main theme of Twain's novel, and the chief agents of its sentimentality are women. In the book they are also the chief agents of cruelty. Examples swarm through the pages of the book. Nigger Jim became a runaway because he was about to be sold into the Deep South, away from his wife and children in Missouri; the pious Mrs. Watson could not resist an offering

---

[7] Mark Twain, *The Adventures of Huckleberry Finn* (New York: Rinehart & Company, 1948), p. 101.

price of $800. Huck and Jim had to flee their Jackson Island sanctuary because Mrs. Judith Loftus sent her husband to capture Jim, for the reward. Sweet and sentimental Mary Jane, on learning from Huck that the Duke and the Dauphin were not her English uncles at all, but confidence men, exclaims: "Come, don't waste a minute—not a second—we'll have them tarred and feathered, and flung in the river!"[8] Thus Twain, who grew up a quarter-century before Bryan and only 150 miles from Salem, implied that many women of the region were simultaneously sentimental and cruel, and that typically the two qualities were a syndrome.

Certainly they were linked in the McGuffey Readers, which alternated maudlin slobbering that virtue is inevitably rewarded (always in hard cash) with ruthlessly harsh formulae of duty and damnation everlasting. Although the evidence conflicts as to whether William Jennings Bryan actually studied in McGuffey, the point is trivial, for if he did not, he must have eaten the same pablum from other spoons. Nor were Bryan's textbooks the only reinforcement that his school provided for the feminine code that ruled his home. His teacher, Mrs. Mary Lemon, was convinced that a spared rod meant a spoiled child. To William she imparted an indelible fear of sin; her impact upon him can be sensed in a fascinating transmogrification that he worked on his childhood. Conventions that he shared with millions of his later auditors required that he refer to mother and school while forbidding him to reflect discredit on either. So, although he could recall very few facts about his school days, he would dilate at length about how lucky he had been in his upbringing. His scriptural training furnished a substitute name for his former teacher; he always called her Mrs. Lamb.

Bryan's stance toward experience was colored by the songs he had heard from his mother, which stayed with him until

---

[8] *Ibid.*, p. 188.

he died. One of his favorites was "Silver Threads Among the Gold." No irrelevancies about aesthetics were permitted to mar his approach to art: What mattered was the moral. He claimed, in a magazine interview with John Reed in 1916, that he had been deeply influenced by four paintings:[9]

> . . ."First, the 'Madonna and Child.' "
> "Which one? Raphael's?"
> "It doesn't make any difference which one. . . . The 'Madonna' is great because it deals with the tenderest human relationship. Next, 'The Breaking of Human Ties' presents the problem of a young man at the critical period of his life—."
> "Whom is that by?"
> "I don't know. But you will find it hanging in every Y.M.C.A. Then, Vereshchagin's 'Apotheosis of War,' which is a powerful peace sermon; and lastly 'Christ Before Pilate,' which contrasts force and love."

To Bryan, every mother was Madonna. His paeans to mother-hood and to woman suffrage (see Document 5) must be read to be believed. A few years before the start of World War I, he bore witness to the growth of intelligence, education, ethics, brotherhood, democracy, and the peace movement. When an Idaho newspaper mewled a summary of his viewpoint—"The era of the brotherhood of man is not coming. It is here now"—Bryan approvingly reprinted the "epigram" in his own journal.[10]

The obverse of Bryan's simpering was his lack of sensitivity. Although his devout father was a Baptist, William, at the age of 14, became a Presbyterian. "I never knew until after his death," admitted Bryan in his *Memoirs,* "that he was disappointed that I did not become a member of his own church."[11]

---

[9] John Reed, "Bryan on Tour," *Collier's,* LVII (May 20, 1916), 11–12.
[10] *The Commoner,* XII (March 8, 1912), 3.
[11] *The Memoirs of William Jennings Bryan,* by Himself and His Wife, Mary Baird Bryan (Philadelphia: The John C. Winston Company, 1925), p. 49.

That insensitivity could drift into callousness is seen in Bryan's summary of his speech to the Presbyterian General Assembly in 1920: "I argued that we should drive all the profiteers out of the Presbyterian church so that, when they go to the penitentiary, they will not go as Presbyterians. There should be no Presbyterian ward in the Profiteer Prison."[12] It was not enough for the state to impose criminal punishment; the church must add a refusal of spiritual solace to lawbreakers. Moreover, while Bryan sought to avoid contamination of his personal purity by association with the sinful, he also wanted the sinful to suffer eternal punishment. One of his Bible sermons wove this thought into the fabric of the case for immortality: "Then, too, a future life is necessary for the administration of any system of justice. The wrongs done by the wicked to their fellows in this world cannot be adequately punished here."[13] The suspicion persists that Bryan would have liked to see Clarence Darrow boil in oil forever (see Document 32).

III

Silas Bryan customarily prayed three times a day. When he was home in Salem, he summoned young William into his office each day a little before noon and read him a chapter from Proverbs. He never missed a chance to urge upon the boy that the Bible was divinely inspired. In 1872, the judge stepped down from the bench and ran unsuccessfully for Congress. Three years later, his son went away to Jacksonville, Illinois. There he stayed for six years, studying at Whipple Academy and at Illinois College. Bryan said in his famous address, "The Prince of Peace," (see Document 15) that at college he had experienced "a period of skepticism." He had joined the church before going to Jacksonville (see Document 31) and his doubts

---

[12] *The Commoner*, XX (September 1920), 8.
[13] M. R. Werner, *Bryan* (New York: Harcourt, Brace and Company, 1929), p. 285.

were neither prolonged nor profound. On his twenty-first birthday he wrote to his future wife that he suffered "some trembling" in thinking of "the unknown future." But he brandished
his rod and his staff: "I would dread to be compelled to set
forth upon this sea with nothing but the light of my reason to
aid me. What a blessing it is that we have that guide, the
Bible."[14] The Holy Writ was beyond challenge.

Bryan saw religion as a body of formulae, the Word. He
quoted approvingly from the Bible: "holy men of God spake as
they were moved by the Holy Ghost."[15] Not only were the
scriptures infallible, but the import of each message was plain.
Nothing needed interpretation. He was not greatly exercised
against atheists or agnostics because he was sure they would
never exert much influence. The true enemy was the modernist believer, who thought that only parts of the Bible were
inspired, and insisted that God had used evolution as his plan
for the creation. "Theistic evolution," declared Bryan, "might
be defined as an anaesthetic that deadens the Christian's pain
while his religion is being removed."[16] Every word of scripture
was scripture: "Give the modernist three words, 'allegorical,'
'poetical,' and 'symbolical,' and he can suck the meaning out of
every vital doctrine of the Christian Church and every passage
in the Bible to which he objects."[17]

Obviously, a person who accepts literally all parts of the
often self-contradictory scriptures will parade many incon-
sistencies in his own beliefs. So with Bryan, who was hardly a
logical thinker and who felt no compulsion to develop his
powers of reasoning. Some recent commentators on his pro-
fessions have stressed his affinities to champions of the Social
Gospel. Admittedly, Bryan would argue in favor of the Golden
Rule: "Love of one's neighbor is the only visible proof that can

---

[14] *Memoirs*, p. 450.
[15] II Peter i:21, quoted in *Seven Questions in Dispute*, p. 17.
[16] *Ibid.*, p. 128.
[17] *Ibid.*, p. 106.

be given of love of God. . . .'How can a man love God whom he hath not seen if he loves not his brother whom he hath seen?' "[18] He would even mount and joust in behalf of a new emphasis for religion:

> . . . People used to read the Bible to find out what it said of heaven; now they read it more to find out what light it throws upon the pathway of today, for they have learned that where Christ spoke once of the world to come, he spoke ten times of man's present relation to his fellow men. People used to search the scriptures, and then retire from society and in seclusion seek to prepare themselves for future bliss; they are coming to understand that to walk in the footsteps of the 'Man of Galilee' they must go about doing good.[19]

This view of Christianity was the wellspring of Bryan's best actions. His sense of the sacredness of human life prompted him to oppose the death penalty for Leo Frank, whether or not Frank was guilty (see Document 24). Bryan's career as Secretary of State, which was not consistently foolish by any means (see Documents 16–22) was shaped in large part by his sense of human brotherhood.

But the Golden Rule was at most half—and I suspect it was considerably less than half—of Bryan's religion. The lessons of his father, mother, and Mrs. Lemon had sunk deep. Bryan really did care about the fate of his immortal soul. When he wrote his will, he began:[20]

> . . . In the name of God, farewell.
>
> Trusting for my salvation to the blood of Jesus Christ, my Lord and Redeemer, and relying on his promise for my hope of resurrection, I consign my body to the dust and commend my spirit to God who gave it.

---

[18] *The Commoner,* XIX (May 1919), 11.

[19] *Ibid.,* XII (June 7, 1912), 2–3.

[20] Paxton Hibben, *The Peerless Leader: William Jennings Bryan* (New York: Farrar and Rinehart, Inc., 1929), p. 388.

While Bryan sincerely enjoined all Christians to do good works, his notion of personal salvation looked elsewhere. It looked to faith and to God's free grace: "He saves, not by the slow process of education, but by a change of heart—the New Birth."[21]

Salvation began with the bodily resurrection of Jesus. It rested upon his substitutionary atonement for the sins of all who believed. With His blood, Christ had paid for all the sins of those who begged forgiveness and testified for Him. They were washed in the blood of the Lamb. "Christianity," wrote Bryan, "has been described as the Gospel of the Second Chance; it is more than that; it is the gospel that offers forgiveness to any who come in true repentance, no matter how often or how deep they may have fallen."[22] He could not bear to think that at death he might simply be snuffed out. Bryan felt any challenge to the total authority of the Gospel to be a menace to his chance for immortality. His outbursts at Darrow in the Scopes trial (see Document 32) expressed not only rage but also terror.

At revival meetings, the front row was reserved for sinners who had come forward to confess. It was called "the anxious bench." Bryan, from early childhood, could seldom get clear of it.

Bryan shared these attitudes with millions of his countrymen. The United States in the late nineteenth century abounded with faith in supernaturalism, in mesmerism, and in the literal occurrence of scriptural miracles. Such beliefs were not confined to the poor and ignorant and unwashed; they were common to all levels of society. Philosopher William James wrote with respect of religious visions, and his brother Henry fashioned tales that were almost ghost stories. Commodore Vanderbilt consulted the dead Jim Fiske about business prob-

---

[21] *Seven Questions in Dispute*, p. 137.
[22] *Ibid.*, p. 83.

lems. Leland Stanford reportedly invested large sums in spiritualism after the death of his only son. J. P. Morgan believed the story of Jonah and the Whale, saying that if he could not trust every word in the Bible he would be unable to trust any of it. Henry George's *Progress and Poverty* (1879) closed with a testimonial to the perpetuity of the soul.

Any testimonial along those lines was good news to Bryan, who had to believe. In his efforts to bolster and defend his faith in life beyond the grave, he resorted to fantastic semantics: "There is only one argument that can be made to one who rejects the authority of the Bible, namely, that the Bible is true."[23] The "strongest evidence possible" for the truths of the Bible was that they had been "vindicated in the lives of thousands of millions of people, millions of whom have died in defense of those truths . . ."[24] The validity of the Blood Atonement "can be proved by experience. Hundreds of millions bear joyful witness to it."[25] In Bryan's view, any opinion held by the majority must be true, and in this view he was a typical American. The process that worked its way with him had been cogently set down by Alexis de Tocqueville:[26]

> . . . At periods of equality men have no faith in one another, by reason of their common resemblance; but this very resemblance gives them almost unbounded confidence in the judgment of the public; for it would seem probable that, as they are all endowed with equal means of judging, the greater truth should go with the greater number. . . . The public, therefore, among a democratic people, has a singular power, which aristocratic nations cannot conceive; for it does not persuade others of its beliefs, but it imposes them and makes them permeate the thinking of everyone by a sort of enormous pressure of the mind of all upon the individual intelligence.

---

[23] *Ibid.*, p. 112.
[24] *Ibid.*, p. 25.
[25] *Ibid.*, p. 83.
[26] Alexis de Tocqueville, *Democracy in America*, ed. Phillips Bradley (New York: Alfred A. Knopf, Inc., 1945), II, 10.

IV

Tocqueville, the most esteemed foreign commentator on American democracy, added that in an egalitarian society even religion held sway "much less as a doctrine of revelation than as a commonly received opinion."[27] But he did not think that it was thereby discredited. Quite the contrary. Where the great body of citizens were on a parity in rights, in education, and in economic condition, each man was tempted to seek material advancement that would lift him even a little above the mass. Each looked only to his own interests. Religion had a special utility in these circumstances because it preached just the opposite viewpoints.

Bryan, while at Whipple Academy, spent three weeks reading George Bancroft's great but teleological history of the United States. Bancroft's perspective was congenial to Bryan, who was persuaded beyond question that God Himself had steered republicanism to success in America. Then, at Illinois College, Bryan reportedly studied Tocqueville for two terms, and scored 100 in the course. As will be seen, Bryan was blind to some crucial insights of *Democracy in America*, but he readily agreed that religion was essential to his country (see Document 31). As the Holy Scriptures were the ultimate sanction of faith in personal immortality, so were they the final ground of hope for social salvation. Bryan erected a ladder of propositions: Civilization depends on morals, morals on religion, religion on faith in God, faith in God on the Bible. Once destroy that foundation, and the ladder will crash. "As the Bible is the only book known to the Christian world whose authority depends upon inspiration, the degradation of the Bible leaves the Christian world without a standard of morals other than that upon which men can agree."[28] But men relying solely on their reasoning powers do not agree. Because their

---

[27] *Democracy in America,* II, 10–11.
[28] *Seven Questions in Dispute,* pp. 15–16, 77, 157.

conclusions differ, a common code of ethics is impossible. Further, morality is learned in childhood, when the powers of reasoning are frail. Further, even the ratiocination of adults is tainted by greed and self-interest; the most impartial of judges is forbidden to try his own case. "Anything that weakens man's faith in God," wrote Bryan, "imperils the future of the race."

These views are far from being silly on their face, and similar convictions have been held by some extremely wise men. But while Bryan's assent to the Fatherhood of God prompted him at times to champion the Brotherhood of Man, it also led him into an intellectual trap that crippled him. He confused the eternal with the temporal, the divine with the secular. In discussing Bryan soon after his death, Walter Lippmann sagaciously observed that majority rule is a worldly device for organizing a government, that it rests ultimately on force rather than on wisdom, and that it is justified chiefly because in general it requires less exercise of force than do alternative systems of government.[29] But an empirical rationale for republicanism did not satisfy Bryan. From the mystical notion that all men are equal in the eyes of God, he lapsed into the absurdity that all men are equal in their competence to set up courses in biology. The voice of the people is the voice of God.

Once again, Holy Writ could be trotted out to sustain Bryan's position. He liked to boast that he was a tribune of Jeffersonianism (see Documents 1, 7), and the divinity himself had left to that cult a heritage of sweeping remarks: "The first principle of republicanism is, that the *lex majoris pariis* is the fundamental law of every society of individuals of equal rights; to consider the will of the society enounced by the majority of a single vote, as sacred as if unanimous, is the first of all lessons in importance, yet the last which is thoroughly learnt."[30] In

---

[29] Walter Lippmann, *Men of Destiny* (New York: The Macmillan Company, 1927), pp. 45–60.

[30] Thomas Jefferson to Baron Alexander von Humboldt, June 13, 1817, in *The Writings of Thomas Jefferson,* ed. Andrew A. Lipscomb, Memorial Edition (Washington, D.C., 1905), XV, 127.

more guarded moments, Jefferson reached for a balance in his injunctions: *"To inculcate on minorities the duty of acquiescence in the will of the majority; and on majorities a respect for the rights of the minority."*[31]

In his gleeful trumpeting of majority rule, Bryan seems never to have suspected that the doctrine contains a great ambiguity, even though the problem had been spelled out by his mentor Tocqueville. On any given question we must identify the group within which a majority shall be decisive (or groups, more inclusive and less so, as in Calhoun's theory of the concurrent majority). When I resist an unjust law, Tocqueville declared in *Democracy in America,* I am not necessarily challenging the right of the majority to rule; I may be appealing from a majority of the state to a majority of the nation or of mankind.[32] One of Tocqueville's most trenchant onslaughts was aimed at "the tyranny of the majority" in the United States. In his day, the powers of government were wielded largely by the states, not by the federal machinery, and within each state the legislative branch was supreme. Legislators, by virtue of popular election and short terms in office, were prey to the whims of a majority of the electorate. The legislatures in turn domineered over the executive officers. Judges, too, were elective in some states, and dependent on the legislature for their salaries in all states; juries were the voices of public opinion as expressed in courtrooms. Nowhere in the system were there organs independent of the majority, to whom a wronged person could go for justice. Absolute and unlimited power, wrote Tocqueville, is tyrannical, even when it is held by a majority. The chief danger in the United States was not anarchy but despotism, which threatened to be more severe than anywhere in Europe. Absolute monarchs in the Old World were fortunate if they could control men's actions, but in the New World the majority

---

31 Thomas Jefferson to Dr. William Bache, February 2, 1800, in *The Life and Selected Writings of Thomas Jefferson,* ed. Adrienne Koch and William Peden (New York: The Modern Library, 1944), p. 556.

32 *Democracy in America,* I, Chap. 15.

seemed on its way to binding men's thoughts as well. The only avenue to power was to become a mere sycophant to the populace, and few indeed were those "who displayed that manly candor and masculine independence of opinion which frequently distinguished the Americans in former times, and which constitutes the leading feature in distinguished characters wherever they may be found."

At the end of his chapter, Tocqueville quoted Bryan's hero against Bryan's views:

> . . . Jefferson also said: "The tyranny of the legislature is really the danger most to be feared, and will continue to be so for many years to come. The tyranny of the executive power will come in its turn, but at a more distant period."
>
> I am glad to cite the opinion of Jefferson upon this subject rather than that of any other, because I consider him the most powerful advocate democracy has ever had.

To all these warnings, Bryan was deaf. He could see no grounds for distinguishing one public office from another; all should be elective. One of his major speeches in Congress was to urge a constitutional amendment making Senators dependent on the popular franchise (see Document 3). "To oppose the popular election of Senators," he said, "is to question the wisdom of our form of Government." He seems not to have noticed that the founders of "our form of Government" had opposed direct election of Senators, or to have known that one of them, James Madison, had wanted Senators to be chosen by the House of Representatives. Bryan wanted the popular will at any moment to be enshrined, instantaneously, in public policy. He went so far as to advocate (see Document 23)— save in cases of invasion—a public referendum on any declaration of war (thus qualifying as an early proponent of a measure that almost passed the lower branch of Congress in January 1938, while the behavior of Japan and Germany was becoming daily more ominous). Civil liberties, too, had to yield to the omniscience of the majority as expressed in government policy (see Document 26). More than two years after World War I had ended, Bryan reiterated his wartime conviction "that citizens should not obstruct the government in the prosecution of the war by the exercise of freedom of speech and press." He was explicit in stating the values that to him justified this viewpoint: "namely, the putting of the government's interests above the interest of the individual."

Although he received a perfect grade in his study of Tocqueville at Illinois College, Bryan had not really mastered his subject. *Democracy in America* might have served as a chart of some shoals and reefs in egalitarianism; to Bryan it was at most a handbook for success at the polls.

V

In Bryan's eyes some men were more equal than others, and farmers were the most equal of all (see Document 9). The yeomen of his rhetoric were always exuding virtue, much as the hibiscus plant gives off fragrance in June. The honest plowmen were the steadfast stanchions of society. By tagging his famous "Cross of Gold" speech with a figure he used in the peroration, we may divert attention from a paragraph that is more fundamental and persistent in his beliefs: "You come to us and tell us that the great cities are in favor of the gold standard; we reply that the great cities rest upon our broad and fertile prairies. Burn down your cities and leave our farms, and your cities will spring up again as if by magic; but destroy our farms and the grass will grow in the streets of every city in the country." (See Document 4.) His idealization of rural life went hand in hand with a dislike and fear of cities. He lived in a metropolis only from 1881 to 1883, while studying at the Union College of Law in Chicago, and the expanding urban area dismayed him. He fled, never to return for long. In one of his rare moments of humility he admitted his lack of identification with the urban poor. Sent to speak at a waterfront mission in

New York, he remarked on his own inadequacy for the job: "It takes a man who has been saved from the depths to reach men like these. I cannot do it. I lack the necessary past."[33]

But he never realized his ignorance of agriculture and its problems. In the "Cross of Gold" speech he did recognize that the typical farmer was a businessman, but Bryan's yeoman was a far cry from the representative rural American landowner. The sturdy tiller of the soil imagined by Bryan did not mine the land, or buy fields on credit as a means of land speculation, or mortgage his property with no intention of repaying the loan. Into a single article on the farm topic (see Document 9) the Great Commoner could pack numerous perversions of language and fact. He wrote that farmers had "an independent way of living compared to city folk." How independent were the men who powered the farm revolt? He claimed that because farmers could grow their own food, they were "less affected" by fluctuations in the prices of foodstuffs than were city folk. How then can we explain the Populist uprising at all? He contended that all members of the family could help on a farm, "without hardship." Had he never witnessed the loneliness of farm wives, or read Hamlin Garland, or seen little children working in the fields? Although Bryan did concede that rural voters were sometimes corrupted, he hurried to add that it was a "well-known fact that repeating and bribe-taking are largely city vices."

Committed to a lifelong panegyric to the agrarian myth, Bryan equated cities with the East, farms with the West and South. (Presumably, Kansas City or Denver was transmuted into a rural area with a congested population.) His affiliation with the Midwest and South seduced him into an effort to head off a denunciation of the Ku Klux Klan by the Democratic party in 1924 (see Document 30). His animosity to cities and the East had fused with his campaign for prohibition a year

---

[33] *Memoirs,* p. 456.

earlier in a shimmering but silly speech when he introduced a
temperance resolution at the Presbyterian General Assembly.
Launching an attack on eastern newspapers, he declared, "I
think the only Bible verse they know is, 'The wise men came
from the East.' They think that if a reform does not start in
New York it does not amount to anything. But no reform ever
does start in New York. . . ."[34]

VI

Historically, the ideal of equality has meant two different things
to Americans. In one of its definitions it signified brotherhood,
and, since this import was derived in large measure from the
primitive Christianity of which Bryan thought himself a dis-
ciple, we may infer that he would have embraced this more
generous sense of the egalitarian vision. But our hopes for him
are vain, because usually he worked from a narrower view.
Equality meant equal rights. It began with the premise that
life was a fight. Thus Bryan rejected the program of his more
radical contemporaries because he thought it falsely assumed
that human beings were or could be made altruistic (see Document 10). "Will socialism purge the individual of selfishness," he asked rhetorically, "or bring a nearer approach to
justice?" He chided the Gold Democrats in 1896, not because
they accepted the goals of the business world, but because
their demarcation of the business world did not include everybody: "The man who is employed for wages is as much a
business man as his employer; . . . the miners who go down
a thousand feet into the earth . . . are as much business men
as the few financial magnates who, in a back room, corner the
money of the world. We come to speak for this broader class
of business men [see Document 4]." Bryan's hero was the self-
made man who remembered that after all, he was God's hum-

---

[34] Hibben, *The Peerless Leader*, p. 378.

ble steward. Bryan's denunciations of governmental favors to the few were a summons not to brotherhood, but to a race in which all started at the same mark and ran the same course.

Even this statement gives too inclusive a definition to Bryan's ruling idea of equality. More precisely, he wanted all Caucasians to have an equal chance in the struggle of life. In his words, "Here the white man and the black man are living together, and while they live together one race must be dominant." Bryan was not by any means a pitiless white supremacist. He thought, for instance, that every individual should receive "all the mental discipline possible." But he added that the notion of social equality was ridiculous. He sanctioned restrictions on suffrage to preserve white rule, and he held up for Negroes a fatuous Horatio Alger ideal (see Documents 8, 30).

VII

If Bryan was woefully unqualified to handle the great problems of the nation, he was superbly equipped to win public office. Many of the traits that were handicaps to him in wielding power were immense assets in gaining popularity. Just look at the muddled medley of notions at the core of his understanding: The Bible is the revealed word of God; the majority of the moment has an unqualified right to rule; the people cannot be wrong; the farmer is the avatar of virtue; personal success is at once token and proof of good character. Bryan had no need to convince his fellow citizens of these shibboleths, for millions of persons already accepted them as self-evident. He shared their acceptance and was a specialist at telling an audience what it already believed (see Document 12). He was young and handsome, eager and energetic. He could turn a phrase, had a rough wit, and automatically used the "loose style" long since singled out by Tocqueville as distinctive to democratic societies. Bryan's rhetoric was loaded with "abstract terms" that "enlarge and obscure the thoughts they are intended to convey. . . ." Above all, his elocution was magnificent. "Among the losses the world has suffered by Mr. Bryan's going," wrote his widow, "the stilling of his voice is to me most irreparable. I speak now of his voice, not of what he said."[35] With these traits Bryan was custom-made for public life, and he had the example of his father to lure him into politics. At college he joined a literary society and concentrated on debating; by becoming a lawyer he completed his preparation.

After practicing law uneventfully in his hometown of Jacksonville for three years, Bryan moved to Lincoln, the capital of Nebraska, in 1887. Only three years later, he won election to the House of Representatives as a Democrat. He was named to the important Committee on Ways and Means, which originated tax bills, and his first major speech in Congress dealt with the tariff. Re-elected to the House in 1892 by a narrow margin, he did not even enter the race in 1894. Indeed, he never held elective office again. But Bryan, while in Congress, had spoken far and wide for the American Bimetallic League, which was financed by western owners of silver mines. Two of the wealthiest, Marcus Daly and William A. Clark, had bought the Omaha *World-Herald* in 1894, and had named Bryan editor-in-chief. He was his party's nominee the next year for the Senate of the United States, but ran only a poor third in the balloting in the legislature.

In a sense Bryan's achievement in 1896 was quite impressive. Although he lost every state north of the Ohio River, he did win nearly a million more votes than had gone to any previous Democratic candidate for the presidency. Following his more decisive loss in 1900 to McKinley, Bryan founded his own weekly paper, *The Commoner,* which continued publication for two decades. The Gold Bugs from the East won the Dem-

---

[35] *Memoirs*, p. 252.

ocratic national convention in 1904 and put up their own man to head the ticket. He was decisively defeated, and Bryan got the nod again four years later, only to suffer a third defeat. After Bryan played a dramatic role in the Democratic convention at Baltimore in 1912, President-elect Wilson picked him to be Secretary of State.

Bryan's performance as Secretary, by far the most important public office he had ever held, was mottled. By refusing to serve wine at diplomatic dinners he evoked incredulous grimaces in chancelleries throughout Europe. He complicated relations with Britain by publicly endorsing Home Rule for Ireland. His "missionary statecraft" let him believe that he was scuttling dollar diplomacy when in fact his actions in Central America promoted it (see Document 17). On the other hand, in 1914 he perceived that American private loans to Allied governments might have calamitous consequences (see Document 19). When faced by British as well as German actions that allegedly violated the rights of the United States as a neutral nation, he patiently urged an even-handed policy (see Document 21) upon President Wilson, whose own self-deceptions made him incapable of accepting it. If Bryan was foolish, he was also sincere in his notion that the arbitration treaties he had signed with many nations could have prevented World War I. He even saw these treaties as a guarantee of perpetual peace and claimed that they were the kernel from which Wilson had cultivated his League of Nations (see Document 27).

When his proposals failed to win acceptance during the *Lusitania* crisis, Bryan resigned as Secretary of State in June 1915. The following winter he wrote bitterly against Wilson's efforts to promote preparedness. He did campaign for the President's re-election in 1916, but soon he was back with the opposition and pursued his efforts to keep his country neutral right up to the war declaration. Then, Bryan became an all-out advocate of American military efforts. But he was never reconciled to the President. Bryan urged reservations in American ratification of the Covenant of the League, and the President's hostility to such a course formed the first charge in Bryan's extended 1921 catalogue of Woodrow Wilson's mistakes (see Document 28).

Prior to the war, Bryan had gotten most of his income from public lectures, often under the auspices of Chautauqua circuits. Later, he profited from two other types of ventures. He invested widely in real estate, and after he took up permanent residence in Florida in 1921, he talked of its delights daily at noon to huge crowds at Coral Gables. His tenure as Secretary of State brought him another type of work; from 1919 until his death he was special representative in Washington for Latin American countries seeking loans in the United States. During or soon after the war, he took up the two causes—against liquor and against Darwinism—that epitomized the rest of his life (see Documents 29–32).

VIII

A public figure in the United States is expected to be a universal oracle. Like other celebrities, Bryan was asked to comment on a huge range of topics. He obliged readily, prognosticating on the impact on world history of prohibition (see Document 29) and of woman suffrage (see Document 5). He waged sincere crusades for Christ (see Documents 15, 16, 31) and for motherhood (see Document 5). He advised young couples to live within their means (see Document 11) and counselled Negroes to cultivate "virtue, sobriety and good sense" (see Document 8). Even a small sampling of Bryan's platitudes will suggest that the contents of his mind resembled cooked oatmeal.

Of course a politician is almost forced to emit reams of senseless words. But even when the Great Commoner brushed against a serious intellectual problem, he failed to grasp it. Seemingly he never considered the possibility that free coinage of silver might reduce the total supply of money instead of increasing it, and thus might aggravate the condition it was supposed to alleviate. When the *North American Review,* in 1911, solicited a long article on the Supreme Court decisions in the Standard Oil and American Tobacco cases, Bryan could discuss the Rule of Reason only in the moralistic terms, unfailing with him, of evil against good and of the trusts against the people (see Document 13). Because several writers in the same symposium spelled out why business combinations had been formed and why the Court had to find some barricades to shield them from strict construction of the Sherman Act, Bryan's failure to probe into the economic origins of the trusts was painfully apparent.

This was only one episode in which Bryan's understanding was far behind that of his more thoughtful contemporaries. Whereas Bryan proclaimed that woman suffrage would "hasten the triumph of every righteous cause" (see Document 5), Edward Alsworth Ross had cogently explained why it seemed to be lessening the influence of "the virile, who see in graft and monopoly and foul politics worse enemies than beer, Sunday baseball, and the army canteen."[36] Again, Bryan wrote that "the socialist regards competition as a hurtful force, to be entirely exterminated." It cannot be denied that some American radicals would have assented to Bryan's formulation, but nonsocialist Charles Horton Cooley had observed that competition can be dispensed with only by instituting a thoroughgoing system of status, since those two modes are the only ones available for allocating personal positions in society. Finally, whereas Bryan declared that "the socialist believes that altruism will take the place of selfishness under an enforced collectivism" (see Document 10), Henry Demarest Lloyd had worked his way into and beyond this polarity in the two chap-

---

[36] Edward Alsworth Ross, *Sin and Society* (Boston: Houghton, Mifflin Company, 1907), pp. 93–97.

ters on "The Old Self–Interest and the New" that conclude his book, *Wealth Against Commonwealth* (1894).

IX

After Bryan died, his widow asserted that "his oratorical power was by no means the sole factor" in "his prolonged political leadership." She recorded in his *Memoirs* that she had repeatedly urged him to be more moderate in his approach to new political issues, and that he had typically replied: "Don't you see, my dear, that a leader must be well in advance. All progress comes through compromise; not a compromise of principle, but an adjustment between the more radical and the less radical positions. If I begin far in advance, when the compromise is made, our position will be much ahead of the place I would have secured by a less advanced standpoint."[37] Bryan himself, in a letter written in 1921, quoted a definition that had "impressed" him "very much": "A leader is one who is going in the same direction as the people and a little bit ahead. He must go in the same direction or he will not lead and he must be near enough to the people to be in sight or they will not follow."[38]

Fair enough. But is this a statement of Bryan's theory and practice? The files of letters received by the Great Commoner suggest a negative answer. Passage after passage of his incoming correspondence reads as if Bryan was the author. Consider this example, from a letter to Mrs. Bryan in May 1914:[39]

. . . There are so many enemies within and without, and so many traitors to good government in official positions within our government, who are not there to serve the people but to further their own selfish interests, at the expense of justice, and righteousness.

---

[37] *Memoirs,* p. 299.

[38] William Jennings Bryan to S. C. Singleton, December 23, 1921. Bryan Papers, Library of Congress.

[39] J. E. Kirk to Mrs. William Jennings Bryan, May 9, 1914. Bryan Papers, Library of Congress.

. . . In most questions of morals and politics it is not so hard to know what is right and best, and 'the greatest good to the greatest number,' as it is to be able to do the thing we know to be right, and as some are only there for self interest, or are the tools of others, they cannot have the courage of their convictions. . . . I consider Wm. J. Bryan the greatest public man in the nation today, the greatest power and the greatest educator the age has known.

By realizing not only that Bryan could have written the first two of these sentences but also that he could not have written anything more profound on the same subjects, we win perspective on the third sentence. An easy route to recognition as an "educator" is to find glittering phrases for widely held beliefs. Posed differently, we can discern historical shifts in emphasis if we decompose Lincoln's famous triad into its parts. Thus we can say broadly that John Winthrop believed in government of the people, the Founding Fathers in government for the people, and Bryan in government by the people.

A clue to Bryan's eminence is contained in the autobiography of Martin Van Buren, who knew well the childhood of egalitarian politics in the United States:[40]

. . . In this matter of personal popularity the working of the public mind is often inscrutable. In one respect only does it appear to be subject to rule, namely, in the application of a closer scrutiny by the People to the motives of public men than to their actions. When one is presented to them possessed of an ardent temperament who adopts their cause, as they think, from sympathy and sincerely regards their interests as his own, they return sympathy for sympathy with equal sincerity and are always ready to place the most favorable construction upon his actions. . . .

Here, perhaps, is the snug relation of Bryan to the people, of the aspirant to leadership to the supposedly led. His supporters

---

[40] "The Autobiography of Martin Van Buren," ed. John C. Fitzpatrick, *Annual Report of the American Historical Association for the Year 1918*, II (Washington, D.C., 1920), 168.

had no reason to doubt that Bryan was one of their own, that he and they were alike in their essential beliefs, that he and they shared "a persuasion: a broad judgment of public affairs informed by common sentiments and beliefs about the good life in America."[41] In the ungenerous words of the editor and writer, William Allen White, "He could not have talked over their heads if he had tried to do so."[42]

One can suspect that Bryan seldom wanted to be in front of the voters, that in a fundamental sense he thought statesmanship of that character was anti-republican. At the beginning of his public career, as he was about to assume his seat in the House of Representatives, he wrote to a political acquaintance in Nebraska: "So far as leadership is concerned, you know what my idea on that subject is. I believe as Jefferson did in the people. They are competent to lead themselves. They will have one man as an exponent today and another man tomorrow. He will simply be the one who best gives expression to their ideas, not the one who assumes to direct their course."[43]

These remarks contain Bryan's essential principles. He was the model of the prominent politician in a democratic society. Among such a people, as Tocqueville knew, Bryan's road to fame was virtually the only route open in politics. But Tocqueville would have been aghast at Bryan's accomplishments.

X

The reputation of any politician is sure to rise and fall, but the divergency in evaluations of Bryan seems unusually great.

---

[41] Marvin Meyers, *The Jacksonian Persuasion* (New York: Vintage Press, 1960), pp. vii–viii.

[42] William Allen White, *Masks in a Pageant* (New York: The Macmillan Company, 1928), p. 260.

[43] William Jennings Bryan to Edgar Howard, October 20, 1891. Bryan Papers, Library of Congress.

However, it must be admitted that the one I give in this volume is very different from those that most commentators have reached.

Two full-length biographies that appeared soon after Bryan's death—M. R. Werner's *Bryan* and Paxton Hibben's *The Peerless Leader*—contained many gibes at their subject, but the thrusts inclined toward geniality and were delivered with a light touch. The tone of each book suggested that Bryan was sometimes ludicrous, even pathetic, but obviously there was nothing sinister about the man. Further, C. Hartley Grattan, who finished *The Peerless Leader* after Hibben died, suggested that Bryan had changed markedly during his career: "A radical all his life, William Jennings was to end his days an ultra-conservative."[44] At the same time Walter Lippmann was remarking that many people had been prompted by the Scopes trial to ask how the Great Commoner could have degenerated from a liberal in 1896 to a reactionary in 1925. Lippmann shrewdly added that the query rested on a false premise, that Bryan's behavior at Dayton was not a quasi-senile aberration but a suitable climax to his career, that the issues of the trial enabled Bryan to manifest what had always been his two central faiths: revealed religion, and unquestioned majority rule.

Meanwhile other well-known writers were projecting a more favorable, and, at times almost majestic, image of Bryan. One such was George Fort Milton, a native of Tennessee who shared many of Bryan's viewpoints, yet had the insight to recognize him as one of those who "utter in shining similes the desires of the people. . . . In Bryan's case, from first to last, in Fundamentalism as in free silver, woman suffrage, and income tax, he was the apostle of the average man."[45] But

---

44 Hibben, *The Peerless Leader,* p. 369.

45 George Fort Milton, "A Dayton Postscript," *The Outlook,* CXL (August 19, 1925), 550–552.

Milton also called Bryan "a great and good man." Similarly William Allen White, although aware that nobody needed to stand in awe of Bryan's intellect, concluded: "That he succeeded tremendously with his life no one can question who realizes how much the Liberalism of his time owed to him."[46] The claim undoubtedly is true in a sense, but in view of Bryan's beliefs as revealed in the documents, it would raise somber reflections about "the Liberalism of his time."

Bryan has often been presented, not by a precise description of what he thought and did, but by means of abstract rhetoric as overblown and vaporous as his own. Many college students for a generation were taught that he was a gallant reformer and leader of progress. Morison and Commager's survey of American history, which was widely (and rightly) regarded twenty-five years ago as being more sophisticated than any competing textbook, said of Bryan: ". . . his career was characterized by utter sincerity, passionate conviction, courage, audacity, genuine faith in the wisdom of the plain people and the processes of democracy, religious belief in the identity of morals and politics, and an unalterable assurance that the right must eventually triumph over the wrong." The chapter ended with these sentences about the 1896 election: "It was not only the last protest of the old agrarian order against industrialism, it was also the first attempt of the new order to clean house. Bryan was the bridge between Andrew Jackson and Franklin D. Roosevelt."[47]

Lest these judgments be dismissed with the cynical comment that their source was "just a textbook," it should be added that Commager wrote of Bryan again in *The American Mind.* I think he went rather far when he wrote: "No one had more faithfully represented the American mind and character than

---

[46] White, *Masks in a Pageant*, p. 261.

[47] Samuel Eliot Morison and Henry Steele Commager, *The Growth of the American Republic*, 2nd ed. (New York: Oxford University Press, 1937), II, 262, 265.

the Great Commoner . . . ," but we can agree when he added: "but it was the mind and character of the mid-nineteenth, not the twentieth century, that he represented . . ." But what is to be made of the following remarks? Bryan "had championed righteousness and morality with a consistency without parallel in modern politics . . ." Further: ". . . his political creed was born of an instinctive understanding of the meaning of American history, and he pioneered in the advocacy of more and more important legislation than any other politician of his generation. The most representative American of his time, he represented what was, on the whole, soundest and most wholesome in the American character."[48]

Before *The American Mind* was published, another historian at Columbia University offered a more valid critique of the Commoner. Richard Hofstadter not only perceived that Bryan was more a follower of the voters than their leader, he also saw through the argument that Bryan suffered a sea change: "He closed his career in much the same role as he had begun it in 1896: a provincial politician following a provincial populace in provincial prejudices."[49] But Hofstadter, too, saw Bryan as more amusing than menacing. He quoted a eulogy of Bryan as "the greatest Klansman of our time," and then called the phrase "a cruel and inaccurate characterization."[50] The label, while oversimplified, was not wholly misleading, although Hofstadter's position was closer to the truth than the more recent assertion that the Commoner's attitude toward southern Negroes "was worthy of any Klan member."[51] Bryan

---

[48] Henry Steele Commager, *The American Mind: An Interpretation of American Thought and Character Since the 1880's* (New Haven: Yale University Press, 1950), pp. 182, 346.
[49] Richard Hofstadter, *The American Political Tradition and the Men Who Made It* (New York: Alfred A. Knopf, Inc., 1948), p. 201.
[50] *Ibid.*, p. 202.
[51] Lawrence William Levine, "William Jennings Bryan: The Last Decade, 1915–1925" (unpublished doctoral dissertation, Columbia University, 1962), p. 380.

was not the man to join the night riders and take part in flogging Negroes, but neither did he crusade for a Federal antilynching law.

My book on the Scopes trial, *Six Days or Forever?*, appearing a decade after Hofstadter's work, was more hostile to Bryan and took him more seriously. It portrayed a politician who was not only a demagogue but also, at times, a dangerous one, in that he activated some of the worst traits of his sympathizers. My portrayal (I admit it sadly) did not win universal assent. Most studies of Bryan published since 1958 have pointed toward the opposite assertion that his impact was greater than I think it was and also that he fought in the main for justice and decency. For instance, Paolo E. Coletta, who reportedly plans a two-volume biography, wrote an informative article on "Bryan, McKinley, and the Treaty of Paris." Having shown that Bryan had little influence in winning ratification by the Senate, Coletta ended with the sentence: "In the long run, history upholds Bryan rather than McKinley."[52] So far as the article showed, the final advertisement for the Commoner rested on nothing more than his advocacy of Philippine independence in 1899 and the fact that it has since been granted. Paul W. Glad, author of two books dealing with parts of Bryan's career prior to 1912, implied two major conclusions when he wrote: "What was the nature of the progressive program which Bryan persuaded his party to accept?"[53] By also referring to "the obstinate—and ludicrous—old man of the Scopes trial,"[54] Glad seemed to be reviving the notion that a great transformation had occurred in Bryan.

This notion was rejected by Lawrence W. Levine, whose

---

[52] Paolo E. Coletta, "Bryan, McKinley, and the Treaty of Paris," *Pacific Historical Review*, XXVI (1957), 146.

[53] Paul W. Glad, *The Trumpet Soundeth: William Jennings Bryan and His Democracy, 1896–1912* (Lincoln: The University of Nebraska Press, 1960), p. 176.

[54] *Ibid.*, p. vii.

investigations focused on Bryan's last decade. While stressing the Commoner's supposed great contributions to the improvement of American life, Levine's dissertation also contained much unfavorable evidence and interpretation. In his Preface he wrote: "In William Jennings Bryan reform and reaction lived happily, if somewhat incongruously, side by side."[55] But a reader who lacks the time and will to subdue more than 500 pages of typescript might get a far different impression if he read only the Abstract:[56]

> . . . The Bryan of the 1920's was essentially the Bryan of the 1890's. He remained a vigorous and optimistic proponent of reform in all aspects of American life. His entry into the ranks of the militant fundamentalist and prohibitionist movements was not a negation of his reform impulse but stemmed from his conception of the good society and his conviction that the role of the reformer was not merely to improve the society in which men lived but to purify the men themselves.

This remarkable line of argument was picked up by Willard H. Smith and offered in a paper presented to the Mississippi Valley Historical Association in 1964: "Even Bryan's fight against modernism and evolution, as Lawrence W. Levine has well pointed out, is to be interpreted partly in the light of his fear of the influence these theories might have had in slowing up the march toward social reform and progressivism."[57] Admittedly, Bryan did think that the anti–evolution law in Tennessee was a heaven-sent reform, but was he right?

This brief review of varied interpretations of Bryan suggests some of the special reasons (in addition to the justifications that can be offered for any thoughtful collection of primary sources on a significant topic) why it has seemed

---

[55] Levine, "William Jennings Bryan," p. i.
[57] Willard H. Smith, "William Jennings Bryan and the Social Gospel"
[56] *Ibid.*, Abstract, p. 1.
(Paper presented to the Mississippi Valley Historical Association, May 1, 1964, multilithed copy in possession of Ray Ginger), p. 19.

worthwhile to edit this volume. First, if Bryan was not a great leader, he was still a sensitive weather vane to certain winds of ideology emanating from millions of Americans, and no collection of his writings spanning his public career has ever been put together. Second, since judgments about him have so often been abstruse and generalized, there is particular value in looking at the concrete record. Third, since opinions on his life clash so sharply, it is unusually appropriate to offer materials that will help each reader to make up his own mind. The documents present a highly selective, but I hope not distorted, sampling of his works.

RAY GINGER

Waltham, Massachusetts
September 1964

Acknowledgments

Efficient and generous help in the preparation of this volume has been provided by four former students at Brandeis University: Phyllis C. Ewen, Joan H. Feinson, Heidi E. Schuhr, and especially David Allan Levine. Leonard W. Levy of the same school made several helpful suggestions. The decisions have all been mine, and I alone am responsible for the result. In my judgment the selections given here are fairly representative of the range of Bryan's speeches, letters, essays, and other writings.

R.G.

Chronology

1860   William Jennings Bryan born on March 19 at Salem, Illinois. His father, Silas Lillard Bryan, having served eight years in the state senate, became a circuit judge.

1865
TO
1896   Huge increases in output, both in United States and abroad, brought a prolonged downward trend in the general level of prices. Especially significant to Bryan's career were the great declines in prices of silver and of such staple crops as wheat and cotton.

1872   Silas Bryan was unsuccessful as the Democratic nominee for United States House of Representatives.

1873   Congress, by the "Crime of '73," eliminated the silver dollar from the list of standard coins.

1875   Bryan sent to Jacksonville, Illinois, where he studied for six years at Whipple Academy and Illinois College.

1878   Congress passed Bland-Allison Act, requiring coinage each month of at least $2,000,000 but not more than $4,000,000 in silver bullion.

1879   The resumption of specie payments, which obligated the Treasury to redeem Federal currency including greenbacks in gold, put the United States on a *de facto* gold standard for the first time.

1881   Bryan graduated from Illinois College. Until 1883 he studied at Union College of Law in Chicago. These two years were his only sustained period of residence in a major city.

1883   Bryan was moderately successful practicing law at Jack-
TO   sonville.
1887

1884   Bryan married Mary Baird. She began to read law under
       his direction.

1887   Seeking greater opportunities at the bar, Bryan resettled
       in Lincoln, Nebraska, the state capital.

1888   With both Nebraska and Lincoln normally controlled
       by Republicans, Bryan was a delegate to Democratic
       state convention.

1890   The farm revolt gathered momentum. Independent par-
       ties backed by the Farmers' Alliances won substantial
       support in several states.
           Sherman Silver Purchase Act increased to 4,500,000
       ounces of silver bullion per month the amount bought
       by the Treasury for conversion into money.
           William Jennings Bryan elected to U. S. House of
       Representatives in a three-way contest.

1891   Bryan named to the Ways and Means Committee of
       House.
           Farmers' Alliances in the South reportedly had 35,000
       agitators in field.

1892   Bryan re-elected to House, but, due partly to redistrict-
       ing of the state, by a greatly reduced plurality.
           Grover Cleveland, Democrat, elected President for
       second time.
           People's party (Populists) organized on Independence
       Day. Its candidates won more than 1,000,000 votes in
       election.

1893   Financial panic sweeps country; becomes grave depres-
       sion.
           Bryan was a leader in House of unsuccessful fight to
       block repeal of Sherman Silver Purchase Act.

1894   With Democratic machine in Nebraska dominated by supporters of President Cleveland and the gold standard, Bryan did not seek re-election to the House.

Bryan's eloquence at Democratic state convention helped win him the nomination for the Senate, but he placed only third in vote by legislature.

Bryan hired as lecturer by Chautauqua and also by American Bimetallic League, the latter being subsidized by silver-mine owners.

Bryan becomes editor-in-chief of Omaha *World-Herald*.

1895   Bryan stumps country for free coinage of silver.

1896   Bryan a delegate to Democratic national convention in Chicago. During debate on platform he delivers "Cross of Gold Speech."

Nominated for President on fifth ballot.

Bryan endorsed also by People's party, but William McKinley defeated him and became President.

1898   Spanish-American War begins.

Bryan named colonel in militia by governor of Nebraska, and raised a regiment to serve in war. Did not get outside of United States, and resigned the day the treaty ending the war was signed. He had served five months.

1899   Although he opposed acquisition of the Philippines, Bryan advocated ratification of Treaty of Paris.

1900   Bryan again nominated for President. McKinley won even more decisively than in 1896; Bryan victorious only in South and in four Western states.

1901   Bryan began publication of *The Commoner,* a weekly magazine, with 17,000 advance subscribers.

1904 Eastern conservatives secured Democratic nomination for Presidency for Alton B. Parker; he was "defeated by acclamation."

1905 Bryan makes around-the-world tour, lecturing in many
TO countries.
1906

1906 *The Commoner* prints the essence of Bryan's plan for international arbitration treaties.

1908 Bryan, nominated for President a third time, wins only 162 electoral votes to 321 for William Howard Taft.

1910 Publication of the first of ten pamphlets called *The Fundamentals*, expounding the Five Points as a test of true Christianity. Bryan still tolerant of Darwinism.

1912 Bryan created sensation at Democratic national convention. Gave backhanded endorsement to Woodrow Wilson, who won nomination on 46th ballot.

Wilson, in four-cornered race, won just over 42 per cent of popular vote to be elected President.

1913 Bryan became Secretary of State. His main objective in the role was to negotiate arbitration treaties, which the United States signed with thirty other nations.

Bryan used his influence with Congress in behalf of domestic measures, especially the Federal Reserve Act.

The Commoner was converted to a monthly periodical.

1914 World War I broke out at beginning of August.

Bryan opposed loans by American nationals or companies to belligerent governments. This policy, adopted at first, was soon dropped.

Bryan supported President Wilson's intervention in Mexico.

1915 Bryan resigned from State Department in dispute with President over proper policy in *Lusitania* crisis.
Bryan established temporary residence in Florida.
Bryan urged clemency for Leo Frank.
Bryan became prominent in campaign for prohibition.

1916 Democratic campaign took on flavor of neutrality and domestic reform, and Bryan supported Wilson's successful race for re-election.

1917 Bryan urged referendum on American entry into war; later became all-out backer of war effort.

1918 World's Christian Fundamentals Association founded.

1919 Bryan supported reservations to Covenant of League of Nations.

1920 A delegate from Nebraska, Bryan orated for prohibition at Democratic national convention.
Fourteenth Census of United States was first to show a majority of Americans living in urban areas (towns or cities with 2,500 or more inhabitants).

1921 Bryan transferred his citizenship to Florida.
Bryan became prominent in campaign against theory of evolution.

1922 Bryan addressed the legislatures of several states urging
TO that Darwinism be banned from public schools.
1923

1923 General Assembly of Presbyterian Church North affirmed validity of Five Points, but elected another candidate than Bryan to be Moderator, the denomination's highest office.

1924   Bryan, delegate from Florida to Democratic national
       convention, opposed explicit denunciation of Ku Klux
       Klan.

1925   Bryan associated with prosecution of John Thomas
       Scopes at Dayton, Tennessee.
       Bryan died on July 26.

Selected Bibliography

ADLER, SELIG. "Bryan and Wilsonian Caribbean Penetration," *Hispanic American Historical Review*, XX (1940), 198–226.

CHALLENER, RICHARD. "William Jennings Bryan." Edited by NORMAN A. GRAEBNER, *An Uncertain Tradition: American Secretaries of State in the Twentieth Century*. New York: McGraw-Hill Book Company, 1961.

COLETTA, PAOLO E. "Bryan, Anti-Imperialism, and Missionary Diplomacy," *Nebraska History*, XLI (1960), 167–187.

———. "Bryan, Cleveland, and the Disrupted Democracy," *Nebraska History*, XLI (1960), 1–27.

———. "Bryan, McKinley, and the Treaty of Paris," *Pacific Historical Review*, XXVI (1957), 131–146.

———. "The Morning Star of the Reformation: William Jennings Bryan's First Congressional Campaign," *Nebraska History*, XXXVII (1956), 103–119.

———. "William Jennings Bryan and the Nebraska Senatorial Election of 1893," *Nebraska History*, XXXI (1950), 183–203.

DIAMOND, WILLIAM. "Urban and Rural Voting in 1896," *American Historical Review*, XLVI (1940–1941), 281–305.

FITE, GILBERT C. "Republican Strategy and the Farm Vote in the Presidential Campaign of 1896," *American Historical Review*, LXV (1959–1960), 787–806.

GINGER, RAY. *Age of Excess: The United States from 1877 to 1914*. New York: The Macmillan Company, 1965.

———. *Six Days or Forever?: Tennessee v. John Thomas Scopes*. Boston: Beacon Press, 1958.

GLAD, PAUL W. *McKinley, Bryan, and the People*. Philadelphia: J. B. Lippincott Company, 1964.

————. *The Trumpet Soundeth: William Jennings Bryan and His Democracy, 1896–1912.* Lincoln: The University of Nebraska Press, 1960.

HERRICK, GENEVIEVE FORBES, and HERRICK, JOHN ORIGEN. *The Life of William Jennings Bryan.* Chicago: Buxton Publishing House, 1925.

HIBBEN, PAXTON, and GRATTAN, C. HARTLEY. *The Peerless Leader: William Jennings Bryan.* New York: Farrar and Rinehart, Inc., 1929.

HOFSTADTER, RICHARD. "William Jennings Bryan: The Democrat as Revivalist," *The American Political Tradition and the Men Who Made It.* New York: Alfred A. Knopf, Inc., 1948.

LEVINE, LAWRENCE WILLIAM. "William Jennings Bryan: The Last Decade, 1915–1925." Unpublished Ph.D. dissertation, Columbia University, 1962.

LINK, ARTHUR S. *Wilson: The New Freedom.* Princeton: The Princeton University Press, 1956.

————. *Wilson: The Road to the White House.* Princeton: The Princeton University Press, 1947.

————. *Wilson: The Struggle for Neutrality.* Princeton: The Princeton University Press, 1960.

LIPPMANN, WALTER. "Bryan and the Dogma of Majority Rule," *Men of Destiny.* New York: The Macmillan Company, 1927.

LONG, J. C. *Bryan: The Great Commoner.* New York: D. Appleton & Company, 1928.

WERNER, M. R. *Bryan.* New York: Harcourt, Brace and Company, 1928.

WHITE, WILLIAM ALLEN. "Bryan," *Masks in a Pageant.* New York: The Macmillan Company, 1928.

WILLIAMS, WAYNE C. *William Jennings Bryan.* New York: G. P. Putnam's Sons, 1936.

Williams Jennings Bryan:

Selections

1. Free Coinage of Silver

Depression struck wheat-farming areas with renewed violence after 1887; and it was the Western Congressmen who were prominent in replacing the Bland-Allison Act of 1878 with the somewhat more inflationary Sherman Silver Purchase Act of 1890. The new law required the Secretary of the Treasury to buy 4,500,000 ounces of silver bullion a month, to be paid for with Treasury notes (silver certificates). The Treasury had to redeem these notes in gold upon request. After financial panic swept the entire nation in 1893, swarms of holders demanded gold for their notes. To prevent the United States from being driven off the gold standard, newly elected President Cleveland in June 1893 called Congress into special session and asked that the Silver Purchase Act be repealed. William Jennings Bryan for some time after his election to the House of Representatives focused on the tariff problem, which had been the chief factor in the Democratic landslide of 1890. As late as September 1892 Bryan said at a meeting, "I don't know anything about free silver. The people of Nebraska are for free silver and I am for free silver. I will look up the arguments later." Here, as delivered in the House less than a year later, are his arguments. Although a limit of one hour per speaker had been set for the debate, Bryan so impressed the House by "his attractive presence, pleasing manner of delivery, and clear, vibrant and beautifully modulated voice" that he was granted unlimited time by unanimous consent. He spoke for three hours. In a passage that is omitted from the selections, he quickly brushed aside the opposition's argu-

---

Speech of August 16, 1893, in *Congressional Record*, XXV, Pt. I (53rd Cong., 1st Sess.), 401–411.

*ment that in a modern economy the most important part of the
total stock of "money" is the credit created by the banking system.
Bryan also scornfully denied that gold alone could provide enough
precious metals to meet the monetary needs of "an increasing population": "Is there some new California or some undiscovered Aus-
tralia yet to be explored?" The answer, had he known it, was yes:
The Rand fields in South Africa were pouring out gold, and would
be joined five years later by the Klondike.*

. . . We hear much about a "stable currency" and an "honest
dollar." It is a significant fact that those who have spoken in
favor of unconditional repeal have for the most part avoided a
discussion of the effect of an appreciating standard. They take
it for granted that a gold standard is not only an honest standard, but the only stable standard. I denounce that child of
ignorance and avarice the gold dollar, under a universal gold
standard, as the most dishonest dollar which we could employ.

I stand upon the authority of every intelligent writer upon
political economy when I assert that there is not and never has
been an honest dollar. An honest dollar is a dollar absolutely
stable in relation to all other things. . . .

I am on sound and scientific ground, therefore, when I say
that a dollar approaches honesty as its purchasing power
approaches stability. If I borrow a thousand dollars to–day
and next year pay the debt with a thousand dollars which will
secure exactly as much of all things desirable as the one thousand which I borrowed, I have paid in honest dollars. If the
money has increased or decreased in purchasing power, I have
satisfied my debt with dishonest dollars. While the Government
can say that a given weight of gold or silver shall constitute a
dollar, and invest that dollar with legal–tender qualities, it can
not fix the purchasing power of the dollar. That must depend
upon the law of supply and demand, and it may be well to

suggest that this Government never tried to fix the exchangeable value of a dollar until it began to limit the number of dollars coined.

DOLLARS RISE AND FALL.

If the number of dollars increases more rapidly than the need for dollars—as it did after the gold discoveries of 1849—the exchangeable value of each dollar will fall and prices rise. If the demand for dollars increases faster than the number of dollars—as it did after 1800—the price of each dollar will rise and prices generally will fall. The relative value of the dollar may be changed by natural causes or by legislation. An increased supply—the demand remaining the same—or a decreased demand—the supply remaining the same—will reduce the exchangeable value of each dollar. Natural causes may act on both supply and demand; as, for instance, by increasing the product from the mines or by increasing the amount consumed in the arts. Legislation acts directly on the demand, and thus affects the price, since the demand is one of the factors in fixing the price.

If by legislative action the demand for silver is destroyed and the demand for gold is increased by making it the only standard, the exchangeable value of each unit of that standard, or dollar, as we call it, will be increased. If the exchangeable value of the dollar is increased by legislation the debt of the debtor is increased, to his injury and to the advantage of the creditor. And let me suggest here, in reply to the gentleman from Massachusetts [Mr. McCALL], who said that the money loaner was entitled to the advantages derived from improved machinery and inventive genius, that he is mistaken. The laboring man and the producer are entitled to these benefits, and the money loaner by every law of justice ought to be content with a dollar equal in purchasing power to the dollar which he loaned, and any one desiring more than that desires a dishonest dollar, it matters not what name he may give to it. [Loud applause.] Take an illustration: John Doe, of Nebraska, has a farm worth $2,000 and mortgages it to Richard Roe, of Massachusetts, for $1,000. Suppose the value of the monetary unit is increased by legislation which creates a greater demand for gold. The debt is increased. If the increase amounts to 100 per cent the Nebraska farmer finds that the prices of his products have fallen one–half and his land loses one–half its value, unless the price is maintained by the increased population incident to a new country.

The mortgage remains nominally the same, though the debt has actually become twice as great. Will he be deceived by the cry of "honest dollar?" If he should loan a Nebraska neighbor a hog weighing 100 pounds and the next spring demand in return a hog weighing 200 pounds he would be called dishonest, even though he contended that he was only demanding one hog—just the number he loaned. Society has become accustomed to some very nice distinctions. The poor man is called a socialist if he believes that the wealth of the rich should be divided among the poor, but the rich man is called a financier if he devises a plan by which the pittance of the poor can be converted to his use. [Laughter and applause.]

The poor man who takes property by force is called a thief, but the creditor who can by legislation make a debtor pay a dollar twice as large as he borrowed is lauded as the friend of a sound currency. [Laughter and applause.] The man who wants the people to destroy the Government is an anarchist, but the man who wants the Government to destroy the people is a patriot. [Applause.]

CONFIDENCE MUST BE RESTORED.

The great desire now seems to be to restore confidence, and some have an idea that the only way to restore confidence is to coax the money loaner to let go of his hoard by making the profits too tempting to be resisted. Capital is represented as a shy and timid maiden who must be courted, if won. Let me suggest a plan for bringing money from Europe. If it be possible, let us enact a law "Whereas confidence must be restored; and whereas money will always come from its hiding place if the inducement is sufficient: Therefore, be it enacted, That every man who borrows $1 shall pay back $2 and interest (the usury law not to be enforced)."

Would not English capital come "on the swiftest ocean greyhounds?" The money loaner of London would say: "I will not loan in India or Egypt or in South America. The inhabitants of those countries are a wicked and ungodly people and refuse to pay more than they borrowed. I will loan in the United States, for *there* lives an honest people, who delight in a sound currency and pay in an honest dollar." Why does not some one propose that plan? Because no one would dare to increase by law the number of dollars which the debtor must pay, and yet by some it is called wise statesmanship to do indirectly and in the dark what no man has the temerity to propose directly and openly.

We have been called cranks and lunatics and idiots because we have warned our fellow–men against the inevitable and intolerable consequences which would follow the adoption of a gold standard by all the world. But who, I ask, can be silent in the presence of such impending calamities? The United States, England, France, and Germany own to–day about $2,600,000,000 of the world's supply of gold coin, or about five-sevenths of the total amount, and yet these four nations contain but a small fraction of the inhabitants of the globe. What will be the exchangeable value of a gold dollar when India's people, outnumbering alone the inhabitants of the four great nations named, reach out after their share of gold coin? What will be the final price of gold when all the nations of the Occident and Orient join in the scramble?

A distinguished advocate of the gold standard said recently, in substance: "Wheat has now reached a point where the English can afford to buy it, and gold will soon return to re-

lieve our financial embarrassment." How delighted the farmer
will be when he realizes what an opportunity he has to save
his country! A nation in distress; banks failing; mines closed;
laborers unemployed; enterprise at a standstill, and behold, the
farmer, bowed with unceasing, even if unremunerative, toil,
steps forth to save his country—by selling his wheat below
the cost of production! And I am afraid he will even now be
censured for allowing the panic to go as far as it has before
reducing his prices.

It seems cruel that upon the growers of wheat and cotton,
our staple exports, should be placed the burden of supplying
us at whatever cost with the necessary gold, and yet the financier quoted has suggested the only means, except the issue of
bonds, by which our stock of gold can be replenished. If it is
difficult now to secure gold, what will be the condition when
the demand is increased by its adoption as the world's only
primary money? We would simply put gold upon an auction
block, with every nation as a bidder, and each ounce of the
standard metal would be knocked down to the one offering
the most of all other kinds of property. Every disturbance of
finance in one country would communicate itself to every other,
and in the misery which would follow it would be of little
consolation to know that others were suffering as much as, or
more than, we. . . .

The opponents of the Bland law in 1878 were waiting for
international bimetallism. Mr. Cleveland mentioned the prospect of it in his message in 1885, and again this year. It was a
valuable weapon in 1890, when the Sherman bill was passed
and the Brussels conference was called in time to carry us
over the last Presidential election. We are still waiting, and
those are waiting most patiently who favor a gold standard.
[Laughter and applause.] Are we any nearer to an international agreement than we were fifteen years ago? The European nations wait on England, and she refused within a year
to even consider the adoption of the double standard. Can we
conquer her by waiting? We have tried the Fabian policy.

Suppose we try bringing her to terms by action. Let me appeal to your patriotism. Shall we make our laws dependent upon England's action and thus allow her to legislate for us upon the most important of all questions? Shall we confess our inability to enact monetary laws? Are we an English colony or an independent people? If the use of gold alone is to make us slaves, let us use both metals and be free. If there be some living along the Eastern coast—better acquainted with the beauties of the Alps than with the grandeur of the Rockies, more accustomed to the sunny skies of Italy than to the invigorating breezes of the Mississippi Valley—who are not willing to trust their fortunes and their destinies to American citizens, let them learn that the people living between the Alleghanies and the Golden Gate are not afraid to cast their all upon the Republic and rise or fall with it. [Loud applause.]

One hundred and seventeen years ago the Liberty Bell gave notice to a waiting and expectant people that Independence had been declared. There may be doubting, trembling ones among us now, but, sirs, I do not overestimate it when I say that out of twelve millions of voters more than ten millions are waiting, anxiously waiting, for the signal which shall announce the financial independence of the United States. [Applause.] This Congress can not more surely win the approval of a grateful people than by declaring that this nation, the grandest which the world has ever seen, has the right and the ability to legislate for its own people on every subject regardless of the wishes, the entreaties, or the threats of foreign powers. [Applause.]

Perhaps the most important question for us to consider is the question of ratio. Comparatively few people in this country are in favor of a gold standard, and no national party has ever advocated it. Comparatively few, also, will be deceived by the promise of international bimetallism annually held out to us. Among those in favor of bimetallism, and in favor of independent action on the part of the United States, there is, however, an honest difference of opinion as to the particular ratio at which the unlimited coinage of gold and silver should be undertaken. The principle of bimetallism does not stand upon any certain ratio, and may exist at 1 to 30 as well as at 1 to 16.

In fixing the ratio we should select that one which will secure the greatest advantage to the public and cause the least injustice. The present ratio, in my judgment, should be adopted. A change in the ratio could be made (as in 1834) by reducing the size of the gold dollar or by increasing the size of the silver dollar, or by making a change in the weight of both dollars. A larger silver dollar would help the creditor. A smaller gold dollar would help the debtor. It is not just to do either, but if a change must be made, the benefit should be given to the debtor rather than to the creditor.

Let no one accuse me of defending the justness of any change; but I repeat it, if we are given a choice between a change which will aid the debtor by reducing the size of his debt and a change which will aid the creditor by increasing the amount which he is to receive, either by increasing the number of his dollars or their size, the advantage must be given to the debtor, and no man during this debate, whatever may be his private wish or interest, will advocate the giving of the advantage to the creditor.

To illustrate the effect of changing the ratio let us take, for convenience, the ratio of 24 to 1, as advocated by some. We could make this change by reducing the weight of the gold dollar one–third. This would give to the holders of gold an advantage of some $200,000,000, but the creditors would lose several billions of dollars in the actual value of their debts. A debt contracted before 1873 would not be scaled, because the new gold dollar would purchase as much as the old gold dollar would in 1873. Creditors, however, whose loans have been made since that time would suffer, and the most recent loans would show the greatest loss. The value of silver bullion has only fallen in relation to gold. But the purchasing power of one ounce of silver has varied less since 1873 than has the purchasing power of one ounce of gold, which would indicate that gold had risen.

If, on the other hand, the ratio is changed by increasing the size of the silver dollar, it would be necessary to recoin our silver dollars into dollars a half larger, or we would have in circulation two legal–tender silver dollars of different sizes. Of the two plans it would be better, in my judgment, to keep both dollars in circulation together, though unequal in weight, rather than to recoin the lighter dollars. The recoinage of more than 500,000,000 of silver dollars, or the bullion representing them, would cause a shrinkage of about $170,000,000 or one-third of our silver money; it would cause a shrinkage of nearly one–sixth of our metallic money and of more than one–tenth of our total circulation. This contraction would increase our debts more than a billion dollars and decrease the nominal value of our property more than five billions.

A change in the ratio made by increasing the size of the silver dollar as above suggested would also decrease by one-third the number of dollars which could be coined from the annual product of silver. If, as Mr. Carlisle has said, the supply of metal, both gold and silver, is none too large to keep pace with population, the increase in the weight of each dollar would make the supply to that extent deficient. A change in ratio, whether secured by decreasing the gold dollar or by in-creasing the silver dollar, would probably make an international agreement more difficult, because nearly all of the silver coin now in existence circulates at a ratio less than ours.

If the change should be made in this country by increasing the size of the silver dollar and an international agreement secured upon the new ratio, to be effected by other nations in the same way, the amount of money in the world, that is, metallic money, would suffer a contraction of more than $1,000,000,000, to the enormous injury of the debtor class and to the enormous advantage of the creditor class. If we believe that the value of gold has risen because its supply has not increased as fast as the demand caused by favorable legislation, then it would be unfair to continue this appreciation by other legislation favorable to gold. It would be a special injustice to the mine owner and to the farmer, whose products have fallen with silver, to make perpetual the injunction against their prosperity.

We often hear our opponents complain of the "cupidity of the mine owner." Let us admit that the mine owner is selfish, and that he will profit by the increased price of silver bullion. Let us, for the sake of argument, go further, and accuse him of favoring the free coinage of silver solely for the purpose of increasing the price of his product. Does that make him worse than other men? Is not the farmer selfish enough to desire a higher price for wheat? Is not the cotton–grower selfish enough to desire a higher price for his cotton? Is not the laboring man selfish enough to desire higher wages? And, if I may be pardoned for the boldness, are not bankers and business men selfish enough to ask for legislation at our hands which will give them prosperity? Was not this extraordinary session called in order to bring back prosperity to our business men?

Is it any more important that you should keep a mercantile house from failing than that you should keep a mine from suspending? Are those who desire free coinage of silver in order that the barren wastes should be made to "blossom like the rose" any worse than those who want the Sherman law repealed in order to borrow foreign gold and retire clearing-house certificates? There is a class of people whose interest in financial legislation is too often overlooked. The money–loaner has just as much interest in the rise in the value of his product —money—as farmers and miners have in the increased price of their products.

The man who has $10,000 in money becomes worth $20,000 in reality when prices fall one–half. Shall we assume that the money–lenders of this and other countries ignore the advantage which an appreciated currency gives to them and desire it simply for the benefit of the poor man and the laborer? What refining influence is there in their business which purges away the dross of selfishness and makes pure and patriotic only their motives? [Laughter.] Has some new dispensation reversed the parable and left Lazarus in torment while Dives is borne aloft in Abraham's bosom? [Laughter.]

But is the silver miner after all so selfish as to be worthy of censure? Does he ask for some new legislation or for some innovation inaugurated in his behalf? No. He pleads only for the restoration of the money of the fathers. He asks to have given back to him a right which he enjoyed from 1792 to 1873. During all those years he could deposit his silver bullion at the mints and receive full legal–tender coins at the rate of $1.29 for each ounce of silver, and during a part of the time his product could be converted into money at even a higher price. Free coinage can only give back to him what demonetization took away. He does not ask for a silver dollar redeemable in a gold dollar, but for a silver dollar which redeems itself.

If the bullion value of silver has not been reduced by hostile legislation, the free coinage of silver at the present ratio can bring to the mine owner no benefit, except by enabling him to pay a debt already contracted with less ounces of silver. If the price of his product has been reduced by hostile legislation, is he asking any more than we would ask under the same circumstances in seeking to remove the oppressive hand of the law? Let me suggest, too, that those who favor an international agreement are estopped from objecting to the profits of the silver mine owner, because an international agreement could only be effected at some ratio near to ours, probably 15½ to 1, and this would just as surely inure to the benefit of the owner of silver as would free coinage established by the independent action of this country.

If our opponents were correct in asserting that the price of silver bullion could be maintained at 129 cents an ounce by international agreement, but not by our separate action, then international bimetallism would bring a larger profit to the mine owner than the free coinage of silver by this country could. Let the international bimetallist, then, find some better objection to free coinage than that based on the mine owner's profit.

But what is the mine owner's profit? Has anyone told you the average cost of mining an ounce of silver? You have heard of some particular mine where silver can be produced at a low cost, but no one has attempted to give you any reliable data as to the average cost of production. I had a letter from Mr. Leech when he was Director of the Mint, saying that the Government is in possession of no data in regard to the cost of gold production and none of any value in regard to silver. No calculation can be made as to the profits of mining which does not include money spent in prospecting and in mines which have ceased to pay, as well as those which are profitably worked.

When we see a wheel of fortune with twenty–four paddles, see those paddles sold for 10 cents apiece, and see the holder of the winning paddle draw $2, we do not conclude that money can be profitably invested in a wheel of fortune. We know that those who bought expended altogether $2.40 on the turn of the wheel, and that the man who won only received $2; but our opponents insist upon estimating the profits of silver mining by the cost of the winning paddle. It is safe to say that taking the gold and silver of the world—and it is more true of silver than of gold—every dollar's worth of metal has cost a dollar. It is strange that those who watch so carefully lest the silver miner shall receive more for his product than the bare cost of production ignore the more fortunate gold miner.

Did you ever hear a monometallist complain because a man could produce 25.8 grains of gold, .9 fine, at any price whatever, and yet take it to our mint and have it stamped into a dollar with full legal–tender qualities? I saw at the World's Fair a few days ago a nugget of gold, just as it was found, worth over $3,000. What an outrage that the finder should be allowed to convert that into money at such an enormous profit! And yet no advocate of honest money raises his hand to stop that crime. . . .

Well has it been said by the Senator from Missouri [Mr. VEST] that we have come to the parting of the ways. To–day the Democratic party stands between two great forces, each inviting its support. On the one side stand the corporate interests of the nation, its moneyed institutions, its aggregations of wealth and capital, imperious, arrogant, compassionless. They demand special legislation, favors, privileges, and immunities. They can subscribe magnificently to campaign funds; they can strike down opposition with their all–pervading influence, and, to those who fawn and flatter, bring ease and plenty. They demand that the Democratic party shall become their agent to execute their merciless decrees.

On the other side stands that unnumbered throng which gave a name to the Democratic party and for which it has assumed to speak. Work–worn and dust–begrimed, they make their sad appeal. They *hear* of *average* wealth increased on every side and *feel* the *inequality* of its distribution. They see an overproduction of everything desired because of the underproduction of the ability to buy. They can not pay for loyalty except with their suffrages, and can only punish betrayal with their condemnation. Although the ones who most deserve the fostering care of Government, their cries for help too often beat in vain against the outer wall, while others less deserving find ready access to legislative halls.

This army, vast and daily vaster growing, begs the party to be its champion in the present conflict. It can not press its claims 'mid sounds of revelry. Its phalanxes do not form in grand parade, nor has it gaudy banners floating on the breeze. Its battle hymn is "Home, Sweet Home," its war cry—"Equality before the law." To the Democratic party, standing between these two irreconcilable forces, uncertain to which side to turn and conscious that upon its choice its fate depends, come the words of Israel's second lawgiver: "Choose you this day whom ye will serve." What will the answer be? Let me invoke the memory of him whose dust made sacred the soil of Monticello when he joined

> The dead but sceptered sovereigns who still rule
> Our spirits from their urns.

He was called a demagogue and his followers a mob, but the immortal Jefferson dared to follow the best promptings of his heart. He placed man above matter, humanity above property, and, spurning the bribes of wealth and power, pleaded the cause of the common people. It was this devotion to their interests which made his party invincible while he lived and will make his name revered while history endures. And what message comes to us from the Hermitage? When a crisis like the present arose and the national bank of his day sought to control the politics of the nation, God raised up an Andrew Jackson, who had the courage to grapple with that great enemy, and by overthrowing it, he made himself the idol of the people and reinstated the Democratic party in public confidence. What will the decision be to–day? The Democratic party has won the greatest success in its history. Standing upon this victory–crowned summit, will it turn its face to the rising or the setting sun? Will it choose blessings or cursings—life or death—which? Which? [Prolonged applause on the floor and in the galleries, and cries of "Vote!" "Vote!"]

2. Reduce Import Duties

As a member of the Ways and Means Committee that had drafted the measure, Bryan had a special role to play in defending the Wilson tariff bill. He played it well. Compared to the usual run of House debates seventy years ago, which disgusted and dismayed many foreign visitors, this speech set a laudable standard. In addition to having done some homework, Bryan had his wits (and occasionally his wit) about him. He gibed amusingly at carpet manufacturer John Sloane; he was effective in rough-and-tumble repartee with the protectionist Representative from Troy, New York. He rebutted the notion that import duties must be proportioned to international differences in wage rates, and he showed how the tariff was a private tax levied in large measure on rural areas for the benefit of favored industries. The Wilson bill, which cut the average tax on dutied imports from 49 per cent to 30 per cent and altogether removed duties from such raw materials as coal, iron ore, and raw wool, passed the House by 204 to 140. But Democratic defections enabled the Senate to vote more than 600 amendments, and the House reluctantly accepted the upward revisions. The Wilson-Gorman Act did bring duties down a bit from the level set by the McKinley Act of 1890, but it did not come anywhere near embodying a "revenue tariff": even before the Senate amendments, according to the Journal of Commerce, *the Wilson bill left the American tariff "more highly protective than that of any other country."*

Speech of January 13, 1894, in *Congressional Record*, XXVI, Pt. I, Appendix (53rd Cong., 2nd Sess.), 219–232.

. . . We have met here as the representatives of our constituents, varying in commercial interests, varying in industrial pursuits, varying in political convictions, to discuss in this, the people's forum, the principles involved, and to declare by our votes either in favor of the protective principle or in favor of a tariff for revenue only.

I ask you to consider for a moment not the details of the present measure, but the principle involved in the protective tariff. The last national platform of the Democratic party is the first one which gave expression to my convictions upon this question. It was fortunate for the country that in the last campaign the platforms were relieved of ambiguity and clearly defined the tariff issue. The question presented to the voters was:

> Shall the revenue laws be framed by those who desire protection first and revenue as an incident thereto, or by those who desire revenue first and protection only as an incident thereto?

On the 7th day of June, 1892, the Republican national convention met at Minneapolis, and upon motion of the author of the McKinley bill, adopted the following declaration upon the tariff question:

> We reaffirm the American doctrine of protection. We call attention to its growth abroad. We maintain that the prosperous condition of our country is largely due to the wise revenue legislation of the Republican Congress. We believe that all articles which can not be produced in the United States, except luxuries, should be admitted free of duty, and that on all imports coming into competition with the products of American labor there should be levied duties equal to the difference between wages abroad and at home.

Two weeks afterward the Democratic national convention met at Chicago. The present chairman of the Committee of Ways and Means (Mr. Wilson) was permanent chairman of the convention, and presided while the following declaration was adopted:

> We denounce Republican protection as a fraud, a robbery of the great majority of the American people for the benefit of the few. We declare it to be a fundamental principle of the Democratic party that the Federal Government has no constitutional power to impose and collect tariff duties, except for the purpose of revenue only, and we demand that the collection of such taxes shall be limited to the necessities of the Government when honestly and economically administered . . .

I call attention to the fact that, according to the Republican platform, revenue is not only incidental but, if the platform is carried out and the purpose of the policy realized, inconsiderable as well. For, if we put upon the free list all articles which we can not produce, no revenue will be derived from their importation, and if a duty is imposed upon those articles which we can produce, and by the aid of such duties we do produce them, there will be no importation, and therefore, no revenue from such duties, however high. This would leave luxuries, the like of which we do not produce, the only articles upon which a duty would be paid. A protective tariff, therefore, can be a success in the production of revenue only when it fails to carry out in practice the intention of its supporters.

A protective tariff assumes that the article upon which it is laid can not be produced as cheaply in this country as abroad. Not only is this difference in cost made the sole justification for a tariff by the Republican platform, but Mr. McKinley, in reporting the present law, said:

> We have recommended no duty above the point of difference between the normal cost of production here, including labor, and the cost of like production in the countries which seek our markets.

To defend a protective tariff, then, our opponents must show a difference in the cost of production here and abroad equal to the tariff which they ask. The Republican platform does not go so far as Mr. McKinley does in his report before mentioned, for while he advocated a protection equal to the whole difference in the "normal cost of production," the platform only demanded a tariff equal to that portion of the increased cost which was due to higher wages. But for the purpose of argument let us adopt the extreme view.

To illustrate, if the foreign cost of a given yard of cloth is $1, and the cost of the same yard of cloth in this country is $1.50, then 50 cents, being the difference in the cost of production, would be the measure of the tariff levied according to the protective system. It needs no argument to prove that cloth can not be manufactured in this country unless it is sold for more than the cost of production; therefore, if the foreign cost is $1 and the difference in cost is 50 cents, the cloth must be sold at $1.50 per yard in this country.

This illustration proves conclusively that the purpose of the tariff is, first, to make the consumer in this country pay the tariff upon the imported article; second, to make the consumer in this country pay a like amount for the home–made article; and, third, that we can not export an article which needs protection. It proves that the consumer pays the tax on the imported article, for upon no other theory can the tariff be a benefit to the home producer. If the consumer here pays no more for the imported article because of the tariff, his purchases will not be affected whether the tariff be high or low, and he will be no more apt to buy at home than before the tariff was imposed. It proves the second proposition, because unless the consumer is compelled to pay the difference in cost he will not do so, and unless he does so the manufacturer can not produce and sell in this country. It proves the third proposition, because if a tariff of 50 per cent is necessary to enable the manufacturer to sell at $1.50 in this country an article which is sold abroad for $1, then the producer of the $1.50 article in this country can not expect to export it and sell in competition with the $1 article in other countries. . . .

The moment it is understood that Congress is about to change the duty upon any article the person interested in the production of a like article at once protests against any reduction of the tariff. He may believe in tariff reform on other things, but seldom does he believe in tariff reform applied to any article from the protection of which he receives a benefit. He is like the man who wrote to Peel when he was attacking the protective system in England. This man was interested in fishing, and he concluded a protest against a reduction of the tariff on his product by saying:

I am a thorough-going free trader in everything but herrings.

Some of these men who have come before the committee have argued earnestly in favor of a reduction of the tariff on the material which they use as they have protested against a reduction of the tariff on their finished products. They forcibly remind one of the merchant who when a thief had stolen a coat and put it on and ran off with it, shouted to the policeman who was about to shoot, "Shoot him in the pants; the coat belongs to me!"

Those who have enjoyed the benefits of protection not only presume to dictate the tariff schedules, but resent the idea that anyone except a manufacturer should know anything about the subject or have anything to do with the making of tariff laws. One of the leading manufacturing newspapers spoke a short time ago contemptuously of the present Ways and Means Committee, because all of its members do not represent city or manufacturing constituencies; and some of the members were ridiculed as being from "rural villages and country court-houses." At a meeting held last week in New York to protest against the Wilson bill, one of the speakers said:

I traveled through the South and went hundreds of miles without seeing a factory. What do these Southern members know about workingmen? What right have these goose-farmers to make laws for us?

Why, sir, 58 per cent of the people of the United States live in the country and in villages having a less population than 1,000. In the name of those who still believe that "all men are created equal;" in the name of those who still believe in "equality before the law;" in the name of those who believe that the harvest hand has the same rights as the hat–maker, and that the farmer is entitled to as much respect as the factory owner, I protest against the arrogant and impudent assumption that it is the privilege of any particular class to make laws for our people, or that any of our citizens, wherever their residence or whatever their occupation, are excluded from an equal voice in the affairs of Government!

No person would think of trying a case before a party to the suit, and yet it is a fact that the present law was framed in accordance with the expressed wishes of the manufacturers, and in many instances the language of the law was written out by those who were to reap the benefits from its passage. . . .

Let me show you that you can not trust the representations made by interested parties any more safely in the framing of tariff laws than you can in the other affairs of life. I read in yesterday morning's paper that a big meeting was held in New York City by the woolen men to protest against the Wilson bill, and among the vice–presidents elected at that meeting was a man by the name of John Sloane. He is, I understand, a member of the firm of W. & J. Sloane. The resolutions adopted at that meeting denounced the pending measure as destructive of the woolen industry, and yet, while this bill leaves 35 per cent ad valorem on Axminster and moquette carpets, the firm of W. & J. Sloane has within three months exported those same carpets and sold them in Ireland in the face of free–trade England without the protection of a single cent of tariff. [Great applause on the Democratic side.] . . .

Let me call attention to another industry. We have had lately presented to this House the lamentable condition of the manufacturers of collars and cuffs in Troy. [Laughter.]

The able Representative from that district [Mr. HAINES] has presented for them as pathetic an appeal as could well be made. The census gives some very interesting statistics in regard to this promising infant industry, which represents itself as now tottering to ruin. It came into existence before the passage of the McKinley bill. Under the tariff of 1883 these manufacturers enjoyed an ad valorem duty upon their product of 40 per cent, while they were taxed 35 per cent upon the material which they used. The pending measure reduces the tariff on the material which they use and still leaves them 35 per cent ad valorem on their product. It is interesting to note the condition of this industry under the tariff of 1883. The census statistics are collected from the manufacturers themselves and are given, not for the purpose of preventing a reduction of the tariff, but in the regular course of business, and I suppose they never thought that these figures would rise up to condemn them. The statement made by the Census department for the year 1890 includes all the establishments in Troy that reported (12 in number) engaged in the manufacture of shirts, collars, and cuffs. The total capital reported is $3,643,-317; average number of employes, 8,713; total wages paid, $2,474,255; miscellaneous expenses (which include all expenses excepting for wages and material) $534,217; cost of material used, $2,476,156; value of products, $6,217,785. The average yearly wages (including officers, firm members, and clerks, as well as ordinary employes) were, therefore, about $283; 39 per cent of the total value of the product was expended in wages, 39 per cent of the total value of the product was expended for material, and 8 per cent of the total value of the product for miscellaneous expenses, leaving a net profit of about 20 per cent upon the capital invested—that is, the nominal capital; we have no way of knowing the real capital.

Mr. Chairman, you can not rely on the statements that come here from protected industries themselves when prepared for effect.

Mr. HAINES rose.

Mr. BRYAN. I will yield to the gentleman a moment for any question.

Mr. HAINES. My esteemed friend from Nebraska makes the statement that the collar, cuff, and shirt industry was protected 40 per cent under the tariff of 1883. That statement I concede to be entirely correct, but in order to thoroughly understand the situation—

Mr. BRYAN. Does the gentleman rise to submit a question?

Mr. PICKLER. Oh, let him explain; this is a matter affecting his district.

The CHAIRMAN. The gentleman from Nebraska [Mr. BRYAN] can not be interrupted without his consent.

Mr. BRYAN. I do not yield for a speech, though I shall gladly answer any question.

Mr. PICKLER. The gentleman from Nebraska [Mr. BRYAN] has unlimited time, I believe.

The CHAIRMAN. The gentleman from Nebraska is entitled to the floor without interruption.

Mr. BRYAN. I yield for a brief statement.

Mr. HAINES. As introductory to what I was about to say, it was necessary for me to remark, as I stated on Tuesday evening last, that the collar and cuff industry, which originated in Troy, had, by the tariff of 1883, under the general schedule, a protection of 40 per cent. In 1886 the general strike then prevailing throughout the country affected the city of Troy, and at that time many of the operatives engaged there, especially foremen, went to Germany and other countries and established factories to make collars, cuffs, and shirts. Between 1883 and 1886 the collar and cuff business of the whole country was practically done in the city of Troy. Between 1886 and 1890, 25 of those factories failed or went out of existence. It was not until they received protection under the tariff of 1890 that they regained their strength. Under the operation of that law they have maintained wages up to to-day.

While I do not intend to make a speech, I wish the gentleman to understand that 90 per cent of all the labor employed in the collar and cuff industry there is performed by women. When he states that the average amount of wages paid is less than $1 a day or $6 a week, I make the statement that the wages paid for the labor of women are between $7 and $8 a week, and I further state that without protection of our tariff that industry would be compelled to compete against foreign labor, which is paid $1 a week in Japan. What I have asked on behalf of that industry is simply such protection as will compensate for the difference of wages paid here and abroad. That is all; and I think I am justified in asking that much. [Applause.]

Mr. BRYAN. Well, Mr. Chairman, I desire to say to the gentleman from New York, when he speaks of these people failing before the passage of the McKinley bill, that there are thousands of farmers in this country who failed who were making a less profit on their capital than 20 per cent. [Applause on the floor and in the galleries.]

The CHAIRMAN. The Chair must remind our visiting friends in the galleries that they are not permitted to make such demonstrations.

Mr. HAINES. In affidavits before———

The CHAIRMAN. Does the gentleman from Nebraska yield?

Mr. BRYAN. I do not yield to the gentleman for a speech. If he desires to correct any statement I have made I shall gladly yield to him for that purpose; but I can not yield to him for a speech. The gentleman made a speech upon this subject the other evening. I understand it has been printed, and I know he would not care to repeat it here; in fact, I think in a few years he will be ashamed to have made it once. [Laughter and applause on the Democratic side.]

The CHAIRMAN. Of course the gentleman from Nebraska can not be interrupted without his consent.

Mr. BRYAN. I will yield to the gentleman one minute.

Mr. HAINES. I merely wished to state that affidavits were presented to your committee, which I had here the other evening, not only from manufacturers in the city of Troy, but from other reliable sources, going to show that those manufacturers did not average over 6 per cent upon their investment and that they would be content with 5 per cent, while in many instances they are only making 2 per cent. [Applause.]

Mr. BRYAN. I am willing that the people of this country shall take their choice and give credence to whichever statement they prefer.

They can decide for themselves whether they will accept the statement furnished by the Census department or an affidavit furnished by interested parties in order to secure a continuation of the advantages which they now possess under the tariff. And more than that, let me say to the gentleman, if these manufacturers are making only 5 per cent now under the McKinley law, and were making 20 per cent before its enactment, common business judgment would suggest that they would try the experiment of going back to the low tariff with 20 per cent profit instead of trying to be satisfied with only 5 per cent under a higher tariff. [Applause on Democratic side.] . . .

The argument now made that the farmer is prosperous contradicts the statement made in the report which accompanied the McKinley bill. In that report we find these words:

> No prosperity is possible to other industries if agriculture languish. In so far as the fostering care of government can be helpful, it must be faithfully and forcefully exerted to build up and strengthen agriculture. That there is wide-spread depression in this industry to–day can not be doubted.

This admission is made by the committee after thirty years of a protective tariff, framed for the ostensible purpose of helping all industries. After three decades of artificial stimulation we are told that there is widespread depression in the great industry of agriculture, and that without prosperity in this industry prosperity in other industries is impossible. But instead of applying an intelligent remedy they piled the burdens still higher on a depressed industry, and tried to blind the eyes of the farmers by raising the tariff on the great articles of export, whose price fixed in foreign markets can not be raised or lowered by a tariff imposed upon them here. . . .

Much has been said in regard to wages during this debate— in fact the protectionist never tires of pleading for a tariff for the benefit of the workingman. We are told that wages are higher in this country only because of the tariff, and that any reduction in the tariff must result necessarily in a reduction of wages. The protectionists entirely overlook the fact that wages differ in this country in different places for the same work more than the average difference between the wages in this country and England. For instance, farm hands without board receive in one State $12.50 per month; in another State $18.75 per month; in another $22.63 per month, and in another $37.50 per month. In one State just three times as much as in another State—and both States under the same system of protection.

I append to my remarks a table (Appendix I) showing the average yearly wages paid in all mechanical and manufacturing industries in several States. From this table it appears that the average wages in Maine are $356.83, while in Connecticut they are $545.04; in New Hampshire, $410.75; in Nebraska, $537.02, and in California, $637.16.

I also append table (Appendix J) prepared by the Census department for my friend from Illinois [Mr. SPRINGER], showing the wages paid in various towns in the boot and shoe industry and also in the woolen industry. In the woolen industry the protection averages 98 per cent and in some instances runs up to 200 or 300, and yet in the table given the wages in the five towns given run from $7.33 per week to $9.16 per week. The boot and shoe industry is protected now by an ad valorem

duty of 25 per cent, and yet the average weekly wages paid
in the cities given in the table range from $11.58 to $14.62. If
protection makes good wages the wages ought to be highest
where the tariff is highest; but, instead of this, those of our
people who export their products and compete in the world's
market with the cheap labor of other countries as a rule pay
higher relative wages than the highly–protected industries.

There is no question that we to–day manufacture shoes at a
lower cost per shoe than any country in the world, and yet
the wages paid per day are probably double the wages paid
in the same industries in any other country. I am wearing a
pair of shoes made by the Morse–Coe Shoe Company of
Omaha, Nebr. No shoe factory in foreign lands approaches
them in wages paid, and yet they can produce a shoe equal in
quality and price to those produced abroad. We have only
left 20 per cent on boots and shoes in the present bill and have
reduced the tariff on upper and sole leather. The farmers of
the United States export their wheat and cotton and meet in
European markets agricultural products raised by labor which
does not receive one–seventh as much per day on an average
as farm labor in the United States, and yet the farmer who is
thus compelled to compete with the cheapest of all labor is
asked to diminish the purchasing power of his income for the
benefit of manufacturers who are far more favorably situated
as to labor than he.

If it is a mere question of wages per day, why is it that we
dread most those countries in which the highest wages are
paid? And why is it that England is able to give free admission to the products of other European and even Asiatic countries, although the daily wages are very much lower in some
of those countries? If protection is the cause of high wages in
this country, protection ought to secure high wages in other
countries. If a low tariff would make wages low here, free
trade in England ought to make the wages lower than in
countries similarly situated, which have a protective tariff.

The advocates of protection do not deign to explain away these facts.

I am reminded of a dialogue between two citizens of our State which illustrates the manner in which a protectionist discusses this question. A Republican, who had just heard a member of his party discuss the subject of wages, accosted a Democrat and demanded of him an answer to the question: "If protection does not make good wages, why is it that America, with protection, pays better wages than England, with free trade?" The Democrat replied: "If protection makes good wages, you tell me why England, with free trade, pays better wages than Germany does with protection?" The Republican worked at his vest until he tore all the buttons off and then shouted: "Who put down the rebellion, anyhow?" [Laughter.] And that is about as relevant an answer as you can get to the question. [Laughter.]

3. Popular Election of Senators

In considering a proposed amendment to the Constitution which would transfer the election of United States Senators from the legislature to the electorate in each state, the issue of Negro suffrage in the South was a crucial problem. The Republicans urged Federal supervision of Federal elections to insure that Negro votes would be counted; the Democrats were adamant for "state rights." Bryan, in this speech, sought a formula that would evade the conflict of party interests. His maneuver had no immediate consequences; not until 1913 was the Constitution amended to provide for direct election of Senators. However, Bryan's statement did reveal his headlong urge toward ubiquitous and unfiltered popular rule. Although he conceded here that a majority vote in a legislature was not equivalent to the will of most of the citizens, the admission did not make him uneasy about his total understanding of majority rule. Not for him were the sorts of misgivings that had been stated about American politics by Michael Chevalier, a French writer and traveller, contemporary to Tocqueville: "The selfishness of royalty, or more correctly speaking of courts, has hitherto begot much mischief and will continue to do so in future; but it has met with its match in the bosom of republics, and above all under a system of absolute equality, which distributes political power in absolutely equal quantities to the intelligent and the ignorant, to the most eminent merchant and author, and the brutal and drunken peasant of Ireland, who is but just enrolled in the list of citizens. An absolute people, as well as an absolute

---

Speech of July 20, 1894, in *Congressional Record*, XXVI, Pt. 8 (53rd Cong., 2nd Sess.), 7775–7776.

*king, may reject for a time the lessons of experience and the coun-
cils of wisdom; a people as well as a king, may have its courtiers.
A people on the throne, whose authority is limited by no checks,
may blindly and recklessly espouse the quarrels of the minions of
the day; let those who doubt it come here and see it."*

Mr. BRYAN. Mr. Speaker, I desire to call the attention of the
House to what I consider a very improtant question involved
in this joint resolution. I shall not consume time in discussing
the general principle of electing Senators by the people. I believe we can take it for granted that not only in the country
at large, but in this body, there is an overwhelming sentiment
in favor of restoring to the people the right to elect their Senators by a direct vote. It matters not by what course of reasoning we reach that conclusion. We may conclude that the Constitution was a compromise in the beginning; that this plan
was inserted as a necessity, and that the necessity having
passed away, we can and ought to change it; or we may conclude that it was wise at that time, because then they had poor
means of communication, and little means of knowing the
character of the men for whom they voted, but that with our
daily newspapers and our telegraph facilities we need not now
delegate our powers. But whatever may have been the reason
for adopting the present plan in the beginning, we realize
to–day that no man can stand upon the floor of this House
and defend the election of United States Senators by State
Legislatures and at the same time defend the election of governors and of State representatives by a vote of the people.
No distinction can be made between this and other representative offices.

If the people of a State have enough intelligence to choose
their representatives in the State legislature; if they have
enough intelligence to choose their executive officers; if they

have enough intelligence to choose their judges and their officials in all the departments of the State and county, they have
enough intelligence to choose the men who shall represent
them in the United States Senate. To oppose the popular election of Senators is to question the wisdom of our form of
Government.

We all recognize that there is a reason for the election of
Senators by a direct vote to–day that did not exist at the time
the Constitution was adopted. We know that to–day great corporations exist in our States, and that these great corporations,
different from what they used to be one hundred years ago,
are able to compass the election of their tools and their agents
through the instrumentality of Legislatures, as they could not
if Senators were elected directly by the people.

It is said that conventions will nominate. Yes, but behind
conventions stand the voters, and the delegate to a convention
dare not support a man whom the member of a Legislature
might vote for with impunity. The candidate nominated by the
convention must appeal to the voters, but the candidate chosen
by a legislative caucus appeals to no one, and is responsible to
no one. Men have been elected to the Senate whom no party
convention would have dared to nominate.

We are told that we must not change the Constitution because it is a sacred instrument. Who is the best friend, he who
flatters and worships, or he who reproves and corrects? He
who would make such alterations as changed conditions nec-
essitate is a better friend to the Constitution and to good government than he who defends faults and is blind to defects.
Besides, the Federal Constitution has already been amended
fifteen times. Amendment was contemplated and provision
made for it in the instrument itself.

Our State constitutions are frequently changed, and necessarily so, since circumstances change from year to year. Pennsylvania has had four constitutions, Missouri four, Texas three,
Virginia five, etc. Each generation is capable of self-govern-

ment, and must suit to its peculiar needs the machinery of government and the laws.

Mr. Speaker, I do not desire, however, to dwell upon this phase of the question, but I want to call attention to what I believe to be a very important paragraph in this bill. This bill makes the election by direct vote compulsory, and includes a protection against Federal interference. We might as well recognize conditions. There is no statesmanship in shutting our eyes to the facts and asking for things which, though we desire them, yet we can not secure. If two–thirds of both Houses and three–fourths of the States were Democratic, we might be able to secure a provision which would protect the election of United States Senators and Representatives against Federal interference.

If two–thirds of both Houses and three–fourths of the States were Republican they might secure an amendment electing Senators by a direct vote and putting the control of such elections under the supervision of the General Government. But there is not to–day, there has not been for years, and probably will not be for years to come, a time when two–thirds of both Houses, and three–fourths of the States will be controlled by one political party. Therefore, it is worse than useless to attempt to engraft upon this measure a political principle which can never be adopted until three–fourths of the States are in the control of one party. . . .

Now, Mr. Speaker, I propose a substitute for this resolution—but I shall not have it read until later—which will simply leave it optional with the State whether it will elect Senators by a direct vote or not. The justification for this substitute is simple and plain. If we leave it optional with the States, we are not compelled either to prohibit Federal interference or to provide for it. The optional plan gives to the Republican party all the protection which it now has.

It gives to the Democrats who want to prohibit Federal interference all the protection which they now have. . . .

Ah, sirs, we go forth to battle with all the allied power of wealth against us, and if we give them a single excuse behind which they can intrench themselves we shall toil in vain for this reform. If we go forth from this Hall with a partisan principle or party tenet tied to the proposition to elect Senators by a popular vote, every railroad corporation, every gigantic aggregation of wealth will be appealing to party prejudice, and they will not appeal in vain. If we attempt to prohibit Federal interference they will go to the Republicans and say, "Are you going to give up the right of the Federal Government to control elections?" If Federal interference is authorized, they will go to the Democrats and say, "Are you going to surrender the right of self–government?"

But, sirs, if we eliminate partisanship, if we eliminate the question of Federal control, and bring it down to the naked question, "Are you in favor of election of Senators by the people?" we can defeat any combinations formed against us.

4. The Cross of Gold Speech

The struggle over the gold standard was marked by bitter sectional and urban-rural conflicts. During the debate on repeal of the Sherman Silver Purchase Act (see Document 1), Representative Richard P. Bland of Missouri offered an amendment providing for free coinage of silver. Party discipline splintered before sectional loyalties. Although the nine seaboard states from Pennsylvania to Maine had sent 54 Republicans and 45 Democrats to the House, only one of the 99 Representatives voted for Bland's amendment. Conversely, the Representatives of the eight states from Colorado to the Pacific voted 13 to 4 for the amendment, although they numbered 9 Republicans, 7 Democrats, and 1 Populist. If the appeal of the Republican program for urban wage earners is considered, it is virtually certain that the protective tariff benefited them in its discrimination against rural areas, and it is probable that maintenance of the gold standard would benefit them by encouraging city banks to follow liberal credit policies. Bryan in the following speech made during the debate on the platform, spoke for the "country town" and the farmer as distinguished from the "great metropolis," for the Western "pioneer" as distinguished from residents of "the Atlantic coast." His rhetoric was the decisive force giving him the Presidential nomination over the rather colorless Bland, who had been the front-runner when the convention opened. During his vigorous campaign Bryan stressed silver coinage to the neglect of the broad reform character of the Democratic platform. William McKinley won 271 electoral votes to 176; his margin in popular

---

William Jennings Bryan, *The First Battle: A Story of the Campaign of 1896* (Chicago: W. B. Conkey Company, 1896), pp. 199–206.

votes was 7,098,474 to 6,379,830. Because of his strong lead in the South and Rocky Mountain region, Bryan carried 1,551 counties in the nation to 1,163 for McKinley. But in the eight states east of the Mississippi River which cast half of the total national vote (New York, New Jersey, Pennsylvania, Ohio, Indiana, Illinois, Michigan, and Wisconsin), McKinley carried 431 counties to 149. Bryan did not carry a single county in New England, whereas in 1892 the Democratic nominee had won six of the 67.

Mr. Chairman and Gentlemen of the Convention: I would be presumptuous, indeed, to present myself against the distinguished gentlemen to whom you have listened if this were a mere measuring of abilities; but this is not a contest between persons. The humblest citizen in all the land, when clad in the armor of a righteous cause, is stronger than all the hosts of error. I come to speak to you in defense of a cause as holy as the cause of liberty—the cause of humanity.

When this debate is concluded, a motion will be made to lay upon the table the resolution offered in commendation of the administration, and also the resolution offered in condemnation of the administration. We object to bringing this question down to the level of persons. The individual is but an atom; he is born, he acts, he dies; but principles are eternal; and this has been a contest over a principle.

Never before in the history of this country has there been witnessed such a contest as that through which we have just passed. Never before in the history of American politics has a great issue been fought out as this issue has been, by the voters of a great party. On the fourth of March, 1895, a few Democrats, most of them members of Congress, issued an address to the Democrats of the nation, asserting that the money question was the paramount issue of the hour; declaring that a majority of the Democratic party had the right to control the action of the party on this paramount issue; and concluding with the request that the believers in the free coinage of silver in the Democratic party should organize, take charge of, and control the policy of the Democratic party. Three months later, at Memphis, an organization was perfected, and the silver Democrats went forth openly and courageously proclaiming their belief, and declaring that, if successful, they would crystallize into a platform the declaration which they had made. Then began the conflict. With a zeal approaching the zeal which inspired the crusaders who followed Peter the Hermit, our silver Democrats went forth from victory unto victory until they are now assembled, not to discuss, not to debate, but to enter up the judgment already rendered by the plain people of this country. In this contest brother has been arrayed against brother, father against son. The warmest ties of love, acquaintance and association have been disregarded; old leaders have been cast aside when they have refused to give expression to the sentiments of those whom they would lead, and new leaders have sprung up to give direction to this cause of truth. Thus has the contest been waged, and we have assembled here under as binding and solemn instructions as were ever imposed upon representatives of the people.

We do not come as individuals. As individuals we might have been glad to compliment the gentleman from New York (Senator Hill), but we know that the people for whom we speak would never be willing to put him in a position where he could thwart the will of the Democratic party. I say it was not a question of persons; it was a question of principle, and it is not with gladness, my friends, that we find ourselves brought into conflict with those who are now arrayed on the other side.

The gentleman who preceded me (ex–Governor Russell) spoke of the State of Massachusetts; let me assure him that not one present in all this convention entertains the least hostility to the people of the State of Massachusetts, but we stand here representing people who are the equals, before the law, of the greatest citizens in the State of Massachusetts. When you (turning to the gold delegates) come before us and tell us that we are about to disturb your business interests, we reply that you have disturbed our business interests by your course.

We say to you that you have made the definition of a business man too limited in its application. The man who is employed for wages is as much a business man as his employer; the attorney in a country town is as much a business man as the corporation counsel in a great metropolis; the merchant at the cross-roads store is as much a business man as the merchant of New York; the farmer who goes forth in the morning and toils all day—who begins in the spring and toils all summer—and who by the application of brain and muscle to the natural resources of the country creates wealth, is as much a business man as the man who goes upon the board of trade and bets upon the price of grain; the miners who go down a thousand feet into the earth, or climb two thousand feet upon the cliffs, and bring forth from their hiding places the precious metals to be poured into the channels of trade are as much business men as the few financial magnates who, in a back room, corner the money of the world. We come to speak for this broader class of business men.

Ah, my friends, we say not one word against those who live upon the Atlantic coast, but the hardy pioneers who have braved all the dangers of the wilderness, who have made the desert to blossom as the rose—the pioneers away out there (pointing to the West), who rear their children near to Nature's heart, where they can mingle their voices with the voices of the birds—out there where they have erected school-houses for the education of their young, churches where they praise their Creator, and cemeteries where rest the ashes of their dead—these people, we say, are as deserving of the consideration of our party as any people in this country. It is for these that we speak. We do not come as aggressors. Our war is not a war of conquest; we are fighting in the defense of our homes, our families, and posterity. We have petitioned, and our petitions have been scorned; we have entreated, and our entreaties have been disregarded; we have begged, and they have mocked when our calamity came. We beg no longer; we entreat no more; we petition no more. We defy them.

The gentleman from Wisconsin has said that he fears a Robespierre. My friends, in this land of the free you need not fear that a tyrant will spring up from among the people. What we need is an Andrew Jackson to stand, as Jackson stood, against the encroachments of organized wealth.

They tell us that this platform was made to catch votes. We reply to them that changing conditions make new issues; that the principles upon which Democracy rests are as everlasting as the hills, but that they must be applied to new conditions as they arise. Conditions have arisen, and we are here to meet those conditions. They tell us that the income tax ought not to be brought in here; that it is a new idea. They criticise us for our criticism of the Supreme Court of the United States. My friends, we have not criticised; we have simply called attention to what you already know. If you want criticisms, read the dissenting opinions of the court. There you will find criticisms. They say that we passed an unconstitutional law; we deny it. The income tax law was not unconstitutional when it was passed; it was not unconstitutional when it went before the Supreme Court for the first time; it did not become unconstitutional until one of the judges changed his mind, and we cannot be expected to know when a judge will change his mind. The income tax is just. It simply intends to put the burdens of government justly upon the backs of the people. I am in favor of an income tax. When I find a man who is not willing to bear his share of the burdens of the government which protects him, I find a man who is unworthy to enjoy the blessings of a government like ours.

They say that we are opposing national bank currency; it is

true. If you will read what Thomas Benton said, you will find he said that, in searching history, he could find but one parallel to Andrew Jackson; that was Cicero, who destroyed the conspiracy of Cataline and saved Rome. Benton said that Cicero only did for Rome what Jackson did for us when he destroyed the bank conspiracy and saved America. We say in our platform that we believe that the right to coin and issue money is a function of government. We believe it. We believe that it is a part of sovereignty, and can no more with safety be delegated to private individuals than we could afford to delegate to private individuals the power to make penal statutes or levy taxes. Mr. Jefferson, who was once regarded as good Democratic authority, seems to have differed in opinion from the gentleman who has addressed us on the part of the minority. Those who are opposed to this proposition tell us that the issue of paper money is a function of the bank, and that the Government ought to go out of the banking business. I stand with Jefferson rather than with them, and tell them, as he did, that the issue of money is a function of government, and that the banks ought to go out of the governing business.

They complain about the plank which declares against life tenure in office. They have tried to strain it to mean that which it does not mean. What we oppose by that plank is the life tenure which is being built up in Washington, and which excludes from participation in official benefits the humbler members of society.

Let me call your attention to two or three important things. The gentleman from New York says that he will propose an amendment to the platform providing that the proposed change in our monetary system shall not affect contracts already made. Let me remind you that there is no intention of affecting those contracts which according to present laws are made payable in gold; but if he means to say that we cannot change our monetary system without protecting those who have loaned money before the change was made, I desire to ask him where, in law or in morals, he can find justification for not protecting the debtors when the act of 1873 was passed, if he now insists that we must protect the creditors.

He says he will also propose an amendment which will provide for the suspension of free coinage if we fail to maintain the parity within a year. We reply that when we advocate a policy which we believe will be successful, we are not compelled to raise a doubt as to our own sincerity by suggesting what we shall do if we fail. I ask him, if he would apply his logic to us, why he does not apply it to himself. He says he wants this country to try to secure an international agreement. Why does he not tell us what he is going to do if he fails to secure an international agreement? There is more reason for him to do that than there is for us to provide against the failure to maintain the parity. Our opponents have tried for twenty years to secure an international agreement, and those are waiting for it most patiently who do not want it at all.

And now, my friends, let me come to the paramount issue. If they ask us why it is that we say more on the money question than we say upon the tariff question, I reply that, if protection has slain its thousands, the gold standard has slain its tens of thousands. If they ask us why we do not employ in our platform all the things that we believe in, we reply that when we have restored the money of the Constitution all other necessary reforms will be possible; but that until this is done there is no other reform that can be accomplished.

Why is it that within three months such a change has come over the country? Three months ago, when it was confidently asserted that those who believe in the gold standard would frame our platform and nominate our candidates, even the advocates of the gold standard did not think that we could elect a president. And they had good reason for their doubt, because there is scarcely a State here today asking for the gold standard which is not in the absolute control of the Republican party. But note the change. Mr. McKinley was nominated at St. Louis upon a platform which declared for the maintenance of the gold standard until it can be changed into bimetallism by international agreement. Mr. McKinley was the most popular man among the Republicans, and three months ago everybody in the Republican party prophesied his election. How is today? Why, the man who was once pleased to think that he looked like Napoleon—that man shudders today when he remembers that he was nominated on the anniversary of the battle of Waterloo. Not only that, but as he listens he can hear with ever–increasing distinctness the sound of the waves as they beat upon the lonely shores of St. Helena.

Why this change? Ah, my friends, is not the reason for the change evident to any one who will look at the matter? No private character, however pure, no personal popularity, however great, can protect from the avenging wrath of an indignant people a man who will declare that he is in favor of fastening the gold standard upon this country, or who is willing to surrender the right of self-government and place the legislative control of our affairs in the hands of foreign potentates and powers.

We go forth confident that we shall win. Why? Because upon the paramount issue of this campaign there is not a spot of ground upon which the enemy will dare to challenge battle. If they tell us that the gold standard is a good thing, we shall point to their platform and tell them that their platform pledges the party to get rid of the gold standard and substitute bimetallism. If the gold standard is a good thing, why try to get rid of it? I call your attention to the fact that some of the very people who are in this convention today and who tell us that we ought to declare in favor of international bimetallism— thereby declaring that the gold standard is wrong and that the principle of bimetallism is better—these very people four months ago were open and avowed advocates of the gold standard, and were then telling us that we could not legislate two metals together, even with the aid of all the world. If the gold standard is a good thing, we ought to declare in favor of its retention and not in favor of abandoning it; and if the gold standard is a bad thing why should we wait until other nations are willing to help us to let go? Here is the line of battle, and we care not upon which issue they force the fight; we are prepared to meet them on either issue or on both. If they tell us that the gold standard is the standard of civilization, we reply to them that this, the most enlightened of all the nations of the earth, has never declared for a gold standard and that both the great parties this year are declaring against it. If the gold standard is the standard of civilization, why, my friends, should we not have it? If they come to meet us on that issue we can present the history of our nation. More than that; we can tell them that they will search the pages of history in vain to find a single instance where the common people of any land have ever declared themselves in favor of the gold standard. They can find where the holders of fixed investments have declared for a gold standard, but not where the masses have.

Mr. Carlisle said in 1878 that this was a struggle between "the idle holders of idle capital" and "the struggling masses, who produce the wealth and pay the taxes of the country;" and, my friends, the question we are to decide is: Upon which side will the Democratic party fight; upon the side of "the idle holders of idle capital" or upon the side of "the struggling masses?" That is the question which the party must answer first, and then it must be answered by each individual hereafter. The sympathies of the Democratic party, as shown by the platform, are on the side of the struggling masses who have ever been the foundation of the Democratic party. There are two ideas of government. There are those who believe that, if you will only legislate to make the well-to-do prosperous, their prosperity will leak through on those below. The Democratic idea, however, has been that if you legislate to make the masses prosperous, their prosperity will find its way up through every class which rests upon them.

You come to us and tell us that the great cities are in favor of the gold standard; we reply that the great cities rest upon our broad and fertile prairies. Burn down your cities and leave our farms, and your cities will spring up again as if by magic; but destroy our farms and the grass will grow in the streets of every city in the country.

My friends, we declare that this nation is able to legislate for its own people on every question, without waiting for the aid or consent of any other nation on earth; and upon that issue we expect to carry every State in the Union. I shall not slander the inhabitants of the fair State of Massachusetts nor the inhabitants of the State of New York by saying that, when they are confronted with the proposition, they will declare that this nation is not able to attend to its own business. It is the issue of 1776 over again. Our ancestors, when but three millions in number, had the courage to declare their political independence of every other nation; shall we, their descendants, when we have grown to seventy millions, declare that we are less independent than our forefathers? No, my friends, that will never be the verdict of our people. Therefore, we care not upon what lines the battle is fought. If they say bimetallism is good, but that we cannot have it until other nations help us, we reply that, instead of having a gold standard because England has, we will restore bimetallism, and then let England have bimetallism because the United States has it. If they dare to come out in the open field and defend the gold standard as a good thing, we will fight them to the uttermost. Having behind us the producing masses of this nation and the world, supported by the commercial interests, the laboring interests, and the toilers everywhere, we will answer their demand for a gold standard by saying to them: You shall not press down upon the brow of labor this crown of thorns, you shall not crucify mankind upon a cross of gold.

5. Homage to Women (Especially Mothers)

While Bryan in 1896 was fighting in defense of the toiling masses, he also played troubador to those who labored and brought forth. The following tribute to motherhood was fittingly made at Fredericksburg in Virginia, a state especially victimized by the chivalric myth. Bryan's softmindedness about women brought him in 1919 to a declaration that female votes would cure the worst problems of the age. But less than a decade earlier he had been cool to this crusade, by the evidence of a letter written to him by Senator Atlee Pomerene. Admitting that he could not be sure of Bryan's "exact words," Pomerene sent a version of a conversation in his native Ohio in 1909 with Bryan as the two men were going from Canton to Columbus. "When I asked what the objection was to woman suffrage," the Senator recalled, "your reply in substance was that you looked upon suffrage as a duty and not a privilege, and that while there were many women who desired the vote, there were more who either did not desire the vote, or were indifferent on the subject, and you did not believe it right for those who favored suffrage to impose this duty upon those who did not want it, or who were indifferent to it."

A. MOTHERHOOD, 1896

Fredericksburg is not a large city and yet it is rich in incidents of great historic value. Here the women of America have reared a monument to Mary the mother of Washington. I am glad to stand on this spot; I am glad to feel the influences

---

Richard L. Metcalf, editor, *The Real Bryan* (Des Moines: Personal Help Publishing Co., 1908), pp. 41–42.

which surround her grave. In a campaign, especially in a campaign like this, there is much of bitterness and sometimes of abuse spoken against the candidates for public office, but, my friends, there is one character, the mother—a candidate for the affections of all mankind—against whom no true man has ever uttered a word of abuse. There is one name, mother, which is never found upon the tongue of the slanderer—in her presence all criticism is silenced. The painter has, with his brush, transferred the landscape to the canvas with such fidelity that the trees and grasses seem almost real; he has even made the face of a maiden seem instinct with life, but there is one picture so beautiful that no painter has ever been able to perfectly reproduce it, and that is the picture of the mother holding in her arms her babe. Within the shadow of this monument, reared to the memory of her who in her love and loyalty represents the mother of each one of us, I bow in humble reverence to motherhood.

B. WOMAN SUFFRAGE

The Suffrage amendment is now before the states for ratification. Several governors have called special sessions and others will. No excuse for delay. EVERY STATE FAVORABLE TO SUFFRAGE SHOULD ACT AT ONCE so that the fight can be concentrated on the states where it is necessary.

Woman's conscience is needed in politics as never before; it is needed here and in other nations which will be influenced by our example. Woman's conscience is needed to make complete and permanent the nation's victory over the saloon; it is needed to deal successfully with the social evil—the next great moral cause; and it is needed to abolish war.

Woman is coming into her own, and her entrance into pol-

The Commoner, XIX (June 1919), 1.

itics will hasten the triumph of every righteous cause. Welcome, woman—"Last to leave the Cross; first to reach the tomb." She will guard the home with her ballot and, by making the young secure, strengthen the next generation for its problems.

6. "Foreign Influence in American Politics"

An estimated $4 billion in American securities was held in 1893 by British investors. Continued adherence to the gold standard by the United States was an economic question for them, as free coinage of silver would unquestionably lower the value in British money of American investments. For the United States too, economic aspects were important, because a steady in-flow of British capital was widely thought to be essential to American progress. But especially among respectable Easterners, less tangible forces were working. Anxious to be seen as proper by the upper classes in England and on the Continent, these people were feverishly marrying their daughters to European nobility, neglecting American novels in favor of British ones, and buying Old Masters in Italy. They also feared that partial repudiation of American debts by means of free silver would bring onto their heads from Europe the stigma of being thieves and pirates. Many Americans, however, entertained just the opposite attitudes. Appeals to fear of and scorn for England were common among Democratic politicians, particularly when they wanted to win Irish votes in Eastern cities or to play upon the provincialisms of Midwesterners. Bryan knew the game. His Cross of Gold speech (see Document 4) accused the opposition of wishing to "place the legislative control of our affairs in the hands of foreign potentates and powers." Three years later he developed the line at length. His sly alarms over foreign investors in our corporations can only be called demagogic, for he did not even hint at his remedy for the putatively sinister situation.

"Foreign Influence in American Politics," *The Arena*, XIX (April 1898), 433–438.

The *Review of Reviews,* which cannot be accused of silver fanaticism, in its February number contained the following comment on the Chinese loan:

> The matter has peculiar interest from the fact that the arrangement is supposed to have been worked out chiefly by the great bankers, who are neither English, French, nor German in their real allegiance, but must be regarded as a law unto themselves and a separate power, gradually but steadily strengthening their grip upon the destiny of nations.
>
> It was this huge, mysterious money power that enabled the continental governments, led by Russia, to circumvent England and place the Chinese loan at the close of the Japanese war. And now it is the same hidden but potent force that declines to allow the continental powers to make the present Chinese loan, but ordains that England shall make it. The issues of the recent Turco–Greek war were decided, unquestionably, by this coalition of European bankers, who improved the opportunity to gain a better hold upon the revenues both of Turkey and of Greece, and cleared up millions of profit out of the hideous conflict between Moslem and Christian. Their influence has slaughtered the Armenians and wrought the discomfiture of Greece. The hand of this coalition of European bankers has been constantly felt in the affairs of Spain and Cuba. Their method is to secure control of great issues of public securities at heavy discounts, bearing high rates of interest, and then so to manipulate diplomacy and the course of international politics as ultimately to make certain the payment in full of interest and principal. It is not pleasant to remember that these foreign gentlemen, with their finger in every diplomatic and international affair, were invited to come to the rescue of the United States Treasury under the last administration.

While the people of the United States have not been blind to the foreign interference which resulted in the dismemberment of Poland, the subjugation of India and Egypt, and the unsuccessful attempt to overthrow the Mexican republic; while they cannot be ignorant of the manner in which foreign influence is affecting Turkey, Greece, and China, and even now propping up the efforts of Spain to continue monarchical institutions in Cuba; they have reason to be indignant at the extent to which foreign influence has interfered in American politics during recent years, and still more reason to be alarmed at the attempt now being made to give foreign financiers absolute control over the financial policy of this nation.

When President Cleveland entered into a contract with the Rothschild–Morgan syndicate, he submitted to Congress a proposition made by this syndicate, which involved a radical change in the policy of the government. The syndicate virtually offered to the United States a sum equal to $16,000,000 (calculated in interest upon the bonds under consideration) to depart from its established custom of issuing coin bonds and to inaugurate an entirely new custom, namely, the issuing of bonds specifically payable in gold. The proposition was supported in the House by the administration Democrats under the leadership of Mr. Wilson and by most of the prominent Republicans under the leadership of Mr. Reed.

If that offer had been accepted it would have been immediately followed by a proposition to make all government bonds payable in gold. In fact, the Lodge amendment to the Teller resolution contemplated this very thing, and there is no doubt that such a proposition would have received the support of a majority of the Republicans in the House, had it been submitted to that body. This amendment did receive the support of a majority of the Republicans of the Senate.

It is difficult to calculate the far–reaching influence of such a change as that proposed by the Rothschild–Morgan syndicate, indorsed by Mr. Cleveland, and later fathered by Senator Lodge. It would have committed the government to payment in a metal the production of which is largely controlled by the English government, and would have been a voluntary abandonment of the nation's contract right to pay in a metal of which this country is one of the largest producers.

On the 17th day of March, 1896, the English House of Commons unanimously adopted the following resolution:

> That this House is of opinion that instability of the relative value of gold and silver since the action of the Latin Union in 1873 has proved injurious to the best interests of this country, and urges upon the government the advisability of doing all in their power to secure by international agreement a stable monetary par of exchange between gold and silver.

Whether the House of Commons, in passing this resolution, contemplated its effect upon American politics, is not known; nor can it be known whether the resolution above quoted inspired the pledge made by the Republican convention to promote international bimetallism; but it is certain that the action of England was used during the campaign to encourage international bimetallists to hope for the reëstablishment of the double standard through the aid of European nations. The election was sufficiently close to justify the assertion that without the promise to promote international bimetallism the Republican party could not have secured a majority of the electoral votes. It is certain, from a speech recently delivered by Mr. Wolcott in the United States Senate, that the resolution above referred to, together with the speeches delivered by Mr. Arthur J. Balfour and Sir Michael Hicks–Beach in support of the resolution, led the commission to expect concessions, and largely guided our commissioners in the proposals made by them to the English government.

Another evidence of the dominant force of foreign influence is to be found in the fact that the refusal of England to give assistance is accepted by the leading advocates of the gold standard as proof positive that international bimetallism is at present impossible. Upon this failure the pronounced monometallists predicate their demand for the permanent maintenance of the gold standard.

The English House of Commons by a brief resolution leads international bimetallists in the United States to hope for relief from the gold standard, and then the English government, by refusing to coöperate with the United States and France, disappoints the hopes aroused, and plunges our international bimetallists into the depths of despair. Was confiding innocence ever so unkindly treated?

The Republican platform of 1896, while so skilfully drawn as to satisfy the most extreme monometallist and at the same time delight the international bimetallist with the phantom of foreign aid, was, in fact, nothing more or less than an acknowledgment of subserviency to European dictation. The restoration of bimetallism in the United States was by that platform made expressly dependent upon the will of foreign nations, and the duration of the gold standard in the United States was left entirely to the decision of foreign nations. The platform pledged the party to oppose "the free coinage of silver, *except by international agreement with the leading commercial nations of the world*" (which the party promised to promote); and then concluded, "*until such agreement can be obtained the existing gold standard must be preserved.*"

So far as I have been able to learn, this is the first American platform to declare it necessary for the United States to have financial policy identical with that of other nations.

It was said that the triumph of that platform would put an end to any further discussion of the money question and revive prosperity by restoring confidence. It seems, however, that Argonaut Gage continues his search for the golden fleece and is advising Congress that something must be done "to commit the country more thoroughly to the gold standard," in order to "strengthen the credit of the United States both at home and *abroad.*" The Secretary is still endeavoring to conciliate foreign financiers.

Within the last few months several American citizens have announced, upon their return from Europe, that confidence in our securities cannot be fully restored until we retire all government paper and substitute National–Bank notes.

Thus it will be seen that European opinion is continually

at work shaping the conduct of an influential portion of our country. When it is remembered that the failure of our commission to secure international bimetallism was largely due to a protest signed by the London bankers, it becomes evident that the financial policy of seventy millions of American citizens is being determined by a handful of persons who owe no allegiance to our government and have no sympathy with our institutions. If this domination is due to the fact that the American people do not realize the manner in which their political independence is slipping from them, the danger will be overcome by the spread of intelligence; but if it is due to actual inability upon the part of the American people to control their own affairs, then, instead of being a nation, we are but a province.

Foreign influence has not only contaminated those whose ears are habitually turned to receive instructions from across the ocean, but it has been directed toward the fears rather than toward the reason or conscience of the people. When foreign financiers have found themselves unable to defend an appreciating dollar; when they have recognized their inability to prove the gold standard a wise standard, they have threatened to visit a panic upon the United States if our people are guilty of the presumptuous sin of independence. This threat, operating first upon the money magnates of the metropolis, then upon the smaller bankers throughout the nation, then upon merchants and manufacturers, and, finally, upon the army of wage–earners, has been a potent influence in our elections. Will anyone defend foreign influence thus exerted upon the destinies of our republic? Most of these financiers live under governments quite unlike ours. With us, governments derive their just powers from the consent of the governed; in Europe most of the people still hold to the doctrine that supreme power descends from the throne, and that the throne should descend from parent to child. The difference between these two ideas of government is so radical that those who believe in the former idea cannot safely entrust political questions to persons who hold to the latter.

No European nation boasts of its willingness to allow its policy upon financial questions, or, indeed, upon any other questions, to be determined by the people of the United States; any party that would advocate such a doctrine in any European nation would be held up to public scorn and contempt; and yet there are many eminently respectable citizens in the United States who assert the helplessness of the American people to restore bimetallism, however much they may desire it, without an international agreement.

But the European money–changer is not the only foreigner who is exerting an influence upon American politics. Foreigners hold a large amount of stock in our railroads and other corporations. A share of stock held abroad is equal in voting power to a share of stock held in this country. When a majority of the stock is owned abroad the foreign holders are able to choose the directors and, through the directors, to select the officials and other employees of the corporation. If a president of a railroad or other corporation owes his elevation to foreign stockholders, is he not apt to be influenced by them? And, if influenced by them, is he not likely to transmit that influence to his subordinates? May he not become so engrossed in his work as to overlook the injury which he is doing to his country?

If foreigners continue to invest in American securities, and their interest in our politics grows with their investments, is it not possible that a time may come, if it has not already arrived, when foreign influence may be sufficient to decide elections, and ultimately to mould our institutions to conform to European ideals?

Washington, in his farewell address, said: "Against the insidious wiles of foreign influence (I conjure you to believe me, fellow citizens) the jealousy of a free people ought to be constantly awake; since history and experience prove that foreign influence is one of the most baneful foes of republican government."

Has the name of Washington lost its charm? Was he a demagogue, seeking to play upon the passions and prejudices of his countrymen? Or has his advice, wise when it was spoken, become folly now? Has the struggle for the almighty dollar become so intense as to obscure the lofty purpose of our forefathers to establish upon the Western Hemisphere a government "dedicated to the doctrine that all men are created equal"?

7. Imperialism

Although by the Treaty of Paris, which terminated the Spanish-American War, Spain ceded the Philippines to the United States, William Jennings Bryan urged ratification by the Senate. In justifying the recommendation he stood upon his unfailing shibboleth; he wanted to see the islands freed "not by a minority of the Senate, but by a majority of the people." The treaty was approved by one vote more than the necessary two thirds, 57 to 27, on February 6, 1899. Then the Senate rejected a resolution for Philippine independence only by the casting vote of the Vice-President.

Eighteen months later, Bryan was notified by the Democratic National Committee that he had again been nominated for President. He replied with the following speech at Indianapolis on August 18, 1900. Bryan's description of the Boer War as involving the stalwart republican Boers fighting for civil liberty against the tyranny of monarchical Britain might well provoke us today to wry or despairing shrugs, but at the time similar views were being expounded through the nation by such liberal Democrats as John Peter Altgeld and Clarence Darrow. Other passages in Bryan's speech can profitably be compared with parts of Documents 8, 16, 24, and 27 in this volume. Even though Bryan stated his hope that the campaign would pose a "clean-cut issue" between imperialism and the right of self-government, it did not, and the outcome was not a mandate for colonialism. But with a plurality of 861,000 votes, the Republicans scored an even more decisive victory than in 1896.

"Mr. Bryan's Address on Imperialism," *The Outlook*, LXV (August 18, 1900), 938–940.

I was among the number of those who believed it better to ratify the treaty and end the war, release the volunteers, remove the excuse for war expenditures, and then give to the Filipinos the independence which might be forced from Spain by a new treaty. In view of the criticism which my action aroused in some quarters I take this occasion to restate the reasons given at that time. I thought it safer to trust the American people to give independence to the Filipinos than to trust the accomplishment of that purpose to diplomacy with an unfriendly nation. Lincoln embodied an argument in the question, when he asked, "Can aliens make treaties easier than friends can make laws?" I believe that we are now in a better position to wage a successful contest against Imperialism than we would have been had the treaty been rejected. With the treaty ratified, a clean-cut issue is presented between a government by consent and a government by force, and Imperialists must bear the responsibility for all that happens until the question is settled. If the treaty had been rejected, the opponents of Imperialism would have been held responsible for any international complications which might have arisen before the ratification of another treaty.

Even now we are beginning to see the paralyzing influence of Imperialism. Heretofore this Nation has been prompt to express its sympathy with those who were fighting for civil liberty. While our sphere of activity has been limited to the western hemisphere, our sympathies have not been bounded by the seas. We have felt it due to ourselves and to the world, as well as to those who were struggling for the right to govern themselves, to proclaim the interest which our people have from the date of their own independence felt in every contest between human rights and arbitrary power. Three-quarters of a century ago, when our Nation was small, the struggles of Greece aroused our people, and Webster and Clay gave eloquent expression to the universal desire for Grecian independence. In 1896 all parties manifested a lively interest in

the success of the Cubans; but now, when a war is in progress
in South Africa which must result in the extension of the
monarchical idea or in the triumph of a republic, the advocates
of Imperialism in this country dare not say a word in behalf
of the Boers. Sympathy for the Boers does not arise from any
unfriendliness toward England; the American people are not
unfriendly toward the people of any nation. This sympathy is
due to the fact that, as stated in our platform, we believe in the
principle of self–government, and reject, as did our forefathers,
the claims of monarchy. If this Nation surrenders its belief in
the universal application of the principles set forth in the Declaration of Independence, it will lose the prestige and influence
which it has enjoyed among the nations as an exponent of
popular government.

Our opponents, conscious of the weakness of their cause,
seek to confuse Imperialism with expansion, and have even
dared to claim Jefferson as a supporter of their policy. Jefferson spoke so freely and used language with such precision
that no one can be ignorant of his views. On one occasion he
declared: "If there be one principle more deeply rooted than
any other in the mind of every American, it is that we should
have nothing to do with conquest." And again he said: "Conquest is not in our principles; it is inconsistent with our government."

The forcible annexation of territory to be governed by arbitrary power differs as much from the acquisition of territory to
be built up into States as a monarchy differs from a democracy.
The Democratic party does not oppose expansion when expansion enlarges the area of the Republic and incorporates
land which can be settled by American citizens, or adds to our
population people who are willing to become citizens, and are
capable of discharging their duties as such. The acquisition of
the Louisiana territory, Florida, Texas, and other tracts which
have been secured from time to time, enlarged the Republic,
and the Constitution followed the flag into the new territory.

It is now proposed to seize upon distant territory already more densely populated than our own country, and to force upon the people a government for which there is no warrant in our Constitution or our laws. Even the argument that this earth belongs to those who desire to cultivate it and have the physical power to acquire it cannot be invoked to justify the appropriation of the Philippine Islands by the United States. If the islands were uninhabited, American citizens would not be willing to go there and till the soil. The white race will not live so near the equator. Other nations have tried to colonize in the same latitude. The Netherlands have controlled Java for three hundred years, and yet to–day there are less than 60,000 people of European birth scattered among 25,000,000 natives. After a century and a half of English domination in India, less than one–twentieth of one per cent. of the people of India are of English birth, and it requires an army of 70,000 British soldiers to take care of the tax–collectors. Spain has asserted title to the Philippine Islands for three centuries, and yet, when our fleet entered Manila Bay, there were less than 10,000 Spaniards residing in the Philippines.

A colonial policy means that we shall send to the Philippines a few traders, a few task–masters, and a few office-holders, and an army large enough to support the authority of a small fraction of the people, while they rule the natives.

Some say that it is our duty to hold the Philippine Islands. But duty is not an argument; it is a conclusion. To ascertain what our duty is in any emergency, we must supply well-settled and generally accepted principles. It is our duty to avoid stealing, no matter whether the thing to be stolen is of great or little value. It is our duty to avoid killing a human being, no matter where the human being lives or to what race or class he belongs. Every one recognizes the obligation imposed upon individuals to observe both the human and moral law, but as some deny the application of those laws to nations, it may not be out of place to quote the opinion of others.

Jefferson, than whom there is no higher political authority, said: "I know of but one code of morality for men, whether acting singly or collectively."

Franklin, whose learning, wisdom, and virtue are a part of the priceless legacy bequeathed to us from the Revolutionary days, expressed the same idea in even stronger language, when he said: "Justice is as strictly due between neighbor nations as between neighbor citizens. A highwayman is as much a robber when he plunders in a gang as when singly; and the nation that makes an unjust war is only a great gang."

Men may dare to do in crowds what they would not dare to do as individuals, but the moral character of an act is not determined by the number of those who join in it. Force can defend a right, but force has never yet created a right. If it was true, as declared in the resolutions of intervention, that the Cubans "are and of right ought to be free and independent" (language taken from the Declaration of Independence), it is equally true that the Filipinos "are and of right ought to be free and independent." The right of the Cubans to freedom was not based upon their proximity to the United States, nor upon the race or races to which they belong. Congress, by a practically unanimous vote, declared that the principles enunciated at Philadelphia in 1776 were still alive and applicable to the Cubans.

If we have an imperial policy, we must have a large standing army, as its natural and necessary complement. The spirit which will justify the forcible annexation of the Philippine Islands will justify the seizure of other islands and the domination of other peoples, and with wars of conquest we can expect a certain, if not rapid, growth of our military establishment. That a large permanent increase in our regular army is intended by the Republican leaders is not a mere matter of conjecture, but a matter of fact. In his message of December 15, 1898, the President asked for authority to increase the standing army to 100,000. In 1896 the army contained about 25,000 men.

Within two years the President asked for four times that many, and a Republican House of Representatives complied with the request after the Spanish treaty had been signed and no country was at war against the United States in any part of the world. If such an army is demanded when an imperial policy is contemplated but not openly avowed, what may be expected if the people encourage the Republican party by indorsing its policy at the polls? A large standing army is not only a pecuniary burden to the people, and, if accompanied by compulsory service, a constant source of irritation, but it is ever a menace to a republican form of government. The army is the personification of force, and militarism will inevitably change the ideals of the people, and turn the thoughts of our young men from the arts of peace to the science of war. The government which relies for its defense upon its citizens is more likely to be just than one which has at call a large body of professional soldiers. A small standing army and a well–equipped and well–disciplined State militia are sufficient in ordinary times; and in an emergency the Nation should in the future, as in the past, place its dependence upon the volunteers who come from all occupations at their country's call, and return to productive labor when their services are no longer required—men who fight when the country needs fighters, and work when the country needs workers.

The Republican platform assumes that the Philippine Islands will be retained under American sovereignty, and we have a right to demand of the Republican leaders a discussion of the future status of the Filipino. Is he to be a citizen or a subject? Are we to bring into the body politic eight or ten million Asiatics, so different from us in race and history that amalgamation is impossible? Are they to share with us in making the laws and shaping the destiny of this Nation? No Republican of prominence has been bold enough to advocate such a proposition. The McEnery resolution, adopted by the Senate immediately after the ratification of the treaty, expressly negatives this idea. The Democratic platform describes the situation when it says that the Filipinos cannot be citizens without endangering our civilizaion. Who will dispute it? And what is the alternative? If the Filipino is not to be a citizen, shall we make him a subject?

On that question the Democratic platform speaks with emphasis. It declares that the Filipino cannot be a subject without endangering our form of government. A republic can have no subjects. A subject is possible only in a government resting upon force; he is unknown in a government deriving its just powers from the consent of the governed. The Republican platform says that "the largest measure of a self-government consistent with their welfare and our duties shall be secured to them [the Filipinos] by law." This is a strange doctrine for a government which owes its very existence to the men who offered their lives as a protest against government without consent and taxation without representation. In what respect does the position of the Republican party differ from the position taken by the English Government in 1776? Did not the English Government promise a good government to the colonists? What king ever promised a bad government to his people? Did not the English Government promise that the colonists should have the largest measure of self-government consistent with their welfare and English duties? Did not the Spanish Government promise to give to the Cubans the largest measure of self-government consistent with their welfare and Spanish duties? The whole difference between a monarchy and a republic may be summed up in one sentence. In a monarchy the king gives to the people what he believes to be a good government; in a republic the people secure for themselves what they believe to be a good government. The Republican party has accepted the European idea and planted itself upon the ground taken by George III., and by every ruler who distrusts the capacity of the people for self-government or denies them a voice in their own affairs.

"Can we not govern colonies?" we are asked. The question is not what we can do, but what we ought to do. This Nation can do whatever it desires to do, but it must accept responsibility for what it does. If the Constitution stands in the way, the people can amend the Constitution. I repeat, the Nation can do whatever it desires to do, but it cannot avoid the natural and legitimate results of its own conduct. The young man, upon reaching his majority, can do what he pleases. He can disregard the teachings of his parents; he can trample upon all that he has been taught to consider sacred; he can disobey the laws of the State, the laws of society, and the laws of God. He can stamp failure upon his life, and make his very existence a curse to his fellowmen, and he can bring his father and mother in sorrow to the grave; but he cannot annul the sentence, "The wages of sin is death." And so with this Nation. It is of age, and it can do what it pleases; it can spurn the traditions of the past, it can repudiate the principles upon which the Nation rests; it can employ force instead of reason; it can substitute might for right; it can conquer weaker people; it can exploit their lands, appropriate their property, and kill their people; but it cannot repeal the moral law, or escape the punishment decreed for the violation of human rights.

For more than a century this Nation has been a world-power. For ten decades it has been the most potent influence in the world. Not only has it been a world-power, but it has done more to affect the politics of the human race than all the other nations of the world combined. Because our Declaration of Independence was promulgated, others have been promulgated; because the patriots of 1776 fought for liberty, others have fought for it; because our Constitution was adopted, other constitutions have been adopted. The growth of the principle of self-government, planted on American soil, has been the overshadowing political fact of the nineteenth century. It has made this Nation conspicuous among the nations, and given it a place in history such as no other nation has ever enjoyed.

Nothing has been able to check the onward march of this idea. I am not willing that this Nation shall cast aside the omnipotent weapon of truth to seize again the weapon of physical warfare. I would not exchange the glory of this Republic for the glory of all the empires that have risen and fallen since time began.

There is an easy, honest, honorable solution of the Philippine question. It is set forth in the Democratic platform, and it is submitted with confidence to the American people. This plan I unreservedly indorse. If elected, I shall convene Congress in extraordinary session as soon as I am inaugurated, and recommend an immediate declaration of the Nation's purpose, first, to establish a stable form of government in the Philippine Islands, just as we are now establishing a stable form of government in the island of Cuba; second, to give independence to the Filipinos, just as we have promised to give independence to the Cubans; third, to protect the Filipinos from outside interference while they work out their destiny, just as we have protected the republics of Central and South America, and are, by the Monroe Doctrine, pledged to protect Cuba. A European protectorate often results in the exploitation of the ward by the guardian. An American protectorate gives to the nation protected the advantage of our strength, without making it the victim of our greed. For three–quarters of a century the Monroe Doctrine has been a shield to neighboring republics, and yet it has imposed no pecuniary burden upon us. After the Filipinos had aided us in the war against Spain, we could not honorably turn them over to their former masters; we could not leave them to be the victims of the ambitious designs of the European nations; and since we do not desire to make them a part of us, or to hold them as subjects, we propose the only alternative, namely, to give them independence and guard them against molestation from without.

8. "The Race Problem"

Knowing that Bryan's father was from Virginia, and knowing Bryan's opinion that the award of American citizenship to Filipinos would endanger our civilization (see Document 7), we are still not adequately prepared for his views stated below. In the year 1898 a white mob in Phoenix, South Carolina, killed six Negroes during a reign of terror, while another mob massacred at least nine Negroes in Wilmington, North Carolina. In 1900 race riots occurred in cities as widely separated as Akron, New Orleans, and New York. From 1882 to 1907, more persons were lynched in the United States than were legally executed. Since Bryan declared that capital punishment was not justified if it was "a punishment for a crime already committed" (see Document 24), we might expect from him an all-out denunciation of vigilantes. However, when he came to confront the question, he applauded President Roosevelt for coupling a statement that lynching was a bad thing with a statement that rape was also a bad thing. Bryan even suggested that, no one's behavior should be judged when one is acting in an excited way. In considering Negro suffrage, as in considering votes for women (see Document 5), he seemingly thought it a "duty" rather than a "privilege"; it certainly was not a right.

On another page will be found a letter recently written by President Roosevelt to Governor Durbin on the subject of lynching. Forgetting for the present the failure of the president to enforce the law against the trust magnates and Governor

---

"The Race Problem," *The Commoner*, III (August 21, 1903), 1–2.

Durbin's refusal to deliver to Kentucky authorities a republican ex-governor charged with murder, let us consider the subject of mob law as it is related to the race question. The president is right in protesting against mob law—it cannot be defended. It is a reflection on the people if legal means of punishment are adequate and effective, and it is a reflection on the government if the people have reason to distrust its ability to enforce the law. All will agree with the president that punishment should not only be sure, but should be as swift as a due regard to the rights of the accused will permit. Whatever punishments are sanctioned by public opinion should be embodied in the law and in the case of crimes against women the laws should be such—even though a constitutional amendment were necessary to secure it—that the victim of the outrage will be protected from the humiliation of having to give testimony before a crowd of curious, but disinterested persons.

The president is also to be commended for having coupled a denunciation of rape with a condemnation of lynching. Too many cry out against the lawless punishment without saying anything about the horrible crime which arouses the anger of the people. If some of the enthusiasm that is spent passing resolutions denouncing mob law was employed in condemning the unspeakable beastiality that provokes summary punishment there would be fewer instances of mob law.

The fact that the president did not specifically mention southern lynchings shows that the lynchings and burnings in northern states have convinced him that race prejudice is as strong in Illinois, Indiana, Delaware, and Kansas as in Mississippi, Georgia, Alabama, or Texas.

It may be well in this connection to consider race prejudice for a moment in connection with mob law. That there is such a thing must be admitted. It is written on every page of history and is not likely to disappear soon. It must be remembered, too, that the negro has as much prejudice against the white man as the white man has against the negro, and if the negro was in a position to rule the white man there is no reason to doubt that the white man would have reason to complain. This was apparent in the carpet–bag days and is apparent today wherever it can find expression.

A sense of justice, however, restrains this prejudice and it is not often that either the white man or the negro says anything in the presence of the other that is calculated to offend. Color is not a matter of choice, neither can it be changed by will or by law. It is, therefore, as unkind to taunt a man with being black as it is unreasonable for a black man to be angered by such a taunt.

A man is to be praised or blamed according to the use he makes of his talents or opportunities, not by his inherited advantages. The fact that a negro is lynched by a mob because of an outrage upon a woman ought not to increase the race prejudice that exists. White men are lynched for the same crime. Neither must the white man's feelings toward the negro be judged when under great excitement. Man mad is an entirely different creature from man deliberate. Men in anger have killed fathers, wives, brothers, sons and friends—they have broken every tie of love and kinship.

Suffrage qualifications cannot be attributed entirely to race prejudice for suffrage qualifications are to be found in nearly all countries and have been employed in many of our own states. They have been employed by white men against members of the white race and by people of every color against people of their own color. Woman suffragists complain that women are disfranchised and such disfranchisement cannot be explained on the ground of race prejudice either, for husband and wife, mother and son, are not only of the same race, but are linked together by the strongest bonds known.

The suffrage amendments in the south, so much complained of by republican politicians, are not nearly so severe as the republican colonial policy in the Philippines.

First—In every southern state some of the negroes can vote

now, and all others can qualify themselves for suffrage; in the Philippines the inhabitants are permanently disqualified.

Second—The negroes in the south, even when they cannot vote, have the protection of federal and state constitutions; the Filipino has no constitutional protection whatever.

Third—The negroes in the south live under the laws that the white man makes for himself; the Filipino lives under laws that we make for him and would not live under ourselves.

While the brown man of the Orient is faring worse than the black man of the south, the republican leaders are stirring up race antagonism in this country in order to keep the colored vote solid for the republican party. Even the president has contributed more than his share to the agitation. When he has appointed a colored man to office he has done it with a flourish of trumpets and a brass band accompaniment that the world might know that the "door" was wide open. When a colored postmistress was objected to he refused to allow her to resign and closed the office—and did it allay race prejudice? No; it did more to excite race prejudice than any ten colored appointments that President McKinley made.

The Booker T. Washington dinner at the White House did more than the Indianola postoffice incident to excite race prejudice.

The president surely did not intend to inject the question of social equality into politics, for on that issue he could not carry a state in the Union; then why arouse the colored people to expect social equality or agitate the whites with the fear of it? It is a grievous mistake to turn the negro's thoughts from the substantial advantages of industrial, intellectual and moral progress to the unsubstantial promises of social recognition. The amalgamation of the races is not the solution of the race question, and that would be the logical result of social equality. In their natural right to life, liberty and the pursuit of happiness the white man and the black man are equal and these rights should be protected with jealous care. Educational advantages should be open to both races and both should be encouraged to secure all the mental discipline possible.

Whether the more advanced race should fix suffrage qualifications for the less advanced is a question to be determined by the facts in the case, but it is safe to say that on this subject the people of the north would be much like the people of the south if they were compelled to meet the same conditions.

As to the social equality there should be a frank and candid understanding. There is no difference on this subject between the white people of the north and the white people of the south. The color line is drawn by the republican families as distinctly as it is by democratic families, as distinctly by northern families as by southern families. There is more friendliness and helpfulness where this is recognized than where it is left in doubt and uncertainty.

The white race ought to recognize the rights of the black race and lend it every possible assistance. The whites of the south are taxing themselves to educate the children of darker skin, while republican politicians in the north are riding into office on black votes and, while they exclude the colored people from their social functions, are constantly trying to array the southern negro against the southern white man.

There is another aspect of the question. The promise of social equality—false as it is—encourages the educated negro to hope to get away from his race and thus the race loses the benefit that the more progressive negroes might bring to it. Instead of trying to bleach the face or to take the kink out of the hair let the colored man recognize that he is black by nature and set to work to show what one of his race can accomplish. No upright, intelligent and law–abiding colored man ever gets into trouble himself or involves his people in a race war. After the colored man has established a reputation for virtue, sobriety and good sense, let him devote himself to the building up of a society that will satisfy his needs. If he has daughters let him make them worthy of the best young men of his race; if he has sons, let him make them examples of industry and good habits. To deserve respect and not enjoy it is better than to enjoy respect without deserving it, but to deserve respect is the best and surest way to secure it.

A good character is more valuable and more permanent than a postoffice, and nothing will do more to kill race prejudice than the building up of character.

The white man needs to be reminded, as the president suggests, that lawlessness is dangerous and torture demoralizing to those who practice it, but the black man must also be cautioned not to judge the white man's life purpose by the passions of an hour and he should be warned not to allow the vices and lusts of the most abandoned of his race to provoke hostility between himself and the whites.

The race question is here and it will require the intelligence and the patriotism of the people north and south to settle it aright. It has too long been used for political advantage.

9. "Farming as an Occupation"

When a popular journal soon after 1900 ran a series on "Making a Choice of a Profession," it chose Bryan, as an expert on agriculture, to write an article. His essay asked rhetorically, "Given a young man with a thorough education, good habits, willingness to work, and a desire to make himself useful, where can he fare better than on a farm?" The answer was simple: In any city, but Bryan could not hear it. In general, townfolk had always enjoyed more economic opportunities than farmers, and in 1896 the cities had proved their political dominance over the countryside. Even in crude numerical terms, rural areas were being superseded during Bryan's lifetime; by 1920 most Americans lived in towns of 2,500 or more people. The family farm became steadily less viable as more and more farmers were displaced by machinery. But Bryan stood firm —the tag-end of the time-honored American tradition of agrarianism. In the words of the chief historian of that tradition, Henry Nash Smith: "The philosophy and the myth affirmed an admirable set of values, but they ceased very early to be useful in interpreting American society as a whole because they offered no intellectual apparatus for taking account of the industrial revolution. A system which revolved about a half-mystical conception of nature and held up as an ideal a rudimentary type of agriculture was powerless to confront issues arising from the advance of technology."

It is with exceeding pleasure that the following suggestions are presented in regard to the desirability of farming as a life-occupation.

"Farming as an Occupation," *Cosmopolitan*, XXXVI (January 1904), 369–371.

First—It is an independent way of living, compared with work in the city. The farmer can supply his table with meat, vegetables, bread, milk, butter and eggs, and he is less affected than the residents of the city by fluctuations in the price of these commodities. The clothing account, too, is less for those who live upon the farm than for those who live in town, so that it is much easier and much less embarrassing to practise economy. Not only in dress but in living, the farmer and his family avoid the rivalry that leads to extravagance, false pretense and the enervating vices.

Second—It requires less capital to begin work upon a farm than to enter any other sort of independent business, and one can usually obtain farm land on the shares, whereas for any mercantile pursuit it is necessary to pay rent, often in advance. If one has not the means to buy horses, and plows and other agricultural implements, he can usually find a small piece of ground near a town or city where he can raise vegetables, and thus make a start that will enable him to equip himself for larger farming.

Third—All the members of the family can assist in farming, and that, too, without hardship. The wife can, without sacrifice of dignity or a great amount of drudgery, look after the milk, make the butter and take care of the chickens. The girls, as they grow up, can assist the mother, and the boys, before and after school and during the vacations, can help with the chores and with the farming. Their work is not only of pecuniary value to the household, but it can be rendered in such a way as not to interfere with their schooling, and is of much more value to them in the way of exercise than any sort of sport in which they can indulge.

Fourth—Life upon the farm is healthful. One has outdoor air and exercise, both of which are strengthening to the body. The vigorous constitution developed upon the farm enables the farmer's boy to outstrip the city-grown boys in the test of endurance that comes later in life.

Fifth—The habits of industry and application acquired upon the farm are valuable capital, no matter to what occupation or profession the mind is turned. The patience, perseverance and energy which are developed in rural life are the foundations upon which one may build in every honorable vocation.

Sixth—Farm life cultivates hospitality and generosity, and, without entirely removing temptation, gives parental influence a chance to strengthen the child before the seeds of disobedience are implanted by evil associations. People who live miles apart in the country are better acquainted with each other and more attached to each other than the neighbors who are huddled together in the same house, and the children who grow up on the farm can be more careful in their company, and are less apt to contract bad habits, than boys in town.

In the city, there is little manual labor for the boy to do, and to keep him from associating with the boys who are by chance thrown in his way requires a constant exercise of parental authority. In the country, darkness shuts out the world and makes the fireside a welcome retreat for all. The farm is also conducive to good morals. Those who till the soil are brought near to nature, and their contact with the earth and its marvelous activities breeds reverence and respect for the Creator of all things. The farmer lives amid miracles and feels each year his dependence upon the unseen Hand that directs the seasons and sends the refreshing showers. Reverence teaches responsibility, and a sense of responsibility is a wholesome restraint upon conduct.

Seventh—The farmer learns early in life the true basis of rewards. By having to give a dollar's worth of labor for a dollar's worth of product, he is taught that service, to be fair, must be reciprocal. He never falls into the demoralizing habit of expecting something for nothing. He teaches by example that labor is honorable, and has that sense of proprietorship in his handiwork which only those have who feel that they have honestly earned all that they receive. His ideals of life are, therefore, apt to be high, and he imparts to others the stimulus which his occupation and environment excite in him.

Eighth—The husbandman is also the most reliable political factor in the nation. He is the best-informed and the most independent of all who take part in political life. While he is conservative and not subject to frequent change, while he has convictions and is usually a strong partizan, yet his opinions are his own, and, as a rule, he can neither be brought nor driven to cast his vote contrary to his judgment.

While it is true that in close states the corruption of voters has sometimes extended to the farm, still it is a well-known fact that repeating and bribe-taking are largely city vices.

The summer days are long, and the fatigue of the harvest leaves little energy for study, but the winter evenings bring compensation, and the Sabbath-day is in the country usually a day for thought and reflection.

While the labor organization has now done much to turn the attention of its members to the study of economic questions, yet, with the growth of great corporations, the laboring man has become more and more dependent upon his employer, and the wage-earner is not so free to make his ballot express exactly what he wants as is the man who works for himself, and sells his products in the open market.

Henry Clay, fifty years ago, in defending the right of the people of South America to self-government, said:

"Were I to speculate in hypotheses unfavorable to human liberty, my speculations would be founded rather upon the vices, refinements, or density of population. Crowded together in compact masses, even if they were philosophers, the contagion of the passions is communicated and caught, and the effect too often, I admit, is the overthrow of liberty. Dispersed over such an immense space as that on which the people of Spanish America are spread, their physical, and I believe also their moral condition, both favor their liberty."

In enumerating the advantages of farm life, it is not necessary to say that the farmer enjoys all the benefits that are now within his reach. There is probably no field in which there is greater room for improvement. But if the farm as it is has been the nursery of merchants and ministers, orators and statesmen, the farm as it may be and should be is still more inviting. The introduction of acetylene and other kinds of gas, and the perfection of electrical apparatus, will enable multitudes of farmers to substitute a modern light for the dim candle and the smoking lamp. The windmill and the supply–tank are not only saving the muscle of the man, but are contributing to the convenience of the housewife. With water running through the house and supplying both the kitchen and the bathroom, the lot of the farmer's wife will be very much improved.

Another invention is likely to have a marked influence upon farm life, namely, the telephone. No one who has not lived remote from a physician can appreciate the anxiety which a mother feels in case of accident or sickness in the family. The telephone reduces by one–half the time between injury and relief, and in addition to this makes it possible for the farmer to communicate with his neighbors, receive and send telegrams, and be in constant touch with the outside world. The writer's attention has been recently called to the telephone as a time–saver among farmers, and one now wonders how people could have done without it so long.

The electric–car line has already begun to link city with city and to supply the farmers along the line with cheap and rapid transportation for themselves and their products. It will be surprising if the electric lines and the telephones do not result in the next few years in a large increase in the value of suburban property.

In this connection, the "Good Roads" movement cannot be overlooked. The value of a permanent and at all times passable road is beginning to be appreciated, and the farmer is likely to demand that this consideration be shown to his material, intellectual and moral welfare. The mud embargo is an expensive one to the farmer's purse, and not less objectionable in other ways. With good roads it is possible to have larger and better schools, and then will follow the joint intermediate school, with its library and its public assembly-room. The rural delivery is another boon which the farmer appreciates. The state universities are giving increasing attention to studies that will fit young men for the intelligent pursuit of agriculture, and what could be more gratifying? If a father is able to start his son in business with ten thousand dollars, what business is so safe as farming? Given a young man with a thorough education, good habits, willingness to work, and a desire to make himself useful, where can he fare better than on a farm? He can apply his brains to the enriching of the soil, to the diversification of his crops, and to the improvement of his stock, and at the same time give reasonable indulgence to his taste for reading and study. He will have all that contributes to health of body, vigor of mind and to cultivation of the heart—what occupation or profession can offer him richer rewards?

True, the soil will not yield him the fabulous wealth that he might secure by cornering the production or supply of some necessary of life, but it will respond to his industry and give him that of which dishonest gains would rob him—"a conscience void of offense toward God and man." If he must forego the sudden gains that sometimes come to the stock-jobber, he is also relieved of fear of the sudden losses that are still more frequent to those whose fortunes rise and fall with the markets; and the terrors of flood and drought and wind and hail are, all combined, less to be dreaded than the conscienceless greed of the monopolists who wreck the business of competitors and swindle confiding stockholders.

To the briefless barrister who is not ashamed to work, to the pale-faced clerk who is not afraid of dirt—to all who can labor and be content with moderate returns, the farm offers a welcome. Even the dumb animals are more wholesome companions than the bulls and bears of Wall Street, and the harvests give back smile for smile.

10. "Individualism versus Socialism"

After Bryan died, Eugene Debs called him "petty, mean and contemptible, . . . this shallow-minded mouther of empty phrases, this pious, canting mountebank, this prophet of the stone age." Debs' invective cannot be attributed solely to his lifelong dispute with Bryan over social philosophy; the Socialist leader had many friends with whom he disagreed about public issues. The following article gives clues to Debs' venom. How is it possible under conditions of modern industrialism, Debs would ask, to adhere to individualism and simultaneously insure that "the competing parties should be placed upon substantially equal footing . . . "? When Bryan writes, "Justice requires that each individual shall receive from society a reward proportionate to his contribution to society," he would be asked how a professed Christian can rest with such a picayune vision. As a more exalted ideal, Debs would offer: From each according to his abilities, to each according to his needs. That and only that, Debs said, was Christian brotherhood.

The words "individualism" and "socialism" define tendencies rather than concrete systems; for, as extreme individualism is not to be found under any form of government, so there is no example of socialism in full operation. All government being more or less socialistic, the contention, so far as this subject is concerned, is between those who regard individualism as ideal, to be approached as nearly as circumstances will permit, and those who regard a socialistic state as ideal, to be established as far and as fast as public opinion will allow.

"Individualism versus Socialism," *The Century Magazine*, LXXI (October 1906), 856–859.

The individualist believes that competition is not only a helpful but a necessary force in society, to be guarded and protected; the socialist regards competition as a hurtful force, to
be entirely exterminated. It is not necessary to consider those
who consciously take either side for reasons purely selfish; it
is sufficient to know that on both sides there are those who with
great earnestness and sincerity present their theories, convinced of their correctness and sure of the necessity for their
application to human society.

As socialism is the newer doctrine, the socialist is often
greeted with epithet and denunciation rather than with argument; but, as usual, it does not deter him. Martyrdom never
kills a cause, as all history, political as well as religious, demon-
strates.

No one can read socialistic literature without recognizing
the "moral passion" that pervades it. The Ruskin Club of Oak-
land, California, quotes with approval an editorial comment
which asserts that the socialistic creed inspires a religious zeal
and makes its followers enthusiasts in its propagation. It also
quotes Professor Nitto of the University of Naples as asserting
that "the morality that socialism teaches is by far superior to
that of its adversaries"; and it quotes Thomas Kirkup as declaring, in the "Encyclopedia Britannica," that "the ethics of socialism are identical with those of Christianity."

It will be seen, therefore, that the socialists not only claim
superiority in ethics, but attempt to appropriate Christ's teachings as a foundation for their creed. As the maintenance of
either position would insure them ultimate victory, it is clear
that the first battle between the individualist and the socialist
must be in the field of ethics. No one who has faith in the
triumph of the right (and who can contend with vigor without
such a faith?) can doubt that that which is ethically best will
finally prevail in every department of human activity.

Assuming that the highest aim of society is the harmonious
development of the human race, physically, mentally, and

morally, the first question to decide is whether individualism or socialism furnishes the best means of securing that harmonious development. For the purpose of this discussion, individualism will be defined as the private ownership of the means of production and distribution where competition is possible, leaving to public ownership those means of production and distribution in which competition is practically impossible; and socialism will be defined as the collective ownership, through the state, of all the means of production and distribution.

One advocate of socialism defines it as "common ownership of natural resources and public utilities and the common operation of all industries for the public good." It will be seen that the definitions of socialism commonly in use include some things which cannot fairly be described as socialistic, and some of the definitions (like the last one, for instance) beg the question by assuming that the public operation of all industries will necessarily be for the general good. As the socialists agree in hostility to competition as a controlling force, and as individualists agree that competition is necessary for the well-being of society, the fairest and most accurate line between the two schools can be drawn at the point where competition begins to be possible, both schools favoring public ownership where competition is impossible, but differing as to the wisdom of public ownership where competition can have free play.

Much of the strength developed by socialism is due to the fact that socialists advocate certain reforms which individualists also advocate. Take, for illustration, the public ownership of waterworks. It is safe to say that a large majority of the people living in cities of any considerable size favor their public ownership,—individualists because it is practically impossible to have more than one water system in a city, and socialists on the general ground that the government should own all the means of production and distribution. The sentiment in favor of municipal lighting-plants is not yet so strong, and the sentiment in favor of public telephones and public street–car lines is still less pronounced; but the same general principles apply to them, and individualists, without accepting the creed of socialism, can advocate the extension of municipal ownership to these utilities.

Then, too, some of the strength of socialism is due to its condemnation of abuses which, while existing under individualism, are not at all necessary to individualism—abuses which the individualists are as anxious as the socialists to remedy. It is not only consistent with individualism, but is a necessary implication of it, that the competing parties should be placed upon substantially equal footing; for competition is not worthy of that name if one party is able arbitrarily to fix the terms of the agreement, leaving the other with no choice but to submit to the terms prescribed. Individualists, for instance, can consistently advocate usury laws which fix the rate of interest to be charged, these laws being justified on the ground that the borrower and the lender do not stand upon an equal footing. Where the money–lender is left free to take advantage of the necessities of the borrower, the so–called freedom of contract is really freedom to extort. Upon the same ground, society can justify legislation against child labor and legislation limiting the hours of adult labor. One can believe in competition and still favor such limitations and restrictions as will make the competition real and effective. To advocate individualism it is no more necessary to excuse the abuses to which competition may lead than it is to defend the burning of a city because fire is essential to human comfort, or to praise a tempest because air is necessary to human life.

In comparing individualism with socialism, it is only fair to consider individualism when made as good as human wisdom can make it and then to measure it with socialism at its best. It is a common fault of the advocate to present his system, idealized, in contrast with his opponent's system at its worst, and it must be confessed that neither individualist nor socialist has been entirely free from this fault. In dealing with any subject, we must consider man as he is, or as he may reasonably be expected to become under the operation of the system proposed, and it is much safer to consider him as he is than to expect a radical change in his nature. Taking man as we find him, he needs, as individualists believe, the spur of competition. Even the socialists admit the advantage of rivalry within certain limits, but they would substitute altruistic for selfish motives. Just here the individualist and the socialist find themselves in antagonism. The former believes that altruism is a spiritual quality which defies governmental definition, while the socialist believes that altruism will take the place of selfishness under an enforced collectivism.

Ruskin's statement that "government and coöperation are, in all things and eternally, the laws of life; anarchy and competition, eternally and in all things, the laws of death," is often quoted by socialists, but, as generalizations are apt to be, it is more comprehensive than clear. There is a marked distinction between voluntary coöperation upon terms mutually satisfactory, and compulsory coöperation upon terms agreeable to a majority. Many of the attempts to establish voluntary coöperation have failed because of disagreement as to the distribution of the common property or income, and those which have succeeded best have usually rested upon a religious rather than upon an economic basis.

In any attempt to apply the teachings of Christ to an economic state, it must be remembered that his religion begins with a regeneration of the human heart and with an ideal of life which makes service the measure of greatness. Tolstoy, who repudiates socialism as a substantial reform, contends that the bringing of the individual into harmony with God is the all–important thing, and that, this accomplished, all injustice will disappear.

It is much easier to conceive of a voluntary association between persons desiring to work together according to the Christian ideal, than to conceive of the successful operation of a system, enforced by law, wherein altruism is the controlling principle. The attempt to unite church and state has never been helpful to either government or religion, and it is not at all certain that human nature can yet be trusted to use the instrumentalities of government to enforce religious ideas. The persecutions which have made civilization blush have been attempts to compel conformity to religious beliefs sincerely held and zealously promulgated.

The government, whether it leans toward individualism or toward socialism, must be administered by human beings, and its administration will reflect the weaknesses and imperfections of those who control it. Bancroft declares that the expression of the universal conscience in history is the nearest approach to the voice of God, and he is right in paying this tribute to the wisdom of the masses; and yet we cannot overlook the fact that this universal conscience must find governmental expression through frail human beings who yield to the temptation to serve their own interests at the expense of their fellows. Will socialism purge the individual of selfishness or bring a nearer approach to justice?

Justice requires that each individual shall receive from society a reward proportionate to his contribution to society. Can the state, acting through officials, make this apportionment better than it can be made by competition? At present official favors are not distributed strictly according to merit either in republics or in monarchies; is it certain that socialism would insure a fairer division of rewards? If the government operates all the factories, all the farms, and all the stores, there must be superintendents as well as workmen; there must be different kinds of employment, some more pleasant, some less pleasant. Is it likely that any set of men can distribute the work or fix the compensation to the satisfaction of all, or even to the satisfaction of a majority of the people? When the government employs comparatively few of the people, it must make the terms and conditions inviting enough to draw the persons

needed from private employment; and if those employed in the
public service become dissatisfied, they can return to outside
occupations. But what will be the result if there is no private
employment? What outlet will there be for discontent if the
government owns and operates all the means of production and
distribution?

Under individualism a man's reward is determined in the
open market, and where competition is free he can hope to sell
his services for what they are worth. Will his chance for reward
be as good when he must do the work prescribed for him on
the terms fixed by those who are in control of the government?

As there is no example of such a socialistic state as is now
advocated, all reasoning upon the subject must be confined to
the theory, and theory needs to be corrected by experience.
As in mathematics no one can calculate the direction of the
resultant without a knowledge of all the forces that act upon
the moving body, so in estimating the effect of a proposed
system one must take into consideration all the influences that
operate upon the human mind and heart; and who is wise
enough to predict with certainty the result of any system before
it has been thoroughly tried? Individualism has been tested by
centuries of experience. Under it there have been progress and
development. That it has not been free from evil is not a sufficient condemnation. The same rain that furnishes the necessary
moisture for the growing crop sometimes floods the land and
destroys the harvest; the same sun that coaxes the tiny shoot
from Mother Earth sometimes scorches the blade and blasts
the maturing stalk. The good things given us by our heavenly
Father often, if not always, have an admixture of evil, to the
lessening of which the intelligence of man must be constantly
directed. Just now there are signs of an ethical awakening
which is likely to result in reforming some of the evils which
have sprung from individualism, but which can be corrected
without any impairment of the principle.

The individualist, while contending that the largest and

broadest development of the individual, and hence of the entire population, is best secured by full and free competition, made fair by law, believes in a spiritual force which acts beyond the sphere of the state. After the government has secured to the individual, through competition, a reward proportionate to his effort, religion admonishes him of his stewardship and of his obligation to use his greater strength, his larger ability, and his richer reward in the spirit of brotherhood. Under individualism we have seen a constant increase in altruism. The fact that the individual can select the objects of his benevolence and devote his means to the causes that appeal to him has given an added stimulus to his endeavors. Would this stimulus be as great under socialism?

Probably the nearest approach that we have to the socialistic state to–day is to be found in the civil service. If the civil service develops more unselfishness and more altruistic devotion to the general welfare than private employment does, the fact is yet to be discovered. This is not offered as a criticism of civil service in so far as civil service may require examinations to ascertain fitness for office, but it is simply a reference to a well–known fact—viz., that a life position in the government service, which separates one from the lot of the average producer of wealth, has given no extraordinary stimulus to higher development.

It is not necessary to excuse or to defend a competition carried to a point where it creates a submerged fifth, or even a submerged tenth, to recognize the beneficial effect of struggle and discipline upon the men and women who have earned the highest places in industry, society, and government.

There should be no unfriendliness between the honest individualist and the honest socialist; both seek that which they believe to be best for society. The socialist, by pointing out the abuses of individualism, will assist in their correction. At present private monopoly is putting upon individualism an undeserved odium, and it behooves the individualist to address himself energetically to this problem in order that the advantages of competition may be restored to industry. And the duty of immediate action is made more imperative by the fact that the socialist is inclined to support the monopoly, in the belief that it will be easier to induce the government to take over an industry after it has passed into the hands of a few men. The trust magnates and the socialists unite in declaring monopoly to be an economic development, the former hoping to retain the fruits of monopoly in private hands, the latter expecting the ultimate appropriation of the benefits of monopoly by the government. The individualist, on the contrary, contends that the consolidation of industries ceases to be an economic advantage when competition is eliminated; and he believes, further, that no economic advantage which could come from the monopolization of all the industries in the hands of the government could compensate for the stifling of individual initiative and independence. And the individualists who thus believe stand for a morality and for a system of ethics which they are willing to measure against the ethics and morality of socialism.

11. "The First Rule for a Husband and Wife"

Here again is Bryan as universal pundit, or Polonius. He is writing for the Ladies' Home Journal. *While he never generated the spiritual intensity of a John Wesley, he had learned many of the phrases and often sounds like Wesley's "Essay on Money." Just as he could preach the stewardship of wealth (see Document 10), so could he advise the newly married to live within their means. Irvin G. Wyllie, the leading student of the American myth of self-help, has remarked that its ideologues taught that success in business was a reward for "industry, frugality, and sobriety—simple moral virtues that any man could cultivate." Bryan was a legitimate apostle of the creed. He shared its idolatry of mothers (see Document 5); he advised each Negro as an individual to build "a reputation for virtue, sobriety and good sense" (see Document 8). Not content to spread the message in popular magazines, he wrote it out in his own hand in 1917 for the edification of his eleven-year-old grandson.*

Only a few begin life with an inheritance so large as to make economy unnecessary. With the vast majority of young men and young women the life plan includes the gradual accumulation of a fortune. If the word "gradual" is objected to it is enough to say that, as a rule, the accumulation is gradual, even though the imagination may picture a rapid rise. And gradual accumulation is better, after all, than getting rich in haste. "That which comes easy goes easy." We need the discipline that struggle brings.

"The First Rule for a Husband and Wife," *Ladies' Home Journal*, XXIV (October 1907), 13.

Of course, some young men will marry rich, and busy themselves with the care of the wife's property; while some young women will marry a fortune and be relieved (if relief it can be called) of the necessity for careful saving. But rules are made for the multitude rather than for the exceptions, and to the multitude long years of patient self–denial and rigid restraint upon expenditures precede the years spent on "Easy Street."

It is not necessary to dwell here upon the demoralizing influence of "great expectations," or to philosophize upon the strengthening effect of wholesome poverty. It is sufficient to take the situation as we find it and consider life as it presents itself to the average young couple. The husband and wife make their plans together, or should; they enter heartily upon their work: she as willing to sacrifice as he is to labor—and her willingness to save is as important a factor in their success as is his ability to earn.

The first rule that they need to learn is to live within their means. In fact, this is so important a rule that for the purpose of this article it may be considered as the only rule necessary. Without its observance other rules are useless. No matter how much money a man may make, he will finally become a bankrupt if his income is less than his outgo. It is possible, of course, that one may by extravagance purchase a business standing that he does not deserve, and by lucky ventures retrieve what he has spent. But such a course has in it all the elements of a lottery, and usually brings in its train the ruin that overtakes the gamester. It is not for the gambler or for those who would play at hazard that these lines are written. The honest, well-meaning young man who is willing to give to society a service equal in value to the reward which he asks, and the real helpmate who becomes his wife because she is willing to share his sorrows as well as his joys, his trials as well as his triumphs—these are the ones whom I have in mind.

When a family lives beyond its means the cause can generally be found in one of three reasons: in false pride, in a lack of honesty or in an unwillingness to make a present sacrifice for a future gain. Of these three a false pride is probably the most frequent. The young people want to commence where the parents left off. The first generation begins modestly, rises slowly, and, by the time the children are grown, lives in comfort. The second generation is often ashamed to begin in the same way, but wants to start with the comforts and then add the luxuries at once. Sometimes the young lady of marriageable age feels that it would be beneath her station to marry one who had to commence at the bottom of the ladder as her father did, and the poor young man, knowing the sentiment that prevails in society, hesitates to ask her to share his privations. He may have ambition, good health, good habits and high ideals: he may feel sure that in a quarter of a century he will be able to provide her a better home than the one she has at present, but will she be willing to wait for these things and endure the slighting remarks of her girl–companions who are looking for more "eligible" suitors?

This question has caused many a lover to pause, and it has prevented many more from reaching the lover–stage. Possibly an injustice is done the girl in assuming that she demands all the comforts of modern life, and it is not straining the truth to say that many a maid has been so hedged about by the influence of her father's wealth that no one but an adventurer will pay court to her.

The mildest indictment that can be made against those who live beyond their means is that they are willing to purchase tomorrow's sorrow with today's enjoyment, or, to state it more accurately, are unwilling to make a little sacrifice today in order to secure a large advantage in the future. And yet, after all, this is quite a severe indictment, for one of the important differences between the savage and the civilized man is that the former must realize upon every investment at once, while the latter provides for tomorrow. Comfort during life's decline is a sort of annuity which one buys with the savings of his earlier years. The student sacrifices an opportunity to make a few dollars when he continues his studies, but he thereby lays up a capital far greater than he could accumulate in any other way. And so, those who save little by little by limiting self-indulgence have not only the pleasure of seeing their fortune grow, but they also have the wellbeing and security from want which come with a competency. Self–indulgence pays no dividends, while self–denial yields an annual return.

There is moral development as well as pecuniary advantage in the avoidance of debt. Control over one's self is essential to character, and regular, systematic saving involves the curbing of the appetite, the suppression of vanity and the strengthening of the will. Of course, this does not mean that economy should be carried to the point of parsimony: the heart is shriveled by the stifling of benevolence. There should be systematic giving in proportion to income, but this is entirely consistent with a scrutiny of expenditures. It may even be asserted that those who are strict with themselves are generally more willing, as well as more able, to give to worthy causes than those who exhaust their resources in the cultivation of their own selfishness.

Even when love has led them into a union the husband and wife sometimes lack the moral courage to admit before the world the meagerness of their income. They pay more rent than they can afford to pay, dress better than they can afford to dress, entertain more than they can afford to entertain, or travel when they cannot spare the money that traveling costs. The effort to live as well, to dress as well, and to spend as much as the richest one in their social set has caused the downfall of many. And what is the use? No one is deceived. The neighbors know, as a rule, about what one's income is, and if we live beyond it those who help us spend our money will criticise us behind our backs and think the less of us because of the deception attempted.

"We cannot afford it" is a valuable phrase; it is often worth a fortune. It is a manly phrase, and a womanly phrase, too. It will alienate no one whose friendship is worth having; as a matter of fact, one is fortunate to lose a friend who takes offense at that admission when spoken in truth. Candor is a virtue which disarms criticism and wins admiration, even from those who lack it themselves.

As against the false pride of the man who conceals his financial condition from his wife, or which leads the wife to adopt a scale of living beyond the husband's means, let us consider the merit of the opposite position. There is a pride that is justifiable: the pride of the man and woman who scorn false pretense and refuse to compromise with self–respect. They earn what they can, and, having done the best they can, look the world in the face. They buy what they can pay for, and are free from the servitude which debt always enforces. Laying aside a little each year they see hope in the future instead of despair. It is no day–dream that pictures a larger house and "provision for a rainy day." In such a family a child is not a dread visitation, but a welcome sharer of an increasing store. Between the false pride that means final disgrace and agonizing suspense before exposure comes—between this and the dignified admission of limited means, who can hesitate to choose the latter? And yet thousands of families today are filling the present with dread and sowing the winds from which whirlwinds spring because they are ashamed to live within their means.

There is an element of honesty in this question, too, which cannot be overlooked. Not that one who lives extravagantly always intends to be dishonest, but is there not lacking a rightly adjusted sense of honor? The embezzler seldom enters deliberately upon the commission of his crime. He borrows the money, expecting to be able to pay it back, but loses it in speculation or squanders it, and, finally, when repayment is demanded he stands forth a violator of the law. So there is incipient embezzlement in purchases made when one is not sure of being able to pay. For is it honest to run accounts and trust to chance to find the means with which to make payment? The landlord, the grocer, the tailor and the dressmaker are in a position to compare the various standards of integrity, and some are deplorably low. There are two ways of being untruthful: saying that which is known to be false, and saying that which is not known to be true. And so there are two kinds of dishonesty: the contraction of a debt with the intention of not paying it, and the contraction of a debt without knowing how it is to be paid.

To be sure, there may be cases of sickness or emergency when a person must buy on credit, and in such cases honesty requires that the creditor shall know the facts and take the risk voluntarily; but these cases should not be confounded with living beyond one's means. A semi–intentional fraud is practiced when to keep up appearances one runs into debt without reasonable prospect of payment, and yet the guilty party would probably indignantly resent the charge of dishonesty.

Dishonesty in financial transactions is a bold relative of falsehood, and there are several other members of the family, large and small. Extravagance is in itself another form of untruthfulness, for it is usually the acting of a lie. Every young lawyer who has commenced the practice of his profession with the collection of accounts gathers some amusing illustrations of the prevarication which is resorted to by those who buy without knowing when or how payment is to be made.

There is, however, a mean between the two extremes illustrated by the miser and the spendthrift, and it is for this mean that one should aim. There is an ideal that avoids both stinginess and wastefulness, and this is the ideal that public opinion should urge upon the newly–married. And that the ideal may be the more readily accepted after marriage, it should be presented to the young before marriage. There are hundreds of thousands of families in this country following this ideal now, and they are the strength and moral fibre of the land. The man and woman drawn together by the indissoluble ties of love—planning and working together, mutually helpful, mutually forbearing and sharing fully in each other's confidence— these represent the home that has given to American domestic life its high position. These people buy only what they have the money to buy; they claim a fair reward for their labor and yet give good measure in their service, and, laying aside year by year, they travel life's path together, their independence increasing as they proceed. Their children are trained to prudence by example as well as precept, and their own position in society and business becomes each day more secure. Such a couple can contemplate old age with serenity, and in their family life present the fittest earthly type of Heaven.

12. The Trust Problem

It is probable that The Commoner, *over the years, devoted more space to the trust question than to any other single issue. The following speech was made at a rather early stage of the combination movement that swept American industry at the turn of the century, symbolized by the formation of U. S. Steel in 1901. Many of the remarks below were an effort to refute a defense of "trusts" by Charles R. Flint, a large rubber importer who had taken the lead in 1893 in forming U.S. Rubber. Bryan, apparently, was not aware that the history of this company showed how a combination could benefit the entire economy as well as its own stockholders. He also erred in declaring that the United States had never had a complete monopoly. Standard Oil, for instance, since 1877 had enjoyed a stranglehold on petroleum refining (and, be it noted, from then until 1884 the wholesale price of illuminating oil fell much more rapidly than did the index of the wholesale prices of all commodities). As a solution, Bryan made specific proposals for concurrent jurisdiction over interstate corporations by the states and the federal government. The latter prescription was not only acceptable but was eagerly sought by some big businessmen, although they were hostile to Bryan's formula in its totality. In a sense Rockefeller and his associates wanted to go even further than Bryan in extending federal power. They testified before the contemporary U.S. Industrial Commission in favor of national rather than state incorporation of companies, with federal supervision of corporate*

Chicago Conference on Trusts: Speeches, Debates, Resolutions, . . . Held September 13th, 14th, 15th, 16th, 1899 (Chicago: The Civic Federation of Chicago, 1900), pp. 496–514.

accounts and with financial publicity. They saw this device as a barrier against variable and often more radical state laws, thus stultifying Bryan and those later ideologists who think that any growth of federal regulation is in itself liberal and progressive. In fact, it often has been reactionary, depending on who does the regulating, and toward what ends.

I appreciate the very kind words spoken by Governor Stanley in presenting me to this audience. I am glad I live in a country where people can differ from one another, differ honestly, express their convictions boldly, and yet respect one another and acknowledge one another's rights. I am not vain enough, however, to think that any good will which has been expressed by the people toward me is due to personal merit. If I have had political friends it is because people believe with me in certain ideas or rather because I believe with them in certain ideas. It is the idea that makes the man. The man is only important as he helps the idea.

I come this morning to discuss in your presence a great question—a question of growing importance to the American people. The trust principle is not a new principle, but the trust principle is manifesting itself in so many ways and the trusts have grown so rapidly that people now feel alarmed about trusts who did not feel alarmed three years ago. The trust question has grown in importance, because within two years more trusts have been organized, when we come to consider the capitalization and the magnitude of the interests involved, than were organized in all the previous history of the country, and the people now come face to face with this question: Is the trust a blessing or a curse? If a curse, what remedy can be applied to the curse?

I want to start with the declaration that a monopoly in private hands is indefensible from any standpoint, and intolerable. I make no exceptions to the rule. I do not divide monopolies in private hands into good monopolies and bad monopolies. There is no good monopoly in private hands. There can be no good monopoly in private hands until the Almighty sends us angels to preside over the monopoly. There may be a despot who is better than another despot, but there is no good despotism. One trust may be less harmful than another. One trust magnate may be more benevolent than another, but there is no good monopoly in private hands, and I do not believe it is safe for society to permit any man or group of men to monopolize any article of merchandise or any branch of industry.

What is the defense made of the monopoly? The defense of the monopoly is always placed on the ground that if you will allow a few people to control the market and fix the price they will be good to the people who purchase of them. The entire defense of the trusts rests upon a money argument. If the trust will sell to a man an article for a dollar less than the article will cost under other conditions, then in the opinion of some that proves a trust to be a good thing. In the first place I deny that under a monopoly the price will be reduced. In the second place, if under a monopoly the price is reduced the objections to a monopoly from other standpoints far outweigh any financial advantage that the trust could bring. But I protest in the beginning against settling every question upon the dollar argument. I protest against the attempt to drag every question down to the low level of dollars and cents.

In 1859 Abraham Lincoln wrote a letter to the Republicans of Boston who were celebrating Jefferson's birthday, and in the course of the letter he said: "The Republican party believes in the man and the dollar, but in case of conflict it believes in the man before the dollar." In the early years of his administration he sent a message to Congress, and in that message he warned his countryman against the approach of monarchy. And what was it that alarmed him? He said it was the attempt to put capital upon an equal footing with, if not above, labor in the structure of government, and in that attempt to put capital even upon an equal footing with labor in the structure of government he saw the approach of monarchy. Lincoln was right. Whenever you put capital upon an equal footing with labor, or above labor in the structure of government you are on the road toward a government that rests not upon reason but upon force.

Nothing is more important than that we shall in the beginning rightly understand the relation between money and man. Man is the creature of God and money is the creature of man. Money is made to be the servant of man, and I protest against all theories that enthrone money and debase mankind.

What is the purpose of the trust or the monopoly? For when I use the word trust I use it in the sense that the trust means monopoly. What is the purpose of monopoly? You can find out from the speeches made by those who are connected with the trusts. I have here a speech made by Charles R. Flint at Boston on the 25th day of last May, and the morning papers of the 26th in describing the meeting said he defended trust principles before an exceedingly sympathetic audience, and then added: "For his audience was composed almost exclusively of Boston bankers." "We thus secure," he says, "the advantages of larger aggregations of capital and ability; if I am asked what they are the answer is only difficult because the list is so long."

But I want now to read to you a few of the advantages to be derived by the trusts from the trust system. "Raw material bought in large quantities is secured at lower prices." That is the first advantage. One man to buy wool for all the woolen manufacturers. That means that every man who sells wool must sell it at the price fixed by this one purchaser in the United States. The first thing is to lower the price of raw material. The great majority of the people are engaged in the production of raw material and in the purchase of finished products. Comparatively few can stand at the head of syndicates and monopolies and secure the profits for them. Therefore, the first advantage of a monopoly is to lower the price of the raw material furnished by the people. Note the next advantage: "Those plants which are best equipped and most advantageously situated are run continuously and in preference to those less favored."

The next thing, after they have bought all the factories, is to close some of them and to turn out of employment the men who are engaged in them. If you will go about over the country you will see where people have subscribed money to establish enterprises, and where these enterprises, having come under the control of the trusts, have been closed and stand now as silent monuments of the trust system.

Behold the next advantage: "In case of local strikes and fires, the work goes on elsewhere, thus preventing serious loss." Do not the laboring men understand what that means? "In case of local strikes or fires the work goes on elsewhere, thus preventing serious loss." What does it mean? It means that if the people employed in one factory are not satisfied with the terms fixed by the employer and strike, the trust can close that factory and let the employees starve while work goes on in other factories without loss to the manufacturers.

It means that when the trust has frozen out the striking employees in one factory and compelled them to return to work at any price to secure bread for their wives and children it can provoke a strike somewhere else and freeze the workmen out there. When a branch of industry is entirely in the hands of one great monopoly, so that every skilled man in that industry has to go to the one man for employment, then that one man will fix wages as he pleases and the laboring men will share the suffering of the man who sells the raw materials.

"There is no multiplication of the means of distribution and a better force of salesmen takes the place of a large number." That is the next advantage named. I want to warn you that when the monopoly has absolute control, brains will be at a discount, and relatives will be found to fill these positions.

When there is competition every employer has to get a good man to meet competition, but when there is no competition anybody can sit in the office and receive letters and answer them because everybody has to write to the same house for anything he wants. There is no question about it. A trust, a monopoly, can lessen the cost of distribution. But when it does so society has no assurance that it will get any of the benefits from that reduction of cost. But you will take away the necessity for skill and brains. You will take away the stimulus that has given to us the quick, the ever alert commercial traveler. These commercial evangelists, who go from one part of the country to the other proclaiming the merits of their respective goods, will not be needed, because when anybody wants merchandise all he has to do is to write to the one man who has the article for sale, and say, "What will you let me have it for to–day?"

And here is another advantage: "Terms and conditions of sale become more uniform and credit can be more safely granted." The trust can not only fix the price of what it sells, but it can fix the terms upon which it sells. You can pay cash, or, if there is a discount, it is just so much discount, and you have to trust to the manager's generosity as to what is fair when he is on one side and you on the other. I have read some of the advantages which a great trust magnate thinks will come to the trust.

What is the first thing to be expected of a trust? That it will cut down expenses. What is the second? That it will raise prices. We have not had in this country a taste of a complete trust, a complete monopoly, and we cannot tell what will be the result of a complete monopoly by looking at the results that have followed from an attempt to secure a monopoly. A corporation may lower prices to rid itself of competitors; but when it has rid itself of competitors, what is going to be the result? My friends, all you have to know is human nature. God made men selfish. I do not mean to say that He made a mistake when He did, because selfishness is merely the outgrowth of an instinct of self–preservation. It is the abnormal development of a man's desire to protect himself; but everybody who knows human nature knows how easy it is to develop that side of a man's being. Occasionally I find a man who says he is not selfish, but when I do, I find a man who can prove it only by his own affidavit.

We get ideas from every source. An idea is the most important thing that a man can get into his head. An idea will control a man's life. An idea will revolutionize a community, a state, a nation, the world. And we never know when we are going to get an idea. Sometimes we get them when we [do] not want to get them, and sometimes we get them from sources which would not be expected to furnish ideas. We get them from our fellow men. We get them from inanimate nature. We get them from the animals about us. I got a valuable idea once from some hogs. I was riding through Iowa and saw some hogs rooting in a field. The first thought that came to me was that those hogs were destroying a great deal in value, and then my mind ran back to the time when I lived upon a farm and when we had hogs.

Then I thought of the way in which we used to protect property from the hogs by putting rings in the noses of the hogs; and then the question came to me, why did we do it? Not to keep the hogs from getting fat, for we were more interested in their getting fat than they were; the sooner they got fat the sooner we killed them; the longer they were in getting fat the longer they lived. But why did we put the rings in their noses? So that while they were getting fat they would not destroy more than they were worth. And then the thought came to me that one of the great purposes of government was to put rings in the noses of hogs. I don't mean to say anything offensive, but we are all hoggish. In hours of temptation we are likely to trespass upon the rights of others.

I believe in self–government. I believe in the doctrines that underlie this government; I believe that people are capable of governing themselves. Why? Because in their sober moments they have helped to put rings in their own noses, to protect others from themselves and themselves from others in hours of temptation. And so I believe we must recognize human nature. We must recognize selfishness and we must so make our laws that people shall not be permitted to trespass upon the rights of others in their efforts to secure advantages for themselves.

I believe society is interested in the independence of every citizen. I wish we might have a condition where every adult who died might die leaving to his widow and children enough property for the education of his children and the support of his widow. Society is interested in this because if a man dies and leaves no provisions for his wife and children the burden falls upon society. But while I wish to see every person secure for himself a competency, I don't want him to destroy more than he is worth while he is doing that. And I believe the principle of monopoly finds its inspiration in the desire of men to secure by monopoly what they cannot secure in the open field of competition. In other words, if I were going to try to find the root of the monopoly evil I would do as I have often had occasion to do—go back to the bible for an explanation— and I would find it in the declaration that the love of money is the root of all evil.

I will not ask you all to agree with me; we have not met here as a body of men who agree. We have met here as a body of men who are seeking light and each ought to be willing to hear what every other person has to say, and each of us should desire the triumph of that which is true more than the triumph of that which he may think be true.

Let me repeat that the primary cause of monopoly is the love of money and the desire to secure the fruits of monopoly, but I believe that falling prices, caused by the rising dollar, have contributed to this desire and intensified it, because peo-

ple, seeing the fall in prices and measuring the loss of investments, have looked about for some means to protect themselves
from this loss, and they have joined in combinations to hold
up prices to protect their investments from a loss which would
not have occurred but for the rise in the value of dollars and
the fall in the level of prices.

Another thing that, in my judgment, has aided monopoly is
a high tariff. Nobody can dispute that a tariff law, an import
duty, enables a trust to charge for its product the price of a
similar foreign product plus the tariff.

Now some have suggested that to put everything on the
free list that trusts make would destroy the trusts. I do not
agree with this statement, as it is made so broadly. I believe
that the high tariff has been the means of extortion and that
it has aided trusts to collect more than they otherwise could
collect. But I do not believe you could destroy all trusts by
putting all trust made articles on the free list. Why? Because,
if an article can be produced in this country as cheaply as it
can be produced abroad the trust could exist without the aid
of any tariff, although it could not extort so much as it could
with the tariff. While some relief may come from modifica-
tions of the tariff, we cannot destroy monopoly until we lay
the axe at the root of the tree and make monopoly impossible
by law.

It has been suggested that discrimination by railroads has
aided the trusts. No question about it. If one man can secure
from a railroad better rates than another man, he will be able
to run the other man out of business. And there is no question
that discrimination and favoritism secured by one corporation
against a rival have been largely instrumental in enabling the
favored corporation to secure practically a complete monopoly.
Now that can be remedied by laws that will prevent this discrimination, but when we prevent the discrimination, when we
place every producer upon the same footing and absolutely
prevent favoritism, monopoly may still exist. The remedy must

go farther. It must be complete enough to prevent the organization of a monopoly.

Now what can be done to prevent the organization of a monopoly? I think we differ more in remedy than we do in our opinion of the trust. I venture the opinion that few people will defend monopoly as a principle, or a trust organization as a good thing, but I imagine our great difference will be as to remedy, and I want, for a moment, to discuss the remedy.

We have a dual form of government. We have a state government and a federal government, and while this dual form of government has its advantages, and to my mind advantages which can hardly be overestimated, yet it also has its disadvantages. When you prosecute a trust in the United States court it hides behind state sovereignty, and when you prosecute it in the state court it rushes to cover under federal jurisdiction—and we have had some difficulty in determining a remedy.

I believe we ought to have remedies in both state and nation, and that they should be concurrent remedies. In the first place, every state has, or should have, the right to create any private corporation which in the judgment of the people of the state is conducive to the welfare of the people of that state. I believe we can safely intrust to the people of a state the settlement of a question which concerns them. If they create a corporation and it becomes destructive of their best interests they can destroy that corporation, and we can safely trust them both to create and annihilate if conditions make annihilations necessary. In the second place the state has, or should have, the right to prohibit any foreign corporation from doing business in the state, and it has or should have the right to impose such restrictions and limitations as the people of the state may think necessary upon foreign corporations doing business in the state. In other words, the people of the state not only should have a right to create the corporations they want, but they should be permitted to protect themselves against any outside corporation.

But I do not think this is sufficient. I believe, in addition to a state remedy, there must be a federal remedy, and I believe Congress has, or should have, the power to place restrictions and limitations, even to the point of prohibition, upon any corporation organized in any state that wants to do business outside of the state. I say that Congress has, or should have, power to place upon the corporation such limitations and restrictions, even to the point of prohibition, as may to Congress seem necessary for the protection of the public.

Now I believe that these concurrent remedies will prove effective. To repeat, the people of every state shall first decide whether they want to create a corporation; they shall also decide whether they want any outside corporation to do business in the state, and if so, upon what conditions; and then Congress shall exercise the right to place upon every corporation doing business outside of the state in which it is organized such limitations and restrictions as may be necessary for the protection of the public. . . .

I am here to hear, to receive information, and to adopt any method that anybody can propose that looks to the annihilation of the trusts.

One method has occurred to me, and to me it seems a complete method. It may not commend itself to you. If you have something better I shall accept it in the place of this which I am about to suggest. But the method that occurs to me is this: That Congress should pass a law providing that no corporation organized in any state should do business outside of the state in which it is organized until it receives from some power created by Congress a license authorizing it to do business outside of its own state. Now, if the corporation must come to this body created by Congress to secure permission to do business outside of the state, then the license can be granted upon conditions which will, in the first place, prevent the watering of stock; in the second place, prevent monopoly in any branch of business, and, third, provide for publicity as to all of the transactions and business of the corporation.

A voice—Colonel, would such a law be constitutional?

Mr. Bryan—I was going to come to that. I am glad you mentioned it. What I mean to say is that Congress ought to pass such a law. If it is unconstitutional and so declared by the Supreme Court, I am in favor of an amendment to the Constitution that will give to Congress power to destroy every trust in the country. The first condition which I suggest is that no water should be allowed in the stock. I do not agree with those who say it is a matter entirely immaterial whether a corporation has water in its stock or not. It may be true that in the long run, if you are able to run as long as the corporation can, the stock will fall to its natural level, but during all that time the harm goes on; during all that time the trust demands the right to collect dividends upon capital represented by no money whatever. I do not believe that any state should permit the organization of a corporation with a single drop of water in the stock of that corporation. The farmer cannot inflate the value of his land by watering the value of that land. The merchant in the store cannot inflate the value of the goods upon his shelves. Why should the corporation be permitted to put out stock that represents no real value? . . .

In my judgment, when you take from monopoly the power to issue stock not represented by money, you will go more than half the way toward destroying monopoly in the United States.

The law should provide for publicity. As has been well said by men who have spoken here, corporations cannot claim that they have a right, or that it is necessary, to cover their transactions with secrecy, and when you provide for publicity so that the public can know just what there is in the corporation, just what it is doing, and just what it is making, you will take another long step toward the destruction of monopoly.

But I am not willing to stop there. I do not want to go one or two steps, I want to go all the way and make a monopoly absolutely impossible. And, therefore, as a third condition, I suggest that this license shall not be granted until the corpora-

tion shows that it has not had a monopoly, and is not attempting a monopoly of any branch of industry or of any article of
merchandise—and then provide that if the law is violated the
license can be revoked. I do not believe in the government
giving privileges to be exercised by a corporation without reserving the right to withdraw them when those privileges become hurtful to the people.

Now, I may be mistaken, but as I have studied the subject
it has seemed to me that this method of dealing with the
trusts would prove an effective method, but if you once establish the system and require the license, then Congress can,
from year to year, add such new conditions as may be necessary for the protection of the public from the greed and
avarice of great aggregations of wealth. I do not go so far as
some do and say that there shall be no private corporations,
but I say this, that a corporation is created by law, that it is
created for the public good and that it should never be permitted to do a thing that is injurious to the public, and that
if any corporation enjoys any privileges to-day which are
hurtful to the public those privileges ought to be withdrawn
from it. In other words, I am willing that we should first see
whether we can preserve the benefits of the corporation and
take from it its possibilities for harm.

A delegate—Would you apply that to rich individuals also,
suppose Rockefeller did it on his own account?

Mr. Bryan—We have not reached a point yet where an individual has been able to do harm, and, in my judgment, if
we would abolish those laws that grant special privileges and
make some men the favorites of the government, no man, by
his own brain and muscle, could ever earn enough money to
be harmful to the people. . . .

When God made man as the climax of creation he looked
upon his work and said that it was good, and yet when God
finished his work the tallest man was not much taller than the
shortest, and the strongest man was not much stronger than

the weakest. That was God's plan. We looked upon his work and said that it was not quite as good as it might be, and so we made a fictitious person called a corporation that is in some instances a hundred times—a thousand times—a million times stronger than the God–made man. Then we started this man–made giant out among the God–made men. When God made man he placed a limit to his existence, so that if he was a bad man he could not do harm long, but when we made our man–made man we raised the limit as to age. In some states a corporation is given perpetual life.

When God made man he breathed into him a soul and warned him that in the next world he would be held accountable for the deeds done in the flesh, but when we made our man–made man we did not give him a soul, and if he can avoid punishment in this world he need not worry about the hereafter.

My contention is that the government that created must retain control, and that the man–made man must be admonished: "Remember now thy Creator in the days of thy youth"—and throughout thy entire life.

Let me call your attention again to this distinction. We are not dealing with the natural man; we are not dealing with natural rights. We are dealing with the man–made man and artificial privileges.

What government gives, the government can take away. What the government creates, it can control; and I insist that both the state government and the federal government must protect the God–made man from the man–made man.

13. The Supreme Court and the Trusts

When the Supreme Court in 1911, in the Standard Oil and American Tobacco Cases, applied the so-called Rule of Reason to the Sherman Anti-Trust Act, a leading journal of opinion asked Bryan to contribute to a symposium on the decisions. Most of the other essays tried to explain the economic problems and the considerations of public policy that had guided the Court's hand. "When the people of the country returned to peaceful pursuits after the Civil War," wrote one contributor to the North American Review, *"competition was unrestrained, unreckoning, and lawless." True, and combinations were formed in many industries in efforts to maintain prices at profitable levels. A populace alarmed at trusts forced Congress to pass the Sherman Act in 1890. The Supreme Court, fearing with reason that abolition of all combinations would lead to the bankruptcy of much of American business, decided in effect in 1895 that Congress could not legislate thus in regard to manufacturing firms because they were not engaged in interstate commerce. This holding proved too unpopular for the Court to stand by it, but several of the Justices retained their old perception of the situation and their old objective. Four Justices in the Trans-Missouri Freight Association Case (1897) held that the Sherman Act banned only unreasonable restraints of trade, but the majority explicitly rejected the doctrine. By 1911 a new majority, speaking through the Chief Justice, accepted it, and declared that their decision "was in accord with all previous decisions of this court." The remark, said dissenting Justice Harlan, "surprises me quite as much as would a statement that black was white or white was black." Harlan's*

"The Reason," *North American Review*, CXCIV (July 1911), 10–24.

logic was indisputable. Neither he nor William Jennings Bryan would be deterred by the argument that strict interpretation and enforcement of the Anti-Trust Act would convert the economy into what Justice Holmes had called "the bellum omnium contra omnes. . . ." *Complex matters of social policy were not for Bryan; for him this problem, like all problems, was a moralistic one.*

The decision of the United States Supreme Court in the Standard Oil case—and the language of the opinion is repeated with emphasis in the Tobacco case—is epoch-making, although people will differ as to the character of the epoch which it ushers in. There are a number of things that impress one as he reads the majority and minority opinions, and the impression made is so deep that feeling increases with contemplation. It is easier for the public to discuss the subject in diplomatic language now than it will be when the far-reaching effect of the decision is fully understood. The position one takes in regard to the majority and minority opinions depends largely upon the point of view from which he looks at the trust question. Those who regard the trust as a benevolent institution, or as a natural and necessary economic development, will be likely to approve of the position taken by the majority of the Court, and if they approve of the position taken by the Court they will quite naturally indorse the reasons given. Those, on the contrary, who look upon the trust as a real menace to economic independence and to our political institutions will applaud Justice Harlan for having so vigorously dissented, even though in dissenting he stood alone.

Let us consider the position taken by the Court and the language in which the Court's position is stated.

First: The opinion was written by Chief-Justice White, and no one can fail to note the tone of triumph that runs through it. It exhibits something of the spirit of the "Battle Hymn of the Republic," "Be swift, my soul," "Be jubilant, my feet." But the Chief Justice can be excused for betraying something of the exultation of the conqueror. Judges are merely human beings, if in saying this I am not guilty of contempt—that is, "unreasonable" contempt—and we must expect to find in them some of the faults that appear in common clay. Fifteen years ago the Chief Justice, then Justice White, wrote the dissenting opinion in the Trans-Missouri Freight case, and in that opinion, in which three other justices joined him, he set forth the same doctrine that he presents with so much emphasis in the Standard Oil and Tobacco cases. His achievement in converting a minority into a majority is being loudly praised by those who agree with his conclusions. . . .

Second: The next thing that impresses the reader of the opinion written by the Chief Justice is that "the rule of reason," which is presented as a great discovery, was not discovered by the Chief Justice, although he is its most distinguished exponent at this time. It was really discovered by those who were violating the law and was presented by the very learned counsel who attempted, at that time unsuccessfully, to convince the Court that the Anti-trust law did not mean what it said, or at least did not say what the Court, after a long hearing, declared that it did say. It does not detract, however, from the prestige of the Chief Justice that he was not the first to think of inserting the word "unreasonable" in a criminal law. The inventor is very often lost sight of—the man who makes the invention a success is the one who becomes known to the public—and the attorneys who attempted to use the word "unreasonable" as a shield to protect the defendants in the Trans-Missouri Freight case and later in the Joint Traffic Association case will have to content themselves with such consolation as they can obtain from the consciousness that they made the discovery (and from their fees), while the Chief Justice bows and smilingly accepts the plaudits of those who desired the repeal of the criminal part of the Anti–Trust law and a paralysis of its usefulness in the civil courts.

Third: The fact that the Chief Justice has now with him all of the new members—those who have come upon the Supreme bench since "the rule of reason" was promulgated by him fifteen years ago—suggests an inquiry which, however interesting, cannot be answered—namely, *why do all of the new judges concur in what was at first the opinion of a minority?* Why is Justice Harlan, the only survivor of those who joined in the majority opinion fifteen years ago, the only dissenter to–day? If it was due to the persuasive powers of the Chief Justice, why is he so much more successful than he was fifteen years ago? If it were proper to assume that judges were appointed to the Supreme Court *because of their known views upon important questions,* it would be easy to explain the change in the Court, for the judges are appointed by the President, and it would not be difficult for a President to select from the large number of well–qualified lawyers those who held a particular view on an important question. Some influence might be exerted in the selection of judges, even without actual knowledge of their views on a particular subject, if the general sympathy of the applicant was known, his bias for or against a certain class. It is no reflection upon a man to say that he possesses one of the biases which run through society, the aristocratic and democratic biases being the most fundamental. The plutocratic bias is also a fact to be dealt with, and a very important fact, too. A man is often unconscious of the bias that he has, and the bias is, as a rule, more pronounced in proportion as the possessor is unconscious of it; and it is more likely to influence him, too, when unconscious. If a man is conscious of a bias for or against a certain class he is on his guard, and in his effort to overcome it he may lean to the other side; it is the man who is unconscious of his bias who is likely to go to an extreme, and that, too, with perfect honesty of purpose. . . .

Opinion on the trust question is largely a matter of bias; it is a question for the heart as well as the head. It is a poor head that cannot find reasons for doing what the heart wants to do. It is a fundamental "rule of reason" that a man can generally find a reason—not always conclusive and sometimes not even plausible, but a reason sufficient for himself—for doing anything upon which his heart is really set. If bias is admitted—bias in the President as well as in the judge—it is entirely possible that a President might unconsciously select judges who would, without any previous pledge, agree quite naturally with those who represent their side of the great fundamental issues that divide society. If it "just happened" that in the selection of eight judges *all* should take the view of Justice White, and if it is *not* accounted for by bias on great subjects, then it shows what a lottery is conducted at the White House when the President blindfolds himself and picks judges at random, only to find that all the prizes have gone to those who do not fear "reasonable" trusts and none to those who oppose all restraint of trade.

Fourth: Another thing that strikes one as he studies the opinion of the Court is that the Court's decree is entirely lost sight of in the reasons set forth. The Court decided that the Standard Oil Company (and also the Tobacco Company) violated the law, and it ordered a dissolution. But even the defendants did not seem to regard the order as of any serious moment, while the reasons given by the Court have aroused the entire nation, and this submerging of the immediate result is the more remarkable when it is remembered that the language which has startled the country *was not necessary to the decision of either case.* Justice Harlan calls attention to this fact quite pointedly. In the oral opinion delivered in the Tobacco case he said:

> "More than that, and still more than that, it is a very serious matter. What does it matter, so far as this case is concerned, whether that act of Congress contains the word 'reasonable' or

does not contain the word 'reasonable'? We all agree—every man
on this bench agrees—that this is an organization in violation of
the act of Congress, whether the 'reasonable' is or is not in the act.
It is a violation of a law of Congress. Then why could not this
Court have said, under these facts, 'This corporation violates a
law of Congress' and stop there—and stop there? Why was it
necessary for us to go into an elaborate and ingenious argument,
worthy of the genius of the Chief Justice, and attempt to show
that this act should be interpreted as if it contained the word
'reasonable' or the word 'unreasonable'? Whether it contains those
words or not is of no consequence in this case under this act.
If there ever was a case since the organization of this Court in
which a vast amount of an elaborate and able opinion is pure
obiter dicta—*obiter dicta* pure and simple—it is the opinion delivered by the Court in this case as to the construction of this
Anti–trust Act of 1890. I cannot escape that conclusion." . . .

Fifth: The decision of the Court is so revolutionary that it
not only reverses a decision that has stood for fifteen years,
but it amends a law, enacted by Congress, which the Court
refused to amend in the Trans–Missouri Freight case. It is
true that Chief–Justice White, then an associate justice, dissented, but according to our law the decision of the majority
of the Court stands as the decision of the Court—even when
that majority rests upon the opinion of one justice; and to
make it stronger still, even when the opinion of that justice
has changed between two arguments of the case, as did the
opinion of one of the justices in the Income Tax case. It is
no slight matter for the Supreme Court of the United States
to reverse itself upon an important question, because a reversal
cannot but affect rights based upon the former decision and
interests built up upon that decision as a foundation. But the
reversal of a former decision is the more serious when such
reversal involves an encroachment upon the legislative branch
of the government. Justice Harlan in his dissenting opinion
very properly calls attention to the language of the Court
when this identical question was before it in the Trans–Mis-

souri Freight case. He quotes the following from the decision in that case:

"To say, therefore, that the act excludes agreements which are not in unreasonable restraint of trade, and which tend simply to keep up reasonable rates for transportation, is subsequently to leave the question of unreasonableness to the companies themselves. But assuming that agreements of this nature are not void at common law and that the various cases cited by the learned courts below show it, the answer to the statement of their validity now is to be found in the terms of the statute under consideration. The arguments which have been addressed to us against the inclusion of all contracts in restraint of trade, as provided for by the language of the act, have been based upon the alleged presumption that Congress, notwithstanding the language of the act, could not have intended to embrace all contracts, but only such contracts as were in unreasonable restraint of trade. Under these circumstances, we are, therefore, asked to hold that the act of Congress excepts contracts which are not in unreasonable restraint of trade and which only keep rates up to a reasonable price, notwithstanding the language of the act makes no such exception. In other words, we are asked to read into the act by way of judicial legislation an exception that is not placed there by the lawmaking branch of the Government, and this is to be done upon the theory that the impolicy of such legislation is so clear that it cannot be supposed Congress intended the natural import of the language it used. This we cannot and ought not to do. If the act ought to read as contended for by defendants, Congress is the body to amend it, and not this Court by a process of judicial legislation wholly unjustifiable."

It will be seen that the Court at that time not only refused to amend the Anti–trust law by inserting the word "reasonable," but declared that it had no constitutional right to do so. The Court now does the very thing which the Court then declared to be unconstitutional. . . .

Under our Constitution the Court has the final word as to a law, and the only way in which the public can protest against judicial legislation is through the legislative branch of the government. While the Constitution divides the Federal Government into three branches, each independent of the other, it gives to the Supreme Court the power of interpretation, and this transcends for the time being the powers vested in the Legislature. But the people are not mocked; they can by legislation restrict the construction of the Court and prohibit a construction which will nullify a statute.

Then, too, the people can reach a Court through the changes that are constantly occurring in the personnel of the Court. It would have been difficult fifteen years ago to conceive of such a change in the Court as would result in an eight–to–one decision overruling the decision of that date, but, since such a change has taken place, it is possible to conceive of another change during the next fifteen years that will bring at least a majority of the Court back to the rule that prevailed before the so–called "rule of reason" took violent possession of the Court. It is possible also that Congress may see fit to express its disapproval of the construction placed upon the Anti–trust law by the Court in the Standard Oil and Tobacco cases. It may see fit to pass some of the bills already introduced by specifically declaring that the law prohibits all restraint of trade—not merely unreasonable restraint.

While I think that this ought to be done in order that the present law may not be robbed of such strength as it possesses, such legislation should be accompanied by further legislation that will fix arbitrarily the percentage of the total product which one corporation can control. The law as it formerly stood and as it was previously construed was uncertain enough—it was difficult for a corporation to know exactly what it might or might not lawfully do, but this uncertainty is greatly increased by the insertion of the word "unreasonable." The Democratic platform of 1908 set forth a remedy which would, in the opinion of those who urge it, afford substantial relief to the public without doing injustice to any corporation. The platform plan contemplates the licensing of any corporation engaged in interstate commerce when that corporation controls as much as twenty–five per cent. of the total product; corporations controlling a less proportion would not be affected by the plan. Corporations taking out the proposed license would be subject to any restrictions that Congress thought necessary to the proper conduct of their business as well as to the laws of any State in which they did business, and no corporation would be permitted to control more than one–half of the total product. We should have this additional legislation clearly and specifically drawing the line between the corporations engaged in legitimate work and the corporations which are engaged in unlawful transactions. Such legislation is demanded in the interest of the public and in the interest of legitimate business as well. It is not right to assume that any large percentage of our business men desire to engage in transactions which are harmful to the public, and those who are engaged in intentional wrongdoing should be segregated and subjected to punishment. Legitimate business has too long had to bear the odium thrown upon it by those guilty of conduct indefensible in morals as well as repugnant to the letter and spirit of the statutes.

Before passing from this branch of the subject, it may be worth while to inquire whether the Court, in entering upon judicial legislation, does not encourage those who favor a change in the method of selecting judges. Whatever may be said in favor of the appointment for life of men engaged in *interpreting* the law, no good reason can be given for the appointment, especially for life, of a *legislative* body. Nothing is more abhorrent to our institutions than an appointive legislative body. Even the United States Senate is elective, and its members hold office for a specified term, and yet the sentiment in favor of popular election is so strong that we are upon the eve of a change which will make Senators elective by direct vote of the people. If the Supreme Court is to become a legislative body, what reason can be given for not making it elective also? The people would submit much more willingly to judicial legislation if they had a chance to elect the judges for fixed terms. Will they consent to legislation on important questions by a Court whose members are not only *appointed* by the President, but appointed *for life?* Justice Harlan thus answers the question:

> "Nobody can tell what will happen. When the American people come to the conclusion that the judiciary of this land is usurping to itself the functions of the legislative department of the Government, and by judicial construction only is declaring what is the public policy of the United States, we will find trouble. Ninety millions of people—all sorts of people with all sorts of opinions— are not going to submit to the usurpation by the judiciary of the functions of other departments of the Government and the power on its part to declare what is the public policy of the United States."

Sixth: Attention has been called to a number of questions raised by the decision of the Court, but there is one point which, above all others, challenges the attention of the public at this time. What will be the effect of the Court's decision on the statute which it *construes* (to use its language) or (to use the language of the dissenting justice) *virtually repeals?* The Anti-trust law of 1890 reads: "*Every* contract, combination in the form of trust or otherwise, or conspiracy in restraint of trade or commerce, etc." The Court declares that the statute should be constructed or amended) to read: "Every contract, combination in the form of trust or otherwise or conspiracy, in *unreasonable* restraint of trade or commerce etc." Of one thing there is no doubt—namely, that this construction or amendment of the law excludes from the penalties of the act *some* corporations that might, by the construction placed upon it fifteen years ago, be found guilty of a violation of the law. That is, it *lessens* the number of corporations to which it applies, and to this extent *weakens* the law as a protection to the public.

To understand this decision we must remember that after the decision of fifteen years ago the great corporations attempted to secure an amendment to the law *exactly in line with the present decision*. While this effort has been continuous, it is only necessary to refer to the attempt cited by Justice Harlan in his dissenting opinion. This instance is used not only because it is a recent attempt (made in 1909), but because the Judiciary Committee of the Senate filed an elaborate report, setting forth the reasons why the word "unreasonable" should not be inserted in the law. No one will accuse our Senate of being *unreasonably* hostile to big business interests even today, and it was still less hostile two years ago. The changes that have occurred during the last two years have very considerably increased the number of Senators who are opposed to the trusts and opposed to the control of industry by them. Yet even two years ago the Judiciary Committee of that body expressed its disapproval so vehemently that the attempt to change the law was abandoned. . . .

In the light of this decision, who is likely to be convicted of a criminal violation of the Anti-trust law? We may as well recognize that *we now have no criminal law against the trusts.* Whatever is left of the Anti-trust law—the only protection against monopolies for twenty-one years—must be enforced as a civil statute, and of what value is that when it requires four and a half years to reach a decision which, when reached, is of but little value when applied to another case? According to the decision of the Court, each case must now be decided upon the facts which it presents, the reasonableness of the restraint being a mere matter of opinion, and, as the value of testimony depends as much upon the manner of the witness as upon what he says, the court deciding upon a printed record may reach a very different conclusion from that reached by a court or jury having living witnesses before it.

If one would understand the effort of the Court's decision on the Anti-trust law, let him apply it to other criminal statutes with which he is more familiar. What would the statute against larceny amount to if it only prohibited "unreasonable" stealing? Or the statute against burglary if it did not prohibit burglary except when carried beyond a "reasonable" extent? What protection would there be in a law against assault and battery if it prohibited only "undue" beating? The average man will regard the report of the Senate Judiciary Committee above referred to as a much more reasonable document than the decision of the Supreme Court, and the opinion of the average man as to what should constitute a crime is an opinion that must be taken into consideration even by the Supreme Court, for in the United States the opinion of the average man sooner or later becomes the law of the land and the controlling force in government.

Seventh: And what shall we say of the Court's action in allowing six months for reorganization? If the defendants have been guilty of violating the law for twenty years, why should they be allowed six months in which to continue to violate the law while they perfect a new combination? In the Tobacco case Justice Harlan protests with feeling against the time given to the defendants, who are, by the decision, declared to be open and notorious violators of the law. He says, "I find nothing in this record from beginning to end that makes me at all anxious to perpetuate any combination among these companies."

Is it not a little strange that such consideration should be shown to men whose crimes are so enormous? If men of less wealth were involved, would the Court hesitate to enforce the law immediately? If the defendants have violated the law—and they could only be convicted upon the theory that they had violated the law—can the Court suspend the law as to them or grant them immunity in advance for future violation during a given period? Nothing can do more to encourage anarchy—no better material for anarchistic speeches can be furnished—than judicial decisions that deal leniently with great offenders. Equality before the law is not the doctrine of the demagogue. Those who believe in it are not disturbers of the peace, nor are they attempting to array class against class. Equality before the law is a fundamental doctrine of free government, and it cannot be disregarded with impunity by any court, however high. It is of the utmost importance that our courts shall deal with the great criminals as they deal with small ones; a man who steals a pocketbook is a violator of the law and deserves punishment, but he is no more a violator of the law than one who conspires against ninety millions of people. To visit swift condemnation upon the poor and friendless and to grant indulgence to the rich and powerful shocks the sense of justice which God has planted in every heart—that sense of justice which is the only foundation of free institutions.

Eighth: The last question to be considered is, what is to be the result of this decision? We have seen one result—namely, rejoicing on the part of every man pecuniarily interested in the corporations which are exploiting the public. But what will be the effect upon the public? This question cannot be answered without entering the realm of prophecy, and prophecy is uncertain. We have seen one decision of the Supreme Court—the decision in the Dred Scott case—hasten a civil war, and we have seen another decision—the decision in the Income Tax case—compel the submission of an amendment to the Constitution. We shall see, as time goes on, whether the people will acquiesce in this decision or be aroused by it to more energetic action against combinations in restraint of trade, and the result will have its effect upon the reputations of the members of the Court. If the revolution which Chief-Justice White has led marks the beginning of a permanent policy he will be accorded a high place among our jurists. If, on the other hand, public sentiment develops along the line of the dissenting opinion we may expect to see Justice Harlan increasingly honored. If his warning is heeded and the people assert their right to protect themselves against trusts and monopolies he will become the forerunner of a great reform, while the flame which the Court mistook for "the light of reason" will be discarded as an illusion.

14. The Trusts and the Democratic Party

Bryan in 1908 absorbed his third—and worst—defeat for the Presidency, running 1,260,000 votes behind the weak Republican candidate. Four years later, when the Bull Moose defection made Democratic victory almost certain, Bryan was clearly unavailable for the nomination, but he was a delegate from Nebraska to the national convention in Baltimore. Unfortunately, in view of the sensational charges made at the time by the Pujo Committee of Congress about domination of the United States by a hierarchy of financiers, two notorious members of that hierarchy also showed up as delegates: investment banker August Belmont from New York, and financial promoter Thomas Fortune Ryan from Virginia. An incensed Bryan introduced the following denunciation of "the privilege-hunting and favor-seeking class." But cooler heads well knew the Democratic need for campaign contributions from members of that class; as Ollie James of Kentucky, permanent chairman of the convention, blurted to Josephus Daniels, "My God, Josephus, what is the matter with Bryan? Does he want to destroy the Democratic Party?" The resolution had no chance to pass, but Bryan's enemies would not allow him to withdraw it. It was Senator-elect James K. Vardaman of Mississippi who came up with the required formula. He proposed that Bryan retract the second part of his resolution which demanded that Belmont and Ryan withdraw from the convention. Bryan agreed. Then Vardaman urged support for the gutted remnant upon the head of the New York delegation, boss Charles Murphy of Tammany. Reportedly Murphy said to August Belmont,

---

Official Report of the Proceedings of the Democratic National Convention, 1912, pp. 129–133.

"Now Augie, listen to yourself vote yourself out of the convention."
With New York's support, the resolution passed by 883 to 201½.

Mr. William Jennings Bryan, of Nebraska: Mr. Chairman, I understand that the rules under which we are acting require that resolutions be referred to the Committee on Resolutions. I have a resolution which I think ought to be acted upon before we begin the nominations. I therefore ask unanimous consent for its immediate consideration.

The Permanent Chairman: Is there objection to the unanimous consent asked for by the gentleman from Nebraska?

Several Delegates: What is the resolution?

The Permanent Chairman: Is there objection to the reading of the resolution? [After a pause:] The Chair hears none. The gentleman from Nebraska (Mr. Bryan) will read the resolution.

Mr. Bryan, of Nebraska: My resolution is as follows:

"Resolved, That in this crisis in our party's career and in our country's history this convention sends greetings to the people of the United States, and assures them that the party of Jefferson and of Jackson is still the champion of popular government and equality before the law. As proof of our fidelity to the people, we hereby declare ourselves opposed to the nomination of any candidate for president who is the representative of or under obligation to J. Pierpont Morgan, Thomas F. Ryan, August Belmont, or any other member of the privilege-hunting and favor–seeking class.

"Be it further resolved, That we demand the withdrawal from this convention of any delegate or delegates constituting or representing the above–named interests."

The Permanent Chairman: Is there objection to the immediate consideration of the resolution? If there is objection, it takes two–thirds to suspend the rules.

Mr. Thomas J. Spellacy, of Connecticut: I object.

Mr. Luke Lea, of Tennessee: Mr. Chairman, I rise to a question of information. So that this convention may know that it is a duly accredited delegate who objects, I ask that the objector give his name.

MR. SPELLACY, of Connecticut: Thomas J. Spellacy, of Connecticut, objects; and moves that the resolution be referred to the Committee on Resolutions.

MR. JAMES V. COLEMAN, of California: As a delegate from California, I do not think it is the duty of this convention to throw dirt upon anybody.

MR. BRYAN, of Nebraska: Objection having been made to unanimous consent, I move to suspend the rules and pass the resolution at this time.

THE PERMANENT CHAIRMAN: The gentleman from Nebraska moves to suspend the rules and pass the resolution. According to the rules under which we are now operating, it takes two–thirds to suspend the rules. The question is, shall the rules be suspended and the resolution passed?

MR. A. GILCHRIST, of Florida: Mr. Chairman, I rise to a point of order.

THE PERMANENT CHAIRMAN: The gentleman will state his point of order.

MR. GILCHRIST, of Florida: I raise the point of order that above all things else for which the Democratic party has stood, the first is home rule and the right of the states to govern themselves. I have been informed that a great state of this nation, Virginia, the great mother of Presidents, has seen fit to elect as a delegate to this convention one of the men named in this resolution.

THE PERMANENT CHAIRMAN: One moment. Governor Gilchrist will state his point of order first. The argument will come afterward.

MR. GILCHRIST, of Florida: I make the point of order that when a state has elected delegates to this convention, we have no right to go behind the election of delegates made by a sovereign state of this nation. [Applause.]

THE PERMANENT CHAIRMAN: The Chair holds that this convention is a sovereign body, and can, by suspending the rules, do whatever it desires. Therefore the motion is in order. Under the rules each side is entitled to twenty minutes for debate.

MR. EMMETT O'NEAL, of Alabama: Mr. Chairman, it is the right of every delegate to hear what the resolution contains, and I ask that it be read again, so that every member of this Convention can vote intelligently upon it.

THE PERMANENT CHAIRMAN: The gentleman from Nebraska will read the resolution.

MR. BRYAN, of Nebraska: I will read the resolution again:

"*Resolved*, That in this crisis in our party's career and in our country's history, this Convention sends greetings to the people of the United States, and assures them that the party of Jefferson and of Jackson is still the champion of popular government and equality before the law. As proof of our fidelity to the people, we hereby declare ourselves opposed to the nomination of any candidate for President who is the representative of or under obligation to J. Pierpont Morgan, Thomas F. Ryan, August Belmont, or any other member of the privilege–hunting and favor–seeking class. Be it further

"*Resolved*, That we demand the withdrawal from this Convention of any delegate or delegates constituting or representing the above–named interests."

MR. J. RANDOLPH ANDERSON, of Georgia: Mr. Chairman, I move to lay the resolution upon the table.

THE PERMANENT CHAIRMAN: The gentleman is out of order. The gentleman from Nebraska (Mr. Bryan) moves to suspend the rules and pass the resolution, and has the floor for the purpose of debate.

MR. DAVID FITZGERALD, of Connecticut: Mr. Chairman, a question for information. Do I understand that Mr. Ryan of Virginia and Mr. Belmont of New York are delegates here in this Convention?

THE PERMANENT CHAIRMAN: That is not a parliamentary inquiry. The gentleman can ascertain that for himself by looking at the printed list of delegates.

MR. BRYAN, of Nebraska: Members of this Convention, this is an extraordinary resolution; but extraordinary conditions need extraordinary remedies. We are now engaged in the conduct of a convention that will place before this country the Democratic nominee, and I assume that every delegate in this convention is here because he wants that nominee elected. [Applause.] It is in order that we may advance the cause of our candidate that I present this resolution.

There are questions of which a court takes judicial notice, and there are subjects upon which we can assume that the American people are informed. There is not a delegate in this convention who does not know that an effort is being made right now to sell the Democratic party into bondage to the predatory interests of this nation. It is the most brazen, the most insolent, the most impudent attempt that has been made in the history of American politics to dominate a convention, stifle the honest sentiment of a people and make the nominee the bond–slave of the men who exploit the people of this country. [Applause.]

I need not tell you that J. Pierpont Morgan, Thomas F. Ryan and August Belmont are three of the men who are connected with the great money trust of this country, who are as despotic in their rule of the business of the country, and as merciless in their command of their slaves, as any man in the country. [Applause.]

Some one has suggested that we have no right to discuss the delegates who come here from a sovereign State.

MR. GILCHRIST, of Florida: I said that.

MR. BRYAN, of Nebraska: I reply that if these men are willing to insult six and a half million Democrats, we ought to speak out against them, and let them know we resent the insult. [Applause.]

I for one am not willing that Thomas F. Ryan and August Belmont shall come here with their paid attorneys and seek secret counsel with the managers of this party. [Applause.] And no sense of politeness or courtesy to such men will keep me from protecting my party from the disgrace that they inflict upon us. [Applause.]

My friends, I cannot speak for you. You have your own responsibility; but if this is to be a convention run by these men, if our nominee is to be their representative and tool, I pray you to give us, who represent constituencies that do not want this, a chance to go on record with our protest against it. [Applause.] If any of you are willing to nominate a candidate who represents these men, or who is under obligation to these men, do it and take the responsibility. I refuse to take that responsibility. [Applause.]

Some have said that we have not a right to demand the withdrawal of delegates from this convention. I will make you a proposition. One of these men sits with New York and the other sits with Virginia. I make you this proposition: If the State of New York will take a poll of her delegates, and a majority of them—not Mr. Murphy, but a majority of the delegates on a roll call, where her delegates can have their names recorded and printed—do not ask for the withdrawal of the name of Mr. Belmont; and if Virginia will on a roll call protest against the withdrawal of Mr. Ryan, I will then withdraw the last part of the resolution, which demands the withdrawal of these men from the Convention. I will withdraw the last part, on the request of the State delegations in which these gentlemen sit; but I will not withdraw the first part, which demands that our candidate shall be free from entanglement with them. [Applause.]

MR. HENRY D. FLOOD, of Virginia: May I interrupt the gentleman?

THE PERMANENT CHAIRMAN: Does the gentleman from Nebraska yield to the gentleman from Virginia?

MR. BRYAN, of Nebraska: Certainly.

MR. FLOOD, of Virginia: In the name of the sovereign State of Virginia, which has 24 votes on this floor, I accept the insolent proposition made by the only man in this convention who wants to destroy the prospects of Democratic success. [Applause.]

MR. JAMES K. VARDAMAN, of Mississippi: Gentlemen of the Convention, I sincerely hope that the members of this organization will preserve order while the discussion of this question, so vital to the Democracy of America, proceeds. You cannot settle anything by the use of your throats. The time has arrived in the history of this organization when reason, good common sense and moderation should control the deliberations of this body. We cannot afford to permit this opportunity, which the Democracy now enjoys, to be squandered. I think the resolution which has been presented to you by Mr. Bryan contains in part some merit.

I most heartily approve the first part of the resolution. I do not want you, nor would I have this convention trench upon the rights of the States in the selection of delegates [applause]; but I also agree with him that the fewer we have of the class he named, the better it will be for Democracy in November. [Applause.]

I am going to ask you to be quiet and preserve order while Mr. Bryan makes a statement to the Convention.

MR. BRYAN, of Nebraska: I yield to Mr. Price, of Virginia.

MR. JOHN W. PRICE, of Virginia: Mr. Chairman and gentlemen of the Convention, on behalf of the sovereign State of Virginia, we protest as to the latter part of the resolution, but no one will accede more heartily and more thoroughly to the first part of the resolution than the State of Virginia.

Virginia has always been able to control her own internal affairs. [Applause.] She has never yet asked aid or help from any outside influence. [Applause.] If there are undesirable citizens on the delegation from Virginia, Virginia will take that responsibility. [Applause.]

15. "The Prince of Peace"

While traveling in January 1914, Secretary of State Bryan (see Document 16) and his wife suffered a delay of four hours in Pittsburgh. Billy Sunday was exhorting the faithful of that city to declare for Christ, and the Bryans went to hear him. The next day Bryan wrote to the evangelist, who was often attacked because his appeals could become so crude as to seem impious: "Do not allow yourself to be disturbed by critics—God is giving you 'souls for your hire,' and that is a sufficient answer. . . . No man can do good without making enemies, but yours will, as a rule, be among those who do not hear you." Bryan had long been working the revival circuit himself.

Although, until he went to Washington in 1913, Bryan continued to publish The Commoner *as a weekly, the magazine was really managed by his brother Charles F. Bryan. William earned most of his income by giving lectures. He repeated the following talk literally hundreds of times, often under the sponsorship of Chautauqua or Y.M.C.A. groups, and in such cities as Montreal, Toronto, Jerusalem, Cairo, Bombay, Manila, and Tokyo. Because of Bryan's later irascibility and dogmatism on the subject, special interest attaches to the amiable toleration of Darwinism that he manifested prior to World War I.*

I offer no apology for speaking upon a religious theme for it is the most universal of all themes. If I addressed you upon the subject of law I might interest the lawyers; if I discussed the science of medicine I might interest the physicians; in like

---

The Prince of Peace, [1908?].

manner merchants might be interested in a talk on commerce, and farmers in a discussion of agriculture; but none of these subjects appeals to all. Even the science of government, though broader than any profession or occupation, does not embrace the whole sum of life, and those who think upon it differ so among themselves that I could not speak upon the subject so as to please a part without offending others. While to me the science of government is intensely absorbing I recognize that the most important things in life lie outside of the realm of government and that more depends upon what the individual does for himself than upon what the government does or can do for him. Men can be miserable under the best government and they can be happy under the worst government.

Government affects but a part of the life which we live here and does not touch at all the life beyond, while religion touches the infinite circle of existence as well as the small arc of that circle which we spend on earth. No greater theme, therefore, can engage our attention.

Man is a religious being; the heart instinctively seeks for a God. Whether he worships on the banks of the Ganges, prays with his face upturned to the sun, kneels toward Mecca or, regarding all space as a temple, communes with the Heavenly Father according to the Christian creed, man is essentially devout.

There are honest doubters whose sincerity we recognize and respect, but occasionally I find young men who think it smart to be skeptical; they talk as if it were an evidence of larger intelligence to scoff at creeds and refuse to connect themselves with churches. They call themselves "liberal," as if a Christian were narrow minded. To these young men I desire to address myself.

Even some older people profess to regard religion as a superstition, pardonable in the ignorant but unworthy of the educated—a mental state which one can and should outgrow. Those who hold this view look down with mild contempt upon such as give to religion a definite place in their thoughts and lives. They assume an intellectual superiority and often take little pains to conceal the assumption. Tolstoy administers to the "cultured crowd" (the words quoted are his) a severe rebuke when he declares that the religious sentiment rests not upon a superstitious fear of the invisible forces of nature, but upon man's consciousness of his finiteness amid an infinite universe and of his sinfulness; and this consciousness, the great philosopher adds, man can never outgrow. Tolstoy is right; man recognizes how limited are his own powers and how vast is the universe, and he leans upon the arm that is stronger than his. Man feels the weight of his sins and looks for One who is sinless.

Religion has been defined as the relation which man fixes between himself and his God, and morality as the outward manifestation of this relation. Every one, by the time he reaches maturity, has fixed some relation between himself and God and no material change in this relation can take place without a revolution in the man, for this relation is the most potent influence that acts upon a human life.

Religion is the basis of morality in the individual and in the group of individuals. Materialists have attempted to build up a system of morality upon the basis of enlightened self-interest. They would have man figure out by mathematics that it pays him to abstain from wrong doing; they would even inject an element of selfishness into altruism, but the moral system elaborated by the materialists has several defects. First, its virtues are borrowed from moral systems based upon religion; second, as it rests upon argument rather than upon authority, it does not appeal to the young and by the time the young are able to follow their reason they have already become set in their ways. Our laws do not permit a young man to dispose of real estate until he is twenty-one—Why this restraint? Because his reason is not mature; and yet a man's life is largely moulded by the environment of his youth. Third, one never knows just how much of his decision is due to reason and how much is due to passion or to selfish interests. We recognize the bias of self-interest when we exclude from the jury every man, no matter how reasonable or upright he may be, who has a pecuniary interest in the result of the trial. And, fourth, one whose morality is based upon a nice calculation of benefits to be secured spends time figuring that he should spend in action. Those who keep a book account of their good deeds seldom do enough good to justify keeping books.

Morality is the power of endurance in man; and a religion which teaches personal responsibility to God gives strength to morality. There is a powerful restraining influence in the belief that an all–seeing eye scrutinizes every thought and word and act of the individual.

There is a wide difference between the man who is trying to conform to a standard of morality about him and the man who is endeavoring to make his life approximate to a divine standard. The former attempts to live up to the standard if it is above him and down to it if it is below him—and if he is doing right only when others are looking he is sure to find a time when he thinks he is unobserved, and then he takes a vacation and falls. One needs the inner strength which comes with the conscious presence of a personal God. If those who are thus fortified sometimes yield to temptation how helpless and hopeless must those be who rely upon their own strength alone!

There are difficulties to be encountered in religion, but there are difficulties to be encountered everywhere. I passed through a period of skepticism when I was in college and I have been glad ever since that I became a member of the church before I left home for college, for it helped me during those trying days. The college days cover the dangerous period in the young man's life; it is when he is just coming into possession of his powers—when he feels stronger than he ever feels afterward and thinks he knows more than he ever does know.

It was at this period that I was confused by the different theories of creation. But I examined these theories and found that they all assumed something to begin with. The nebular hypothesis, for instance, assumes that matter and force existed —matter in particles infinitely fine and each particle separated from every other particle by space infinitely great. Beginning with this assumption, force working on matter—according to this hypothesis—creates a universe. Well, I have a right to assume, and I prefer to assume a Designer back of the design— a Creator back of creation; and no matter how long you draw out the process of creation, so long as God stands back of it you can not shake my faith in Jehovah. In Genesis it is written that, in the beginning, God created the heavens and the earth, and I can stand on that proposition until I find some theory of creation that goes farther back than "the beginning."

I do not carry the doctrine of evolution as far as some do; I have not yet been able to convince myself, that man is a lineal descendant of the lower animals. I do not mean to find fault with you if you want to accept it; all I mean to say is that while you may trace your ancestry back to the monkey if you find pleasure or pride in doing so, you shall not connect me with your family tree without more evidence than has yet been produced. It is true that man, in some physical qualities, resembles the beast, but man has a mind as well as a body and a soul as well as a mind. The mind is greater than the body and the soul is greater than the mind, and I object to having man's pedigree traced on one-third of him only—and that the lowest third. Fairbairn lays down a sound proposition when he says that it is not sufficient to explain man as an animal; it is necessary to explain man in history—and the Darwinian theory does not do this. The ape, according to this theory, is older than man and yet he is still an ape while man is the author of the marvellous civilization which we see about us.

One does not escape from mystery, however, by accepting this theory, for it does not explain the origin of life. When the follower of Darwin has traced the germ of life back to the lowest form in which it appears—and to follow him one must exercise more faith than religion calls for—he finds that scientists differ. Some believe that the first germ of life came from another planet and others hold that it was the result of spontaneous generation.

If I were compelled to accept one of these theories I would prefer the first, for if we can chase the germ of life off this planet and get it out into space we can guess the rest of the way and no one can contradict us, but if we accept the doctrine of spontaneous generation we can not explain why spontaneous generation ceased to act after the first germ was created.

Go back as far as we may, we can not escape from the creative act, and it is just as easy for me to believe that God created man as he is as to believe that, millions of years ago, He created a germ of life and endowed it with power to develop into all that we see today. But I object to the Darwinian theory, until more conclusive proof is produced, because I fear we shall lose the consciousness of God's presence in our daily life, if we must assume that through all the ages no spiritual force has touched the life of man or shaped the destiny of nations. But there is another objection. The Darwinian theory represents man as reaching his present perfection by the operation of the law of hate—the merciless law by which the strong crowd out and kill off the weak. If this is the law of our development then, if there is any logic that can bind the human mind, we shall turn backward toward the beast in proportion as we substitute the law of love. How can hatred be the law of development when nations have advanced in proportion as they have departed from that law and adopted the law of love?

But while I do not accept the Darwinian theory I shall not quarrel with you about it; I only refer to it to remind you that it does not solve the mystery of life or explain human progress.

I fear that some have accepted it in the hope of escaping from the miracle, but why should the miracle frighten us? It bothered me once, and I am inclined to think that it is one of the test questions with the Christian.

Christ can not be separated from the miraculous; His birth, His ministrations, and His resurrection, all involve the miraculous, and the change which His religion works in the human heart is a continuing miracle. Eliminate the miracles and Christ becomes merely a human being and His gospel is stripped of divine authority.

The miracle raises two questions: "Can God perform a miracle?" and, "Would He want to?" The first is easy to answer. A God who can make a world can do anything He wants to do with it. The power to perform miracles is necessarily implied in the power to create. But would God want to perform a miracle?—this is the question which has given most of the trouble. The more I have considered it the less inclined I am to answer in the negative. To say that God would not perform a miracle is to assume a more intimate knowledge of God's plans and purposes than I can claim to have. I will not deny that God does perform a miracle or may perform one merely because I do not know how or why He does it. The fact that we are constantly learning of the existence of new forces suggests the possibility that God may operate through forces yet unknown to us, and the mysteries with which we deal every day warn me that faith is as necessary as sight. Who would have credited a century ago the stories that are now told of the wonder working electricity? For ages man had known the lightning, but only to fear it; now, this invisible current is generated by a man–made machine, imprisoned in a man–made wire and made to do the bidding of man. We are even able to dispense with the wire and hurl words through space, and the X–ray has enabled us to look through substances which were supposed, until recently, to exclude all light. The miracle is not more mysterious than many of the things with which man now deals—it is simply different. The immaculate conception is not more mysterious than any other conception—it is simply unlike; nor is the resurrection of Christ more mysterious than the myriad resurrections which mark each annual seed–time.

It is sometimes said that God could not suspend one of His laws without stopping the Universe, but do we not suspend or overcome the law of gravitation every day? Every time we move a foot or lift a weight, we temporarily interfere with the operation of the most universal of natural laws and yet the world is not disturbed.

Science has taught us so many things that we are tempted to conclude that we know everything, but there is really a great unknown which is still unexplored and that which we have learned ought to increase our reverence rather than our egotism. Science has disclosed some of the machinery of the universe, but science has not yet revealed to us the great secret—the secret of life. It is to be found in every blade of grass, in every insect, in every bird and in every animal, as well as in man. Six thousand years of recorded history and yet we know no more about the secret of life than they knew in the beginning. We live, we plan; we have our hopes, our fears; and yet in a moment a change may come over any one of us and this body will become a mass of lifeless clay. What is it that, having, we live and, having not, we are as the clod? We know not and yet the progress of the race and the civilization which we now behold are the work of men and women who have not solved the mystery of their own lives.

And our food, must we understand it before we eat it? If we refused to eat anything until we could understand the mystery of its growth, we would die of starvation. But mystery does not bother us in the dining room; it is only in the church that it is an obstacle.

I was eating a piece of watermelon some months ago and was struck with its beauty. I took some of the seed and dried them and weighed them, and found that it would require some five thousand seed to weigh a pound. And then I applied mathematics to that forty pound melon. One of these seeds, put into the ground, when warmed by the sun and moistened by the rain, goes to work; it gathers from somewhere two hundred thousand times its own weight and, forcing this raw material through a tiny stem, constructs a watermelon. It covers the outside with a coating of green; inside of the green it puts a layer of white, and within the white a core of red, and all through the red it scatters seeds each one capable of continuing the work of reproduction. Where did that little seed get its tremendous power? Where did it find its coloring matter? How did it collect its flavoring extract? How did it build a watermelon? Until you can explain a watermelon, do not be too sure that you can set limits to the power of the Almighty or say just what He would do or how He would do it. I can not explain the watermelon but I eat it and enjoy it.

Everything that grows tells a like story of infinite power. Why should I deny that a divine hand fed a multitude with a few loaves and fishes when I see hundreds of millions fed every year by a hand which converts the seeds scattered over the field into an abundant harvest? We know that food can be multiplied in a few months' time; shall we deny the power of the Creator to eliminate the element of time, when we have gone so far in eliminating the element of space?

But there is something even more wonderful still—the mysterious change that takes place in the human heart when the man begins to hate the things he loved and to love the things he hated—the marvellous transformation that takes place in the man who, before the change, would have sacrificed the world for his own advancement but who, after the change, would give his life for a principle and esteem it a privilege to make sacrifice for his convictions. What greater miracle than this, that converts a selfish, self centered, human being into a center from which good influences flow out in every direction! And yet this miracle has been wrought in the heart of each one of us—or may be wrought—and we have seen it wrought in the hearts of those about us. No, living in the midst of mystery and miracles I shall not allow either to deprive me of the benefits of the Christian religion.

Some of those who question the miracle also question the theory of atonement; they assert that it does not accord with their idea of justice for one to die for others. Let each one bear his own sins and the punishments due for them, they say. The doctrine of vicarious suffering is not a new one; it is as old as the race. That one should suffer for others is one of the most familiar of principles and we see the principle illustrated every day of our lives. Take the family, for instance; from the day the mother's first child is born, for twenty-five or thirty years they are scarcely out of her waking thoughts. She sacrifices for them, she surrenders herself to them. Is it because she expects them to pay her back? Fortunate for the parent and fortunate for the child if the latter has an opportunity to repay in part the debt it owes. But no child can compensate a parent for a parent's care. In the course of nature the debt is paid, not to the parent, but to the next generation, each generation suffering and sacrificing for the one following.

Nor is this confined to the family. Every step in advance has been made possible by those who have been willing to sacrifice for posterity. Freedom of speech, freedom of the press, freedom of conscience and free government have all been won for the world by those who were willing to make sacrifices for their fellows. So well established is this doctrine that we do not regard any one as great unless he recognizes how unimportant his life is in comparison with the problems with which he deals.

I find proof that man was made in the image of his Creator in the fact that, throughout the centuries, man has been willing to die that blessings denied to him might be enjoyed by his children, his children's children and the world.

The seeming paradox: "He that saveth his life shall lose it and he that loseth his life for my sake shall find it," has an application wider than that usually given to it; it is an epitome of history. Those who live only for themselves live little lives, but those who give themselves for the advancement of things greater than themselves find a larger life than the one surrendered. Wendell Phillips gave expression to the same idea when he said: "How prudently most men sink into nameless graves, while now and then a few forget themselves into immortality."

Instead of being an unnatural plan, the plan of salvation is in perfect harmony with human nature as we understand it. Sacrifice is the language of love, and Christ, in suffering for the world, adopted the only means of reaching the heart, and this can be demonstrated, not only by theory but by experience, for the story of His life, His teachings, His sufferings and His death has been translated into every language and everywhere it has touched the heart.

But if I were going to present an argument in favor of the divinity of Christ, I would not begin with miracles or mystery or theory of atonement. I would begin as Carnegie Simpson begins in his book entitled, "The Fact of Christ." Commencing with the fact that Christ lived, he points out that one can not contemplate this undisputed fact without feeling that in some way this fact is related to those now living. He says that one can read of Alexander, of Caesar or of Napoleon, and not feel that it is a matter of personal concern; but that when one reads that Christ lived and how He lived and how He died he feels that somehow there is a chord that stretches from that life to his. As he studies the character of Christ he becomes conscious of certain virtues which stand out in bold relief—purity, humility, a forgiving spirit and an unfathomable love. The author is correct. Christ presents an example of purity in thought and life, and man, conscious of his own imperfections and grieved over his shortcomings, finds inspiration in One who was tempted in all points like as we are, and yet without sin. I am not sure but that we can find just here a way of determining whether one possesses the true spirit of a Christian. If he finds in the sinlessness of Christ an inspiration and a stimulus to greater effort and higher living, he is indeed a follower; if, on the other hand, he resents the reproof which the purity of Christ offers he is likely to question the divinity of Christ in order to excuse himself for not being a follower.

Humility is a rare virtue. If one is rich he is apt to be proud of his riches; if he has distinguished ancestry, he is apt to be proud of his lineage; if he is well educated, he is apt to be proud of his learning. Some one has suggested that if one becomes humble, he soon becomes proud of his humility. Christ, however, possessed of all power, was the very personification of humility.

The most difficult of all the virtues to cultivate is the forgiving spirit. Revenge seems to be natural to the human heart; to want to get even with an enemy is a common sin. It has even been popular to boast of vindictiveness; it was once inscribed on a monument to a hero that he had repaid both friends and enemies more than he had received. This was not the spirit of Christ. . . .

A belief in immortality not only consoles the individual but it exerts a powerful influence in bringing peace between individuals. If one really thinks that man dies as the brute dies, he may yield to the temptation to do injustice to his neighbor when the circumstances are such as to promise security from detection. But if one really expects to meet again, and live eternally with, those whom he knows today, he is restrained from evil deeds by the fear of endless remorse. We do not know what rewards are in store for us or what punishments may be reserved, but if there were no other punishment it would be enough for one who deliberately and consciously wrongs another to have to live forever in the company of the person wronged and have his littleness and selfishness laid bare. I repeat, a belief in immortality must exert a powerful influence in establishing justice between men and thus laying the foundation for peace.

Again, Christ deserves to be called The Prince of Peace because He has given us a measure of greatness which promotes peace. When His disciples disputed among themselves as to which should be greatest in the Kingdom of Heaven, He rebuked them and said: "Let him who would be chiefest among you be the servant of all." Service is the measure of greatness; it always has been true; it is true today, and it always will be true, that he is greatest who does the most of good. And yet, what a revolution it will work in this old world when this standard becomes the standard of life. Nearly all of our controversies and combats arise from the fact that we are trying to get something from each other—there will be peace when our aim is to do something for each other. Our enmities and animosities arise from our efforts to get as much as possible out of the world—there will be peace when our endeavor is to put as much as possible into the world. Society will take an immeasurable step toward peace when it estimates a citizen by his output rather than by his income and gives the crown of its approval to the one who makes the largest contribution to the welfare of all. It is the glory of the Christian ideal that, while it is within sight of the weakest and the lowliest, it is yet so high that the best and the noblest are kept with their faces turned ever upward.

Christ has also led the way to peace by giving us a formula for the propagation of good. Not all of those who have really desired to do good have employed the Christian method—not all Christians even. In all the history of the human race but two methods have been employed. The first is the forcible method. A man has an idea which he thinks is good; he tells his neighbors about it and they do not like it. This makes him angry and, seizing a club, he attempts to make them like it. One trouble about this rule is that it works both ways; when a man starts out to compel his neighbors to think as he does, he generally finds them willing to accept the challenge and they spend so much time in trying to coerce each other that they have no time left to be of service to each other.

The other is the Bible plan—be not overcome of evil but overcome evil with good. And there is no other way of overcoming evil. I am not much of a farmer—I get more credit for my farming than I deserve, and my little farm receives more advertising than it is entitled to. But I am farmer enough to know that if I cut down weeds they will spring up again, and I know that if I plant something there which has more vitality than the weeds I shall not only get rid of the constant cutting but have the benefit of the crop besides.

In order that there might be no mistake about His plan of propagating good, Christ went into detail and laid emphasis upon the value of example—"so live that others seeing your good works may be constrained to glorify your Father which is in Heaven." There is no human influence so potent for good as that which goes out from an upright life. A sermon may be answered; the arguments presented in a speech may be disputed, but no one can answer a Christian life—it is the unanswerable argument in favor of our religion.

It may be a slow process—this conversion of the world by the silent influence of a noble example, but it is the only sure one, and the doctrine applies to nations as well as to individuals. The Gospel of the Prince of Peace gives us the only hope that the world has—and it is an increasing hope—of the substitution of reason for the arbitrament of force in the settlement of international disputes.

But Christ has given us a platform more fundamental than any political party has ever written. We are interested in platforms; we attend conventions, sometimes traveling long distances; we have wordy wars over the phraseology of various planks and then we wage earnest campaigns to secure the endorsement of these platforms at the polls. But the platform given to the world by the Nazarene is more far-reaching and more comprehensive than any platform ever written by the convention of any party in any country. When He condensed into one commandment those of the ten which relate of man's duty toward his fellows and enjoined upon us the rule, "Thou shalt love thy neighbor as thyself," He presented a plan for the solution of all the problems that now vex society or may hereafter arise. Other remedies may palliate or postpone the day of settlement but this is all–sufficient and the reconciliation which it effects is a permanent one.

If I were to attempt to apply this thought to various questions which are at issue, I might be accused of entering the domain of partisan politics, but I may safely apply it to two great problems. First, let us consider the question of capital and labor. This is not a transient issue or a local one. It engages the attention of the people of all countries and has appeared in every age. The immediate need in this country is arbitration, for neither side to the controversy can be trusted to deal with absolute justice, if allowed undisputed control; but arbitration, like a court, is a last resort. It would be better if the relations between employer and employee were such as to make arbitration unnecessary. Just in proportion as men recognize their kinship to each other and deal with each other in the spirit of brotherhood will friendship and harmony be secured. Both employer and employee need to cultivate the spirit which follows from obedience to the great commandment.

The second problem to which I would apply this platform of peace is that which relates to the accumulation of wealth. We can not much longer delay consideration of the ethics of money–making. That many of the enormous fortunes which have been accumulated in the last quarter of a century are now held by men who have given to society no adequate service in return for the money secured is now generally recognized. While legislation can and should protect the public from predatory wealth, a more effective remedy will be found in the cultivation of a public opinion which will substitute a higher ideal than the one which tolerates the enjoyment of unearned gains. No man who really knows what brotherly love is will desire to take advantage of his neighbor, and the conscience when not seared will admonish against injustice. My faith in the future rests upon the belief that Christ's teachings are being more studied today than ever before and that with this larger study will come an application of those teachings to the every day life of the world. In former times men read that Christ came to bring life and immortality to light and placed the emphasis upon immortality; now they are studying Christ's relation to human life. In former years many thought to prepare themselves for future bliss by a life of seclusion here; now they are learning that they can not follow in the footsteps of the Master unless they go about doing good. Christ declared that He came that we might have life and have it more abundantly. The world is learning that Christ came not to narrow life but to enlarge it—to fill it with purpose, earnestness and happiness.

But this Prince of Peace promises not only peace but strength. Some have thought His teachings fit only for the weak and the timid and unsuited to men of vigor, energy and ambition. Nothing could be farther from the truth. Only the man of faith can be courageous. Confident that he fights on the side of Jehovah he doubts not the success of his cause. What matters it whether he shares in the shouts of triumph? If every word spoken in behalf of truth has its influence and every deed done for the right weighs in the final account it is immaterial to the Christian whether his eyes behold victory or whether he dies in the midst of the conflict. . . .

16. "A Single Standard of Morality"

The Nebraska delegation to the Democratic convention of 1912 was instructed to support Champ Clark of Missouri, Speaker of the House of Representatives, for the Presidential nomination. It did so until the fourteenth ballot, when Bryan led a switch to Woodrow Wilson (who was not actually nominated until the 46th ballot). Bryan justified his action by pointing to the support of Clark by the allegedly plutocratic New York delegation, and promised to go back to Clark if New York deserted him. This left-handed endorsement by Bryan was hardly pleasing to Wilson, as he found himself on the verge of becoming a minority President, having won less than 42 per cent of the popular vote. He desperately needed support, and the Great Commoner had a large following in the party inside Congress as well as among the electorate. Thus it came about that Bryan was named Secretary of State. "For nineteen hundred years," he wrote, "the gospel of the Prince of Peace has been making its majestic march around the world, and during these centuries the philosophy of the Sermon on the Mount has become more and more the rule of daily life. It only remains to lift that code of morals from the level of the individual and make it real in the law of nations, and this, I believe, is the task that God has reserved for the United States." Such sentiments would be hard to credit had they been written before World War I, but in fact the quotation is from a book published in 1917. The notion is expanded in the following article, which was also written after Bryan had left the Department of State.

"A Single Standard of Morality," *The Commoner*, XVI (March 1916), 9.

In a speech to his Birmingham constituents, delivered in 1858, John Bright, the great English statesman, said:

> ... The moral law was not written for men alone in their individual character, but it was written as well for nations, and for nations great as this of which we are citizens. If nations reject and deride that moral law, there is a penalty which will inevitably follow. It may not come at once, it may not come in our lifetime; but, rely upon it, the great Italian is not a poet only, but a prophet, when he says:
>
> "The sword of Heaven is not in haste to smite, Nor yet doth linger."

The rule for which Bright so eloquently pleads is the ideal toward which the world has been moving, all too slowly, but moving, for centuries and the need for this single standard of morality—a standard applicable alike to individuals and to nations—is emphasized by every war that stains the hands of man. It is the supreme international need at the present time.

The universally recognized standard of morals for individuals is built upon the Ten Commandments, and no one disputes the validity of the Commandments against killing, stealing, bearing false witness and covetousness, when applied to individuals; but these commandments are not sufficiently applied to the large groups, called nations and because they are not applied there is no standard of morals which can be authoritatively invoked for the regulation of international affairs.

Men whose consciences would not permit them to take a neighbor's life, as an individual act, think it is entirely proper to take life by wholesale, either through those whom they command or at the command of others—and that, too, without regard to the cause of the war. Nations which long since ceased to imprison their own citizens for debt, do not hesitate to bombard foreign cities and slaughter the inhabitants of foreign countries as a means of enforcing the re-payment of international loans—sometimes loans of questionable validity.

Men who would not think of stealing from a neighbor are

taught to believe that it is patriotic to defend the taking of territory, if their nation gains by the act. Men who would shrink from slandering a neighbor seem to feel no compunctions of conscience when they misrepresent the purposes and plans of other nations; and covetousness, which is regarded as sinful in the individual, seems to be transformed into a virtue when it infects a nation. This attempt to limit the application of these commandments to small transactions has cost an enormous quantity of blood and has brought confusion into international councils.

The false philosophy which is responsible for the blurring of the line between right and wrong in international affairs, is the old, brutal barbarous doctrine that might makes right—the doctrine that a nation is at liberty to seize whatever it has the strength to seize and the power to hold. This doctrine not only leads to cruelty and inhumanity as between belligerents, but it leads to the ignoring of the rights of neutrals. Belligerent nations which make might the test of right, exalt "military necessity" to a position of supreme importance and demand that neutral nations submit to any dangers or damage that the belligerent nations think will contribute to the success of belligerent arms.

International law is a series of precedents and, since precedents relied upon are the wrongs perpetrated, or the rights respected, by nations at war, international law has the appearance of being written upon the theory that war and not peace is the normal relation between nations. The remedy for this very unsatisfactory condition is to be sought upon five lines.

First. The substitution of arbitration for force in the settlement of all differences which are arbitrable in character. The leading nations, however, do not regard all questions as arbitrable. For illustration, the most advanced arbitration treaties to which the United States is a party contains four exceptions, viz., questions of honor, of independence, of vital interests and questions which affect the interests of third parties.

Second. The investigation, by an international tribunal, of all disputes which are not declared by treaty to be arbitrable. This closes the gap left by the arbitration treaties and leaves nothing which can become the cause of war until after a period of delay which gives opportunity for passion to subside, for the separation of questions of honor from questions of fact and for the peace of the estranged nations to bring their influence to bear on their respective governments.

These treaties are framed upon the theory that diplomacy, at its best, is the art of keeping cool. Man should deal with his fellows, not when he is angry, but when he is calm. When he is angry he talks of what he can do, and usually overestimates it; when he is calm he thinks of what he ought to do, and listens to the voice of conscience. The settlement of international disputes should, therefore, be postponed until the parties can dispassionately consider the questions at issue.

The thirty treaties above mentioned, negotiated in 1914 and 1915, with governments exercising authority over three–fourths of the inhabitants of the globe, contain three provisions which promise to make wars between the contracting parties a remote possibility; first, they include disputes of every kind and character; second, they allow a year's time for investigation and report; and, third, they pledge the contracting nations not to declare war or begin hostilities until the investigation is concluded and the report made.

Third. It is not sufficient to provide the machinery for the preservation of peace. Much depends upon the tone of diplomatic communications—they may be persuasive or irritating. When the moral code now recognized among individuals becomes binding between nations, the rules which make lifetime attachments possible between neighbors will be followed in the chancellories of the world and the threat and the ultimatum will give way to the maxim: Nothing is final between friends.

Fourth. Back of this change in the language of diplomacy must be a change in the dominant national thought—a change which can not come until limitations are no longer placed upon the operation of moral principles. The individual, if his ideals are worthy, is as careful to respect the rights of others as he is to enforce his own rights, and it is this respect for the rights of others that makes neighborhood peace possible.

The same scrupulous regard for the rights of other nations will go far toward promoting international peace. Respect for the rights of others requires a higher form of courage than is required for the enforcement of one's own rights, and the heroism of self–restraint is superior, therefore to the heroism of conquest. "He that is slow to anger is better than the mighty; and he that ruleth his spirit than he that taketh a city."

Fifth. Still more fundamental in building a permanent peace is the spirit of brotherhood. Love, and love only, can take man from the "tooth and claw" class, make him conscious of kinship with all the race and conform his conduct to the Golden Rule. It is this, and this only, that will make it possible to plan for a limitless period of peace, with a nearer and nearer approach toward perfect justice. This is the solid rock "all else is shifting sand."

Carlyle, in the closing chapter of his French Revolution, presents this philosophy when he says:

> Hast thou considered how Thought is stronger than artillery parks, and (were it fifty years after death and martyrdom, or were it two thousand years) writes and unwrites acts of Parliament, removes mountains; models the world like soft clay? Also how the beginning of all Thought, worth the name, is love?

International relations, like all other human relations, rest on moral philosophy, and, in constructing an ethical code for the direction of governments in their dealings with each other, we must begin with a sense of kinship—the spirit of brotherhood.

Obedience to the injunction, "Thou shalt love thy neighbor as thyself" will lead to self-restraint; indeed, the motive for wrong doing being removed, self–restraint will become easy.

Then nations will be as careful to avoid doing injustice as they are now to enforce what they call their rights, but which are sometimes more selfish interests, sometimes the promptings of brutal instincts and sometimes the supposed requirements of a false standard of morality. When love is on the throne, nations will accept the measure of greatness to which the individual is expected to conform and seek to cultivate respect, not by exciting fear, but by rendering service.

Love, the wisest of instructors, will also soften the language of diplomacy, purge it of the phrases that intimate a resort to force, infuse into it the living spirit of good will and make it an irresistable power for the promotion of peace.

The lasting friendships, not formal but real, thus created will lead us to investigate with fairness all disputes which may arise and, constantly enlarging the number of controversies which can be submitted to arbitration, finally include ALL and usher in the day for which the Christian world has so long prayed, when "They shall beat their swords into plowshares, and their spears into pruning–hooks; nation shall not lift up sword against nation, neither shall they learn war any more."

17. Dollar Diplomacy in Latin America

Explaining why the administration had refused to ask American bankers to participate in 1913 in the Six Power Loan to China, Bryan pointed out that the United States would "not have a controlling voice" in the consortium. Some of his actions in Central America are also hard to reconcile with his supposed repudiation of dollar diplomacy. With the Panama Canal about to open, he was especially eager to reduce European influence and build up American power in the Caribbean. He supported the President's Mexican policies and, in 1921, even had the nerve to say of himself and of Wilson: "We both opposed intervention in Mexico." His message to the American minister in Santo Domingo (item "A") justified sweeping intervention by the United States in the internal affairs of that nation. The case of Nicaragua was even more extreme. President Taft had sent the marines there, and in 1912 they helped to suppress a revolution, and remained there throughout the Wilson years. Bryan's original proposal for a treaty with Nicaragua would have given the United States a canal right of way in perpetuity (shades of Jefferson), the right to establish a naval base, and the right to intervene with armed force to preserve Nicaraguan independence or to maintain life and property. The last Bryan-Chamorro Treaty, signed August 5, 1914, constituted a Platt Amendment for Nicaragua; many of its more arbitrary features were stricken out by the Senate before ratification occurred on February 18, 1916. True, Bryan did propose to Wilson (item "B") that the United States lend its public credit to Nicaragua to make that government less dependent on foreign bankers. But when Wilson proved cool to the idea, Bryan had to rely on private American capital. While working to get a million dollars for Nicaragua in 1913, he suggested that as collateral the country should give the last 49 per cent of its railroad system to American bankers.

A. SANTO DOMINGO

Your March 2, 3 p. m. and March 4, 1 a. m. Communicate with President Bordas on board *Petrel* and inform him that this Department advises him to point out to Arias (1) that the Government of the United States will not permit revolutionary methods to be employed in Santo Domingo, (2) that no money will be paid to him by the Dominican Government unless there is just claim for services actually rendered, (3) that patriotic services rendered to the people are the only bases upon which to seek public honors, (4) and that the influence of the United States Government will be used to reward those who show themselves deserving and will be used against those who attempt to misuse governmental power for personal ambition or private gain, and that (5) the only methods through which public office should be sought are those upon which the Constitutional Assembly is now at work in perfecting.

B. NICARAGUA†

. . . A new necessity for the application of the principle [of the Monroe Doctrine] has arisen, and the application is entirely in keeping with the spirit of the doctrine and carries out the real purpose of that doctrine. The right of American republics to work out their own destiny along lines consistent with popular government, is just as much menaced today by foreign

---

Secretary Bryan to Minister Sullivan (Dominican Republic), March 5, 1914. U.S. Department of State, *Papers Relating to the Foreign Relations of the United States, 1914* (Washington, D.C.: Government Printing Office, 1922), p. 215.

† Secretary Bryan to President Wilson, October 28, 1913. Bryan Papers, Library of Congress.

financial interests as it was a century ago by the political aspirations of foreign governments. If the people of an American republic are left free to attend to their own affairs, no despot can long keep them in subjection; but when a local despot is held in authority by powerful financial interests, and is furnished money for the employment of soldiers, the people are as helpless as if a foreign army had landed on their shores. This, we have reason to believe, is the situation in Mexico, and I cannot see that our obligation is any less now than it was then. We must protect the people of these republics in their right to attend to their own business, free from external coercion, no matter what form that external coercion may take.

Your utterance in regard to conquest was timely. We must be relieved of suspicion as to our motives. We must be bound in advance not to turn to our own advantage any power we employ. It will be impossible for us to win the confidence of the people of Latin America, unless they know that we do not seek their territory or ourselves desire to exercise political authority over them. If we have occasion to go into any country, it must be as we went into Cuba, at the invitation of the Government, or with assurances that will leave no doubt as to the temporary character of our intervention. Our only object must be to secure to the people an opportunity to vote, that they may themselves select their rulers and establish their government.

It has occurred to me that this might be an opportune time to outline the policy which I suggested a few months ago in connection with Nicaragua, namely, the loaning of our credit to the Latin American states. They have to borrow money, and it is the money borrowed by those Governments that has put them under obligations to foreign financiers. We cannot deny them the right to borrow money, and we cannot overlook the sense of gratitude and the feeling of obligation that come with a loan. If our country, openly claiming a paramount influence in the Western Hemisphere, will go to the rescue of these countries and enable them to secure the money they need for education, sanitation and internal development, there will be no excuse for their putting themselves under obligations to financiers in other lands. I believe it is perfectly safe and will make absolutely sure our domination of the situation. . . .

18. Plan for Peace:
Compulsory Investigation of International Disputes

Bryan printed his proposal for international arbitration in The Commoner *nearly a decade before World War I. As he explained to a correspondent in January 1915: "You will notice that the first editorial, February 17, 1905, includes two suggestions: First, that this nation should take the initiative in framing a system of arbitration so comprehensive that 'all differences will be submitted to the arbitration court' and; Second, 'reserving to each nation the right to refuse to accept the finding if it believes it affects its honor or integrity.' It would be impossible to make the plan include 'all differences' without this reservation—the two, therefore, are necessary parts of the one plan." He frequently agitated for the idea prior to becoming Secretary of State. Then his plan, promptly accepted by the President, was presented to other nations in April 1913. The initial treaty was signed with Salvador on August 8, 1913. By the anniversary of this first agreement, twenty treaties had been signed, eighteen of which were ratified by the Senate on August 13, 1914. By the time Bryan left the Department of State, thirty of his treaties had been consummated. But his attempt to evade the problem of sovereignty had been in vain. While Bryan was willing to let each nation retain its freedom to reject the recommendations of the arbitration panel in cases involving "honor or integrity," the agreement with Russia (on which the final signature was dated October 1, 1914) reserves to both parties "full liberty" in regard to any and all findings by the panel (item "A"). Even so,*

U.S. Department of State, *Papers Relating to the Foreign Relations of the United States, 1915* (Washington, D.C.: Government Printing Office, 1924), pp. 1283–1285.

a treaty with Germany was never written into the books. But Bryan did not give up hope for one and continued his efforts even after the war broke out in Europe (item "B").

A. TREATY WITH RUSSIA

TREATY FOR THE SETTLEMENT OF DISPUTES

The President of the United States of America and His Majesty the Emperor of all the Russias, desiring to strengthen the friendly relations which unite their countries and to serve the cause of general peace, have decided to conclude a Treaty for these purposes and have consequently appointed their Plenipotentiaries designated hereinafter, to wit:

The President of the United States of America, the Honorable William Jennings Bryan, Secretary of State of the United States; and

His Majesty the Emperor of all the Russias, His Excellency G. Bakhmeteff, Master of His Court and His Ambassador Extraordinary and Plenipotentiary to the United States of America;

Who, after exhibiting to each other their Full Powers found to be in due and proper form, have agreed upon the following articles:

ARTICLE I.

Any differences arising between the Government of the United States of America and the Imperial Government of Russia, of whatever nature they may be, shall, when diplomatic proceedings have failed, be submitted for examination and report to a Permanent International Commission constituted in the manner prescribed in the following article; likewise the High Contracting Parties agree not to resort, with respect to each other, to any acts of force during the examination to be made by the Commission and before its report is handed in.

ARTICLE II.

The International Commission shall be composed of five members appointed as follows: Each Government shall designate two members; the fifth member shall be designated by common consent and shall not belong to any of the nationalities already represented on the Commission; he shall perform the duties of President.

The two Governments shall bear by halves the expenses of the Commission.

The Commission shall be organized within six months from the exchange of ratifications of the present Convention.

The members shall be appointed for one year and their appointment may be renewed. They shall remain in office until superseded or reappointed, or until the work on which they are engaged at the time their office expires is completed.

Any vacancies which may arise shall be filled in the manner followed for the original appointment.

ARTICLE III.

In case a difference should arise between the High Contracting Parties which is not settled by diplomatic methods, each Party shall have a right to ask that the examination thereof be intrusted to the International Commission charged with making a report. Notice shall be given to the President of the International Commission, who shall at once communicate with his colleagues.

As regards the procedure which it is to follow, the Commission shall as far as possible be guided by the provisions contained in articles 9 to 36 of Convention I of The Hague of 1907.

The High Contracting Parties agree to afford the Commission, as fully as they may think possible, all means and all necessary facilities for its examination and its report.

The work of the Commission shall be completed within one year from the date on which it has taken jurisdiction of the case, unless the High Contracting Parties should agree to set a different period.

The conclusion of the Commission and the terms of its report shall be adopted by a majority. The report, signed only by the President acting by virtue of his office, shall be transmitted by him to each of the Contracting Parties.

The High Contracting Parties reserve full liberty as to the action to be taken on the report of the Commission.

ARTICLE IV.

The present Treaty shall be ratified by the President of the United States of America, with the advice and consent of the Senate of the United States, and by His Majesty the Emperor of all the Russias.

It shall go into force immediately after the exchange of ratification and shall last five years.

If it has not been denounced at least six months before the expiration of this period it shall be tacitly renewed for a period of twelve months after either party shall have notified the other of its intention to terminate it.

In witness whereof, the respective Plenipotentiaries have signed the present Treaty and have affixed thereunto their seals. . . .

B. PROPOSED TREATY WITH GERMANY

Eighteen treaties providing for investigation in all cases were ratified last Thursday, Netherlands form being one most favored by Senate. Four more signed and will be ratified within a few days. British and French treaties agreed upon and will

---

Secretary Bryan to Ambassador Gerard (Germany), August 17, 1914. U.S. Department of State, *Papers Relating to the Foreign Relations of the United States, 1914, Supplement: The World War* (Washington, D.C.: Government Printing Office, 1928), p. 6. The reply to Bryan on August 21, 1914, required exactly eight words: "Sorry to report no hope peace treaty. Gerard"

be signed same day, but day cannot be fixed as British treaty is being submitted Colonies for approval. If German Government will authorize its Ambassador to sign similar treaty its ratification can be secured before Congress adjourns. If verbal changes are desired shall be glad to consider them, as we are willing to make any reasonable concession in details provided principles are retained. War makes us especially anxious to negotiate treaties with European countries, so that the treaties will cover any disputes that may arise between us and European governments during war. Possibility of dispute is remote, but still possibility. These treaties provide for investigation in all cases before hostilities begin. It would be a great triumph in diplomacy if it could be so arranged that treaty with Germany could be signed on same day as British and French, or before or after. If a favorable opportunity presents itself, please bring matter to attention Foreign Office.

19. American Private Loans to Allied Governments

All too seldom do important government officials have a chance to isolate themselves in order to ponder a single issue. Not only are they subject most of the time to an inchoate barrage of public questions, but they are, of course, prey to problems and dilemmas and griefs stemming from their private affairs. A remarkable conjunction of events played upon Wilson and Bryan in August of 1914. On the first day of the month, Germany declared war on Russia. On the sixth, Bryan drafted a letter of condolence to the President about the death of his wife. Meanwhile the administration was preparing to launch a new policy in Mexico, aimed at deposing Venustiano Carranza and installing Pancho Villa. On the tenth, Bryan drafted an outline of possible courses in Mexico for the President, and declared: "The Mexican question has been in my mind today to the exclusion of all else . . ." On the same day the Secretary of State drafted another letter to the President, printed below, dealing with a very different problem. The government of France had approached J. P. Morgan & Company about floating a war loan in the United States. Would the administration approve such action by the banking firm? On the afternoon of August 15, Secretary Bryan gave a statement to the press: "There is no reason why loans should not be made to the governments of neutral nations, but in the judgment of this Government loans by American bankers to any foreign nation which is at war is inconsistent with the true spirit of neutrality."

Secretary Bryan to President Wilson, August 10, 1914. Bryan Papers, Library of Congress. A substantially similar statement was published in *The Commoner* in September. Bryan's official release of August 15 was printed by the New York *Times* on the next day.

I beg to communicate to you an important matter which has come before the Department. Morgan Company of New York have asked whether there would be any objection to their making a loan to the French Government and also the Rothchilds—I suppose that is intended for the French Government. I have conferred with Mr. Lansing and he knows of no legal objection to financing this loan, but I have suggested to him the advisability of presenting to you an aspect of the case which is not legal but I believe to be consistent with our attitude in international matters. It is whether it would be advisable for this Government to take the position that it will not approve of any loan to a belligerent nation. The reasons that I would give in support of this proposition are:

First: Money is the worst of all contrabands because it commands everything else. The question of making loans contraband by international agreement has been discussed, but no action has been taken. I know of nothing that would do more to prevent war than an international agreement that neutral nations would not loan to belligerents. While such an agreement would be of great advantage, could we not by our example hasten the reaching of such an agreement? We are the one great nation which is not involved and our refusal to loan to any belligerent would naturally tend to hasten a conclusion of the war. We are responsible for the use of our influence through example and as we cannot tell what we can do until we try, the only way of testing our influence is to set the example and observe its effect. This is the fundamental reason in support of the suggestion submitted.

Second: There is a special and local reason, it seems to me, why this course would be advisable. Mr. Lansing observed in the discussion of the subject that a loan would be taken by those in sympathy with the country in whose behalf the loan was negotiated. If we approved of a loan to France we could not, of course, object to a loan to Great Britain, Germany, Russia, Austria or to any other country, and if loans were made to these countries our citizens would be divided into groups, each group loaning money to the country which it favors and this money could not be furnished without expressions of sympathy. These expressions of sympathy are disturbing enough when they do not rest upon pecuniary interests—they would be still more disturbing if each group was pecuniarily interested in the success of the nation to whom its members had loaned money.

Third: The powerful financial interests which would be connected with these loans would be tempted to use their influence through the newspapers to support the interests of the Government to which they had loaned because the value of the security would be directly affected by the result of the war. We would thus find our newspapers violently arrayed on one side or the other, each paper supporting a financial group and pecuniary interest. All of this influence would make it all the more difficult for us to maintain neutrality, as our action on various questions that would arise would affect one side or the other and powerful financial interests would be thrown into the balance.

I am to talk over the telephone with Mr. Davidson of the Morgan Company at one o'clock, but I will have him delay final action until you have time to consider this question.

It grieves me to be compelled to intrude any question upon you at this time, but I am sure you will pardon me for submitting a matter of such great importance.

With assurances of high respect, I am, My dear Mr. President,

Yours very truly,

W J Bryan

P. S. Mr. Lansing calls attention to the fact that an American citizen who goes abroad and voluntarily enlists in the army of a belligerent nation loses the protection of his citizenship while so engaged, and asks why dollars, going abroad and enlisting in war, should be more protected. As we cannot prevent American citizens going abroad at their own risk, so we cannot prevent dollars going abroad at the risk of the owners, but the influence of the Government is used to prevent American citizens from doing this. Would the Government not be justified in using its influence against the enlistment of the nation's dollars in a foreign war? [Added at the bottom in ink in Bryan's handwriting is the following] The Morgans say that the money would be spent here but the floating of these loans would absorb the loanable funds & might affect our ability to borrow

20. British Infringements of American Neutrality

Within a few months the Wilson administration, partly by the device of a meaningless distinction between war loans to the Allies and commercial credits granted to them, scrapped the policy laid down by Bryan in August 1914. The British also deftly played on American sensibilities to forestall action that would make effective our protests against violations of the rights of neutrals on the high seas. Cecil Spring-Rice, the ambassador in Washington, reported on September 8, 1914 to Foreign Minister Sir Edward Grey about a conversation with the President. Wilson, wrote Spring-Rice, had said in the event of a German victory "the United States would have to give up its present ideals and devote all its energies to defense, which would mean the end of its present system of government. . . . I said, 'You and Grey are fed on the same food and I think you understand.'" Spring-Rice managed to link Bryan's peace treaties to the outbreak of the war in a series of flattering notes to the Secretary of State. In October 1914 Bryan could proudly read in the ambassador's own hand that "even one week's enforced delay would probably have saved the peace of the world." Two years later Spring-Rice was less restrained: "probably" became "doubtless." By January 1915 Bryan was persuaded that, in his words, adherence to his plan by all the nations of Europe would have made it "quite certain that the present war would not have commenced." But while trying by his treaties to strengthen international law, the Secretary in other respects conceded major breaches in it. In the following

---

Secretary Bryan to Ambassador Page, December 26, 1914. U.S. Department of State, *Papers Relating to the Foreign Relations of the United States, 1914, Supplement: The World War* (Washington, D.C.: Government Printing Office, 1928), pp. 372–375.

*note of December 26, 1914, he contended that a belligerent should
not encroach upon the rights of neutral commerce "unless such interference is manifestly an imperative necessity to protect their
national safety, and then only to the extent that it is a necessity."
Thus, in the course of a supposed protest against British policy,
Bryan inadvertently undercut the grounds of his protest and held
out to Britain a ready-made justification for whatever she chose
to do.*

The present condition of American foreign trade resulting from
the frequent seizures and detentions of American cargoes destined to neutral European ports has become so serious as to
require a candid statement of the views of this Government in
order that the British Government may be fully informed as to
the attitude of the United States toward the policy which has
been pursued by the British authorities during the present war.

You will, therefore, communicate the following to His
Majesty's Principal Secretary of State for Foreign Affairs, but
in doing so you will assure him that it is done in the most
friendly spirit and in the belief that frankness will better serve
the continuance of cordial relations between the two countries
than silence, which may be misconstrued into acquiescence in
a course of conduct which this Government can not but consider to be an infringement upon the rights of American
citizens.

The Government of the United States has viewed with growing concern the large number of vessels laden with American
goods destined to neutral ports in Europe, which have been
seized on the high seas, taken into British ports and detained
sometimes for weeks by the British authorities. During the
early days of the war this Government assumed that the policy
adopted by the British Government was due to the unexpected
outbreak of hostilities and the necessity of immediate action to

prevent contraband from reaching the enemy. For this reason it was not disposed to judge this policy harshly or protest it vigorously, although it was manifestly very injurious to American trade with the neutral countries of Europe. This Government, relying confidently upon the high regard which Great Britain has so often exhibited in the past for the rights of other nations, confidently awaited amendment of a course of action which denied to neutral commerce the freedom to which it was entitled by the law of nations.

This expectation seemed to be rendered the more assured by the statement of the Foreign Office early in November that the British Government were satisfied with guarantees offered by the Norwegian, Swedish, and Danish Governments as to non–exportation of contraband goods when consigned to named persons in the territories of those Governments, and that orders had been given to the British fleet and customs authorities to restrict interference with neutral vessels carrying such cargoes so consigned to verification of ship's papers and cargoes.

It is, therefore, a matter of deep regret that, though nearly five months have passed since the war began, the British Government have not materially changed their policy and do not treat less rigorously ships and cargoes passing between neutral ports in the peaceful pursuit of lawful commerce, which belligerents should protect rather than interrupt. The great freedom from detention and seizure which was confidently expected to result from consigning shipments to definite consignees, rather than "to order," is still awaited.

It is needless to point out to His Majesty's Government, usually the champion of the freedom of the seas and the rights of trade, that peace, not war, is the normal relation between nations and that the commerce between countries which are not belligerents should not be interfered with by those at war unless such interference is manifestly an imperative necessity to protect their national safety, and then only to the extent that it is a necessity. It is with no lack of appreciation of the momentous nature of the present struggle in which Great Britain is engaged and with no selfish desire to gain undue commercial advantage that this Government is reluctantly forced to the conclusion that the present policy of His Majesty's Government toward neutral ships and cargoes exceeds the manifest necessity of a belligerent and constitutes restrictions upon the rights of American citizens on the high seas which are not justified by the rules of international law or required under the principle of self–preservation.

The Government of the United States does not intend at this time to discuss the propriety of including certain articles in the lists of absolute and conditional contraband, which have been proclaimed by His Majesty. Open to objection as some of these seem to this Government, the chief ground of present complaint is the treatment of cargoes of both classes of articles when bound to neutral ports.

Articles listed as absolute contraband, shipped from the United States and consigned to neutral countries, have been seized and detained on the ground that the countries to which they were destined have not prohibited the exportation of such articles. Unwarranted as such detentions are, in the opinion of this Government, American exporters are further perplexed by the apparent indecision of the British authorities in applying their own rules to neutral cargoes. For example, a shipment of copper from this country to a specified consignee in Sweden was detained because, as was stated by Great Britain, Sweden had placed no embargo on copper. On the other hand, Italy not only prohibited the export of copper, but, as this Government is informed, put in force a decree that shipments to Italian consignees or "to order," which arrive in ports of Italy, can not be exported or transshipped. The only exception Italy makes is of copper which passes through that country in transit to another country. In spite of these decrees, however, the British Foreign Office has thus far declined to affirm that copper shipments consigned to Italy will not be molested on the high seas. Seizures are so numerous and delays so prolonged that exporters are afraid to send their copper to Italy, steamship lines decline to accept it, and insurers refuse to issue policies upon it. In a word, a legitimate trade is being greatly impaired through uncertainty as to the treatment which it may expect at the hands of the British authorities.

We feel that we are abundantly justified in asking for information as to the manner in which the British Government propose to carry out the policy which they have adopted, in order that we may determine the steps necessary to protect our citizens, engaged in foreign trade, in their rights and from the serious losses to which they are liable through ignorance of the hazards to which their cargoes are exposed.

In the case of conditional contraband the policy of Great Britain appears to this Government to be equally unjustified by the established rules of international conduct. As evidence of this, attention is directed to the fact that a number of the American cargoes which have been seized consist of foodstuffs and other articles of common use in all countries which are admittedly relative contraband. In spite of the presumption of innocent use because destined to neutral territory, the British authorities made these seizures and detentions without, so far as we are informed, being in possession of facts which warranted a reasonable belief that the shipments had in reality a belligerent destination, as that term is used in international law. Mere suspicion is not evidence and doubts should be resolved in favor of neutral commerce, not against it. The effect upon trade in these articles between neutral nations resulting from interrupted voyages and detained cargoes is not entirely cured by reimbursement of the owners for the damages which they have suffered, after investigation has failed to establish an enemy destination. The injury is to American commerce with neutral countries as a whole through the hazard of the enterprise and the repeated diversion of goods from established markets.

It also appears that cargoes of this character have been seized by the British authorities because of a belief that, though not originally so intended by the shippers, they will ultimately reach the territory of the enemies of Great Britain. Yet this belief is frequently reduced to a mere fear in view of the embargoes which have been decreed by the neutral countries to which they are destined on the articles composing the cargoes.

That a consignment "to order" of articles listed as conditional contraband and shipped to a neutral port raises a legal presumption of enemy destination appears to be directly contrary to the doctrine previously held by Great Britain and thus stated by Lord Salisbury during the South African War:

> Foodstuffs, though having a hostile destination, can be considered as contraband of war only if they are for the enemy forces; it is not sufficient that they are capable of being so used, it must be shown that this was in fact their destination at the time of their seizure.

With this statement as to conditional contraband the views of this Government are in entire accord, and upon this historic doctrine, consistently maintained by Great Britain when a belligerent as well as a neutral, American shippers were entitled to rely.

The Government of the United States readily admits the full right of a belligerent to visit and search on the high seas the vessels of American citizens or other neutral vessels carrying American goods and to detain them *when there is sufficient evidence to justify a belief that contraband articles are in their cargoes;* but His Majesty's Government, judging by their own experience in the past, must realize that this Government can not without protest permit American ships or American cargoes to be taken into British ports and there detained for the purpose of searching generally for evidence of contraband, or upon presumptions created by special municipal enactments which are clearly at variance with international law and practice.

This Government believes and earnestly hopes His Majesty's Government will come to the same belief, that a course of conduct more in conformity with the rules of international usage, which Great Britain has strongly sanctioned for many years, will in the end better serve the interests of belligerents as well as those of neutrals.

Not only is the situation a critical one to the commercial interests of the United States, but many of the great industries of this country are suffering because their products are denied long–established markets in European countries, which, though neutral, are contiguous to the nations at war. Producers and exporters, steamship and insurance companies are pressing, and not without reason, for relief from the menace to transatlantic trade which is gradually but surely destroying their business and threatening them with financial disaster.

The Government of the United States, still relying upon the deep sense of justice of the British nation, which has been so often manifested in the intercourse between the two countries during so many years of uninterrupted friendship, expresses confidently the hope that His Majesty's Government will realize the obstacles and difficulties which their present policy has placed in the way of commerce between the United States and the neutral countries of Europe, and will instruct their officials to refrain from all unnecessary interference with the freedom of trade between nations which are sufferers, though not participants, in the present conflict; and will in their treatment of neutral ships and cargoes conform more closely to those rules governing the maritime relations between belligerents and neutrals, which have received the sanction of the civilized world, and which Great Britain has, in other wars, so strongly and successfully advocated.

In conclusion, it should be impressed upon His Majesty's Government that the present condition of American trade with the neutral European countries is such that, if it does not improve, it may arouse a feeling contrary to that which has so long existed between the American and British peoples. Already it is becoming more and more the subject of public criticism and complaint. There is an increasing belief, doubtless not entirely unjustified, that the present British policy toward American trade is responsible for the depression in certain industries which depend upon European markets. The attention of the British Government is called to this possible result of their present policy to show how widespread the effect is upon the industrial life of the United States and to emphasize the importance of removing the cause of complaint.

21. Proposals on the *Lusitania* Crisis

On February 4, 1915, Germany proclaimed a war zone around the British Isles, within which she would sink enemy ships on sight. She added that since British vessels were flying neutral flags, neutrals would enter the zone at their peril. At the time Colonel Edward M. House was en route to Europe as the President's personal emissary to determine if it might be possible to negotiate an end to the war. He traveled aboard the Cunard liner Lusitania, *the fastest and largest steamship on the Atlantic at that time. As the vessel neared Ireland, the captain began to fear attack and ran up the American flag. "Every newspaper in London has asked me about it," wrote House in his diary, "but, fortunately, I was not an eye-witness to it and have been able to say that I only knew it from hearsay." The United States reacted to the German policy by stating that the Imperial Government would be held to strict accountability for assault on American ships and lives. Three months later, on May 7, the* Lusitania *was torpedoed and sunk. Nearly 1,200 civilians, including 128 Americans, were killed. The ship was carrying large quantities of contraband including munitions. It was not armed, but the British had armed some of their merchant vessels. Although Theodore Roosevelt and other jingoes wanted war against Germany, the President sought to calm public opinion. In a speech at Philadelphia on May 10 he boldly asserted, "There is such a thing as a man being too proud to fight." Most of the nation approved. But he was also drafting a note to Germany in which he virtually demanded that she give up submarine warfare against unarmed merchantmen. The two handwritten letters that follow, both dated May 12, explained Bryan's reservations to the President.*

179

A. THE RELEVANCE OF THE ARBITRATION TREATIES

I am so fearful of the embarassment which the jingoes will cause by *assuming* that your note means war—an interpretation which might affect the *tone* of Germany's reply, as well as make it more difficult to postpone final settlement, that I venture to suggest the propriety of meeting the issue *now* by a statement given out at the time the statement is published or before. To explain what I mean I give the following—*not* as a draft of such a notice or interview but as an illustration: "The words 'strict accountability' having been construed by some of the newspapers to mean an *immediate* settlement of the matter I deem it fitting to say that that construction is not a necessary one. In individual matters friends some times find it wise to postpone the settlement of disputes until such differences can be considered calmly and on their merits. So it may be with nations. The United States and Germany, between whom there exists a long standing friendship, may find it advisable to postpone until peace is restored any disputes that do not yield to diplomatic treatment. Germany has endorsed the principle of investigation embodied in the thirty treaties signed with as many nations. These treaties give a years time for investigation and apply to *all* disputes of every character."

From this nations stand point there is no reason why this policy should not control as between the United States and Germany. I believe such a statement would do great good.

B. A POLICY OF TRUE NEUTRALITY

Your more than generous note received with draft of protest to Germany. I have gone over it very carefully and will give it to Mr. Lansing at once, for I agree with you that it is well to act without delay in order to give direction to public opinion.

Secretary Bryan to President Wilson, May 12, 1915. Wilson Papers, Library of Congress. (This citation applies to both documents above.)

I do not see that you could have stated your position more clearly or more forcibly. In one sentence I suggest addition of words "as the last few weeks have shown," so that it will read: "Submarines, we respectfully submit, can not be used against Merchantmen, as the last few weeks have shown, without an inevitable violation of many sacred principles of justice and humanity." The only other amendment that occurs to me relates to the Cushing and Gulflight. Would it not be wise to make some reference to the rules sent us and the offer to apologize and make reparation in case a neutral ship is sunk by mistake? I suggest something like this: "Apology and reparation for destruction of neutral ships, sunk by mistake, while they may satisfy international obligations, if no loss of life results, can not justify or excuse a practice, the natural and almost necessary effect of which is to subject neutral nations to new and innumerable risks, for it must be remembered that peace, not war, is the normal state, and that nations that resort to war to settle disputes are not at liberty to subordinate the rights of neutrals to the supposed, or even actual, needs of belligerents." I am in doubt of the propriety of referring to the note published by Bernsdorf [*sic*].

But, my dear Mr. President, I join in this document with a heavy heart. I am as sure of your patriotic purpose as I am of my own, but after long consideration both careful and prayerful, I can not bring myself to the belief that it is wise to relinquish the hope of playing the part of a friend to both sides in the role of peace maker, and I fear this note will result in such a relinquishment—for the hope requires for its realization the retaining of the confidence of both sides. The protest will be popular in this country, for a time at least and possibly permanently, because public sentiment, already favorable to the allies, has been perceptibly increased by the *Lusitania* tragedy, but there is peril in this very fact. Your position, being the position of the government, will be approved—the approval varying in emphasis in proportion to the feeling against Germany. There being no information that the final accounting will be postponed until the war is over, the jingo element will not only predict, but demand, war—see enclosed editorial from Washington Post of this morning—and the line will be more distinctly drawn between those who sympathize with Germany and the rest of the people. Outside of the country the demand will be applauded by the allies, and the more they applaud the more Germany will be embittered, because we unsparingly denounce the retaliatory methods employed by her without condemning the announced purpose of the allies to starve the non–combattants of Germany and without complaining of the conduct of Great Britain in relying on passengers, including men, women and children of the United States, to give immunity to vessels carrying munitions of war—without even suggesting that she should convoy passenger ships as carefully as she does ships carrying horses and gasoline. This enumeration does not include a reference to Great Britain's indifference to the increasing dangers thrown upon us by the misuse of our flag or to her unwarranted interference with our trade with neutral nations. Germany can not but construe the strong statement of the case against her, coupled with silence as to the unjustifiable action of the allies, as partiality toward the latter—an impression which will be deepened in proportion to the loudness of the praise which the allies bestow upon this government's statement of its position. The only way, as I see it, to prevent irreparable injury being done by the statement is to issue simultaneously a protest against the objectionable conduct of the allies which will keep them from rejoicing and show Germany that we are defending our rights from aggression from both sides.

I am only giving you, my dear Mr. President, the situation as it appears to me—and am praying all the while that I may be wholly mistaken and that your judgment may be vindicated by events.

22. Henry Ford's Peace Ship

In spite of Bryan's reservations, the President sent to Germany his harsh note protesting against submarine warfare. When Germany procrastinated in replying, Wilson drew up another strict message. The Secretary of State reacted by suggesting arbitration of the Lusitania issues, steps to prevent passenger vessels from carrying ammunition, and moderating the language of the proposed second note to Germany. As his views were rejected, Bryan resigned early in June 1915 from the State Department and announced himself opposed to the President's drive for military preparedness. By October he was writing in The Commoner: *"Don't let the jingoes confuse the issue. It is not a question of defense—this country will defend itself if it is ever attacked—and if that time ever comes the common people will furnish the soldiers—* . . . *the jingoes will be too busy making army contracts and negotiating usurious war loans to go to the front. The preparedness now demanded will provoke war instead of preventing it." Two months later Bryan got involved in the most quixotic episode of the neutrality struggle. Mme Rosika Schwimmer, a pacifist and feminist, convinced Henry Ford that the war could be halted by the intervention of a congress of peace delegates from the neutral countries. Ford financed a Peace Ship to carry the American group to Europe. Although Bryan favored the project, he did not embark on the Peace Ship. The following telegram to Ford explained his reasons.*

I am in hearty sympathy with your proposed peace plan. It is worthy of all praise and will I trust accomplish much good.

Bryan to Henry Ford (late November 1915). Bryan Papers, Library of Congress.

I deeply appreciate invitation and would accept without hesitation but after earnest consideration of subject am impressed with the belief that just now I can render a greater service here opposing the plan to commit this country to a large and indefinite increase in expenditures for Army and Navy—a plan which would not only be oppressive to the taxpayers but would I believe be a menace to our nations' peace and influence. I hope it may be possible to join your party at the Hague if not earlier. Shall if agreeable to you meet you in New York next Friday morning or evening and explain more fully—

23. On the Eve of War

While President Wilson was pushing through Congress the biggest naval appropriation in the nation's history, Bryan continued his strident opposition to preparedness. Writing to Postmaster General Albert S. Burleson on March 8, 1916, the Great Commoner declared: "I may see you soon for I expect to come to Washington if the President's diplomacy leads to the verge of war as I fear it will. My one supreme purpose at this time is to do what I can to prevent war. I believe that the interests of our party as well as the interests of the country and the world demand that we shall not enter this war. *Any 'honor' that would require it is a sham honor and as for 'humanity' we have a higher mission than to go around the world looking for an opportunity to help one European monarch fight out his quarrels with another." Although he supported President Wilson for reelection in 1916 (see Documents 25 and 26), Bryan held to these views right up to American entry into the conflict. On the very eve of war he addressed to every member of Congress a public appeal for arbitration of the issues with Germany (item "A"). On April 3, 1917 he suggested to a Representative a popular referendum on any declaration of war (item "B"). During the next three days Congress exercised its constitutional right to take action without any mandate from the electorate.*

A. THE RELEVANCE OF THE ARBITRATION TREATIES

Gentlemen:

Exercising the citizen's right of petition, I appeal to you. The dispute with Germany has passed beyond the domain of di-

Bryan to the members of the U.S. Senate and House of Representatives, 28 March, 1917. Flyer in Bryan Papers, Library of Congress.

plomacy and some advise settlement by the sword. The metropolitan press, which tried to prevent the re–election of the President and failed, undismayed by a popular verdict of more than one–half million, now seeks to lash the country into a fury and urges the Government to take part in the European conflict.

To you, and to you only, is given constitutional authority to declare war—war which, in this case, may mean the signing of the death warrant of thousands, even millions, of your countrymen, and the laying of grievous burdens upon future generations. Before you take this blood upon your hands, consider, I pray you, first, that the wrongs which you would punish, cruel and unjustifiable as they are, are not intended primarily against this country, but are acts of desperation directed against other nations with which the offenders are at war. Second, that our land is not threatened with invasion, but that we are asked to go three thousand miles for a chance to fight. Third, that we have not the excuse for going to war that the European nations had. They had no machinery for peace; we have a peace plan offered by this nation to the globe and now embodied in thirty treaties with three–quarters of the population of the globe. The plan has the endorsement of the President, the commendation of the Senate and the approval of the people at the polls. It provides for investigation of all disputes by an international tribunal before resort to war.

Fortunately, these treaties compel us to employ the plan with Great Britain, France, Italy, and Russia before going to war with them. Germany formally approved the plan, although no treaty has yet been concluded with her. Shall we repudiate our own plan the first time we have an opportunity to employ it?

If, as the President recently declared, the American people do not want war, is it not worth while to try the peace plan before bringing upon the people the horrors of war? Until an attempt is made and fails, no one is able to say that it would be impossible to secure the suspension of "ruthless" submarine warfare during the investigation for which the plan provides? Shall we deny to ourselves the credit of trying to settle the dispute with the treaty plan?

And, is it not worth while to do our part in trying to avoid injury? Would it not be better, as well as cheaper, for the Government to carry on its own vessels such Americans as must go to Europe, rather than engage in war to vindicate the right of citizens to disregard all risks and ride upon belligerent ships?

Is it not worth while to separate passengers from contraband cargoes, so that the captains of passenger ships can give their entire attention to the safety of the passengers? Our nation is the world's foremost advocate of peace; if we go to war it should be for a cause which history will justify.

If you reach the conclusion that nothing but war will satisfy the nation's honor, is it too much to ask that, by a referendum, you consult the wishes of those who must, in case of war, defend the nation's honor with their lives?

As one who expects to live up to a citizen's duties, if war comes, I plead with you to use all honorable means to preserve peace before you take the responsibility of plunging our beloved land into this unprecedented struggle, begun without any sufficient cause and conducted by both sides in utter disregard of the well settled rights of neutrals.

B. A REFERENDUM ON WAR

My published appeal presents my views. They have not changed. Believing in right of people to rule, even on question of war, I favor referendum as means of ascertaining public will. If referendum refused each representative must conscine-

---

Bryan to Representative B. C. Hilliard, April 3, 1917. Bryan Papers, Library of Congress.

tiously try to find out for himself the wishes of his constituents and then obey them or resign. In such a crisis as this no one can advise another. Each must decide his duty for himself. That is the rule upon which I have acted and am acting. I am so strongly opposed to entering this war that I have felt it my duty to do all in my power to counteract the influence of the metropolitan press. If I were a representative and convinced that my constituents desired war, I would resign and leave them to speak through someone in harmony with their views. I would not share responsibility for this Nations entering the War.

24. Capital Punishment and the Frank Case

During the twenty–two months when Bryan was waging his gallant fight for neutrality, he also showed a heightened sensitivity on certain questions of domestic policy. One occasion originated in April 1913, when the dead body of a 14–year–old girl was found in a pencil factory in Atlanta, Georgia, which was managed by Leo Frank. Frank, a Jew from New York, was indicted for murder, and, in a courthouse surrounded by a mob, he was convicted by a terrorized jury. Every appellate court that reviewed the case, including the Supreme Court of the United States, was divided about it. But the conviction was not overturned. With Frank in prison awaiting execution, the once great Populist leader Tom Watson launched a scurrilous campaign in his Jeffersonian against "the typical young libertine Jew" motivated by "a lustful eagerness enhanced by the racial novelty of the girl of the uncircumcised." On June 21, 1915, the day before the execution was to occur, Bryan wrote the following endorsement of clemency. As this letter indicates, the governor of Georgia did commute the sentence to imprisonment, but two months later, Frank was abducted from the penitentiary and lynched.

In thinking over the Frank case last night I decided to write you in favor of a commutation of the sentence: seeing in the morning papers that the execution was set for tomorrow I decided to wire you instead of writing, but upon reaching Asheville I learned of the action you have taken. Although I

Bryan to Governor John M. Slaton, June 21, 1915. Bryan Papers, Library of Congress.

have not read your reasons I hasten to congratulate you on the decision reached. I had not had time to follow the evidence and therefore have not formed an opinion as to the guilt or innocence of the accused. My approval of your action in commuting the sentence to imprisonment is based entirely upon the conviction that the government can not afford to violate the sacredness of human life as a punishment for a crime already committed In putting a human being to death—not to prevent loss of life but to avenge a death the Government does not restore the life taken by the condemned man but it does, in my judgment, take the risk of teaching its citizens to underestimate the value of life. I approve the doctrine that no one, not even the Government is justified in extinguishing the spark of life in any human being except to prevent the taking of another life Whatever may be the feeling now I believe the clemency which you extend will find increasing endorsement as the years go by, and I am sure that you feel relieved not to share in the responsibility for the death of a fellow man.

25. Compulsory Investigation of Labor Disputes

However much he might be repelled by the preparedness program of Woodrow Wilson, Bryan would have found it difficult to oppose his reelection in 1916 (see Document 23). Lifelong fidelity to the Democratic party was reinforced by the undeniable truth that most of the outspoken warmongers were backing the Republican nominee, Charles Evans Hughes. Perhaps too, Bryan was lured by the resurgent progressivism that overcame the President during the campaign, of which the most startling outburst was his handling of a threatened railroad strike. The 400,000 locomotive engineers, firemen, trainmen, and conductors had been almost unanimous in voting for a walkout, but their demands for an eight-hour day at the same pay plus time and a half for overtime were bitterly opposed by the railroads. In conferences at the White House the President asked the Brotherhoods to drop their insistence on punitive overtime, but endorsed the other demand. They accepted the compromise. The railroads rejected it. Then on August 29 Wilson asked Congress to enact the eight-hour day for railroads, along with compulsory suspension of any strike while the issues were investigated by a federal commission. (The Adamson Act of September 3 embodied the former proposal.) A similar proposal for a cooling-off period and compulsory investigation before a rail strike had been made by Bryan in the following letter. In domestic labor disputes more than in international disputes the idea was fitting, for the issue of sovereignty seemed to be solved by the interstate commerce clause of the Constitution. But that issue was nearly fatal in

---

Bryan to Senator Francis G. Newlands, August 27, 1916. Bryan Papers, Library of Congress.

*this instance also: the Supreme Court upheld the Adamson Act by
the narrow margin of 5 to 4.*

The morning papers report the prospects unfavorable for an
amicable adjustment of dispute between railroads & their employees. As you are the chairman of the Senate Committee
having charge of such matters, I venture to write you in regard to the general subject. The Brotherhoods are opposed to
arbitration and there is much to be said against any plan that
would bind them to *accept in advance* any finding that a
board might make. It is too much of a gamble. As both sides
would probably be represented on the board the decision
would really rest upon *one man* or at most upon two or three,
and the parties would have to take their chances, first, on the
bias of the man (as the man would be supposed to be without
bias—an impossibility—his bias would be unknown) and, second, on his being influenced, consciously or unconsciously, by
prospect of future advantage. As the railroads are in a much
better position to extend favors of value they would have a
decided advantage over the employees in the matter of future
favors. I enclose copy of a telegram sent to the heads of the
Brotherhoods suggesting the plan embodied in our treaties.
The 30 treaties provide for *investigation,* instead of arbitration,
each party reserving the right to act independently. (See the
Netherlands Treaty enclosed)

   You may be interested to know that I advocated this plan
for labor disputes many years ago—before I thought of pro-
posing it for international disputes. I believe the plan will be
almost sure to secure a settlement. Why not have arbitration
where *both parties* are willing and investigation in *all cases*
where arbitration is not resorted to. We have our arbitration
treaties with 26 nations and the 30 treaties cover questions
which can not be submitted to arbitration. Why not use both
methods in labor disputes, making the same distinctions. There

are questions which neither side might be willing to submit
to arbitration, but *all* questions can be investigated. The fact
that the findings are *not* binding on either party but rest upon
their merits, increases the probability of absolute fairness. The
question of *hours* is not a matter for arbitration. Congress
can fix the length of a working day. The *public* as well as the
employees are interested in the employees having hours short
enough to insure maximum efficiency and to allow time for
the enjoyment of home and preparations for proper performance of civic duties. Congress can fix hours & penalty for overtime, but investigation may be necessary to determine what,
at present freight and passenger rates, should be paid per hour.
I think the demands of the men are just but this is a matter
of opinion. Nothing but an investigation of the facts will determine what is really just in the matter of pay, and each side
should be left free to decide its course *after* the report of the
commission. The power to *fix wages* involves the power to fix
the status of those who toil and to vitally affect their future.
The employees can not be asked to surrender this power into
the hands of either their employers or a commission. If after
all the necessary facts are before the public either side attempts
to ignore the public's rights or to jeopardize public welfare
Congress can take such action as the situation may require.
Pardon this long letter. I hope the Presidents plan will be accepted, but if it is rejected and Congressional action becomes
necessary you may find it of advantage to consider the principle embodied in the treaty plan.

26. Freedom of Thought and Freedom of Speech

The declaration of war in 1917 prompted Bryan to write to the President: "Believing it to be the duty of the citizen to bear his part of the burden of war and his share of its perils I hereby tender my services to the government. Please enroll me as a private whenever I am needed and assign me to any work that I can do." Whereas the preceding period of the struggle for neutrality had showed Bryan at his most creative, the war years revealed him at his most repressive. His adulation of the majority had often been tied to a hostility to dissenting minorities. In the anti-anarchist clamor following the assassination of President McKinley, Bryan proposed that immigrants swear their allegiance to the Declaration of Independence (item "A"). During World War I he denounced "unpatriotic" utterances (item "B"). Item "C" was prompted by an unquestionably serious cluster of bomb plots at the end of April 1919. In item "D" we are again confronted by an almost incredible document. It was addressed to a man who during the war had edited a pro-German newspaper subsidized by the Imperial Government. Writing after the Palmer Raids, nearly thirty months after the Armistice, Bryan reiterated his belief "that citizens should not obstruct the government in the prosecution of the war by the exercise of freedom of speech and press."

A. OATH OF ALLEGIANCE FOR IMMIGRANTS

There is so much talk now about so amending the immigration laws as to exclude anarchists, and it is to be hoped that this will be done. The law should be strict on this point and

The Commoner, I (October 4, 1901), 6.

the immigrant should be compelled to assert his belief, not only in some form of government but his belief in our form of government. And, while he is swearing, it would not hurt him to declare that he accepts the Declaration of Independence as his political creed.

B. "UNPATRIOTIC" UTTERANCES

Before our nation enters a war it is perfectly proper to discuss the wisdom of going to war, but the discussion is closed when congress acts. After that, no one should be permitted to cloak attacks upon his government or to aid to the enemy under the claim that he is exercising freedom of speech. No sympathy, therefore, will be wasted upon those who have been arrested for unpatriotic utterances. They abuse free speech. And this applies to attacks on the Allies as well as attacks on the United States. We can no more allow our allies to be crushed than we can afford to be crushed ourselves. The defeat of our allies would throw the whole burden of the war upon us. We must stand together and fight it through. There are only two sides to a war—every American must be on the side of the United States.

C. BOMB PLOTS[†]

The increase in the use of the bomb compels the nation to consider the matter at once. Ours is the freest country in the world. Here, more nearly, than anywhere else, THE PEOPLE RULE. We have made revolution unnecessary by making evolution easy. If any citizen has an improvement to propose let it be considered, but we have no room for those who advocate the torch and the bomb. Open murder and secret assassination are alike un–American and cannot be tolerated. We must pro-

---

tect the liberty loving and the law abiding from the lawless, whether the lawless be the desperate poor or the predatory rich. The plutocrat is the forerunner of anarchy—Democracy must guard society against him as well as against his victims. Lawlessness must go.

D. MAJORITY RULE AND FREEDOM OF SPEECH

Your favor at hand. I do not know that we differ on so many things but we may differ quite radically on a few things. I am glad to have a copy of Deb's statement and am pleased to note that he has not advocated violence. As I told you I draw the line at the advocating of violence.

I favor the absolute freedom of speech and of the press in the proposal of remedies provided they are to be secured by constitutional methods and this includes constitutional amendments to be adopted in accordance with the provisions of the Constitution. I do not concede the right of revolution in a country like ours where the government is in the hands of the people as ours is. Having the right to choose our Senators, Congressmen and President the people can control the government. I think that the Constitution should be more easily amended and am advocating an amendment that would permit a majority of Congress to submit an amendment and a majority of the states to ratify providing the total vote for the amendment is a majority of the total vote cast in the country.

I am in favor of the Initiative and Referendum, including the referendum on war. I have been trying for twenty–five years to give the *majority* absolute control of the government, including the right of the majority of the Senate to close debate and compel a vote, but, as I have said, I do not concede to anyone the right to advocate the overthrow of the government

---

Bryan to George Sylvester Viereck, March 15, 1921. Bryan Papers, Library of Congress.

by violence, and I make no distinction between advising violence and acts of violence.

I repeat that I am glad to learn from Mr. Deb's statement that he did not advise revolution. The case seems to have been the use of language, the natural effect of which was to discourage support of the government during the war and to encourage the enemies to believe that the government was acting contrary to the wishes of the people.

I urged the President to forbid Americans riding on belligerent ships, not because it was contrary to international law but because I thought the Americans ought to suspend this right rather than risk drawing their country into a war. After the war began I though that citizens should not obstruct the government in the prosecution of the war by the exercise of freedom of speech and press. I thought that they should suspend the right to such criticism rather than risk prolonging the war. My views rested upon the same ground in both cases, namely, the putting of the government's interests above the interest of the individual.

This letter is not for publication but a personal response to your favor. I was very glad to see you and Mrs. Viereck.

27. World Disarmament

Two months before the Scopes trial (see Document 32) Bryan told a fundamentalist conference, "For the first time in my life I'm on the side of the majority." He was wrong of course. Probably in his campaign for neutrality (see Documents 19–23) he spoke for a majority in the vast region from the Alleghenies to the Rockies if not in the entire nation, and there can be no doubt that he sided with the overwhelming mass of Americans on the subject of disarmament after the war. In the same month in 1921 that saw Bryan write the following letter to the Educational Secretary of the World Alliance for International Friendship Through the Churches, Senator William E. Borah of Idaho introduced a resolution asking the administration to open disarmament talks with Britain and Japan. The resolution swept majestically through Congress, helping to coerce a reluctant President Harding into acceptance of the Washington Naval Conference. As a result the major powers actually agreed to cut back their equipment for war.

Your favor at hand. I enclose some editorials which express my views on the subject. I am in favor of disarmament by agreement if we can get agreement, by example, if we can not reach agreement, in fact I go so far as to advocate use of the ten billions of indebtedness of our allies to us to purchase disarmament. I do not favor giving the debt to the allies unconditionally—to do so would simply encourage them to spend the money in getting ready for another war. If we give it on

---

Bryan to Frederick Lynch, February 9, 1921. Bryan Papers, Library of Congress.

condition that they so revise the treaty as to permit disarmament by agreement, it may mean world peace.

While I feel hopeful of government action, still I feel so deeply on the subject that if government action is delayed in said favor, a search conference on the subject to pass resolutions demanding action, such a conference aught to be held in Washington if it is found necessary. This is the time for the Christians of the world to unite with a view to building universal peace on the basis of friendship and co–operation.

28. A Judgment of Woodrow Wilson

While the great debate was taking place about the League of Nations, Bryan drew up a statement calling it "the greatest step toward peace in a thousand years. . . . Deliberation before war—the investigation of all disputes . . . before hostilities begin. This almost ends war. The idea is taken from the thirty treaties negotiated by the United States with three-quarters of the world." The statement called for American reservations to the Covenant of the League, including protection for the Monroe Doctrine. "Another matter that should be made clear . . . is that each nation has the right to decide for itself whether it will undertake the things advised by the general council. . . . This nation cannot afford to allow a council in which it has so small a voice to carry it into war against its will." Thus Bryan sought to end war without infringing in the slightest upon the sovereignty of any nation, and he was embittered when the President continued to insist on unqualified ratification of the Covenant. Against this background, Bryan was asked in 1921 to serve on a committee to raise funds for the Woodrow Wilson Foundation. He wrote the following reply, but across the bottom of it he pencilled the instruction: "File this or hold."

I appreciate the honor you do me but I feel that this committee should be made up of those who can endorse with enthusiasm his *entire* record. I can not. His refusal to permit ratification with reservations, his veto of the resolution to reduce the army, his endorsement of universal compulsory military train-

Bryan to Hamilton Holt, September 17, 1921. Bryan Papers, Library of Congress.

ing and his refusal to send a representative to confer on disarmament—these and other international acts, with his opposition to war prohibition, his advocacy of the repeal of the excess profits tax, his action in turning over the Reserve Bank to the control of Wall Street and other acts on domestic questions, make it impossible for me to join with you with the heartiness that a committeeman should. I yield to none in appreciation of his great qualities and of the many splendid things he has done but I cannot commend without reservations, and reservations would offend him as well as the other members of the committee. Time will enable us to measure with more accuracy than we can now the value of his service and the seriousness of his mistakes.

29. Worldwide Crusade for Prohibition

Bryan in 1890 campaigned against prohibition. A recent biographer contends that he did so because he "believed that the question was a moral and not a political one," but it has also been alleged that liquor interests helped finance his race for Congress. When a prohibition amendment to the Constitution came before the House of Representatives during his first term, he voted against it. In 1904 he came out for local option, but until 1910 he refused to join the temperance movement; reportedly he signed up after hearing a little girl recite "The lips that touch liquor shall never touch mine." In 1913, even when his boycott of wine at state functions caused a hubbub, we find a correspondent writing him "in the hope that some day you may afford us national leadership." But the preceding year the Federal Council of the Churches of Christ in America, uniting denominations with 17 million communicants, had set up its Commission on Temperance, which in 1915 launched a nationwide campaign for total abstinence. At this time Bryan began to speak at mass rallies; 16,000 people came to his meeting in Philadelphia, and an estimated 12,000 of them took the pledge. His address at Carnegie Hall (item "A") to the National Abstainers Union on the last day of April 1915 was soaked in the sentimentality that we have already observed (see Document 5). He urged the Democratic party to take up prohibition not only because it was righteous but also because it was expedient (item "B"). After the Volstead Act and the Eighteenth Amendment brought at least a paper victory domestically, Bryan urged that liquor be banned from the entire globe (item "C").

A. "SUPPORT TO THE CAUSE OF WATER"

The world is aroused to the menace of alcohol—war has been declared against it in every civilized land and there is no neutral ground. I call you to the colors—to the standard raised by the National Abstainers Union for "Health and Home and Humanity." Rise! Let us pledge our support to the cause of water—in water, the daily need of every living thing. It ascends from the seas, obedient to the summons of the sun, and, descending, showers blessing upon the earth; it gives of its sparkling beauty to the fragrant flower; its alchemy transmutes base clay into golden grain; it is the canvas upon which the finger of the Infinite traces the radiant bow of promise. It is the one drink that refreshes and adds no sorrow with it— Jehovah looked upon it at Creation's dawn and said—"It is good."

B. POLITICAL EXPEDIENCY OF A
PROHIBITION PLATFORM†

You may quote me as saying the first reason why the Democratic Party should take the dry side of the prohibition question is that it is the right side, and parties as well as individuals should do what is right without stopping to count the cost, or advantages, but as is generally always the case, the best do right, and the Democratic Party would find it expedient to take the dry side. It is the growing side and has even now become the popular side.

When more than two-thirds of the Senate and about two-thirds of the House united in making the District of Columbia dry, and when a considerable majority in both Senate and House stand ready to vote in favor of submitting a national prohibition amendment, the saloon becomes an outlaw—a

fugitive from justice, and from this time on no party can afford to be the champion of the saloon, nor its defender.

As an additional reason, it must be remembered that the South, the strong hold of Democracy, is almost dry. There are only four wet states: Florida, Texas, Kentucky and Louisiana. The Florida Legislature that meets in April is sure to submit the prohibition amendment, and there is no question about the adoption of the amendment when submitted. A majority of the Democrats in Texas declared in favor of prohibition at a primary election last summer and the Legislature has called a Constitutional Convention which will deal with this subject. There is no doubt that the amendment will be submitted in Kentucky next year, and little doubt of its adoption.

The South is leading the nation on this moral issue of the generation and is being enthusiastically supported by the Western States which joined with the South in the re–election of the President.

The fate of the Democratic Party in Indiana last fall ought to be a warning. It allowed the liquor interests to force a wet plank into its platform. The result was, it lost the state and Indiana is now dry, by statute and will be made dry by a constitutional amendment when the new constitution is written.

The Democratic Party owes nothing to the wet cities of the east—it owes everything to dry communities of the South and of the West.

It would be fatal to the prospects of the Democratic Party in dry territory to take the side of the saloon and dry territory is growing every day.

C. "PROHIBITION"

Responding to The Outlook's invitation, I beg to submit a few observations in regard to enforcement of the Prohibition

The Outlook, CXXXIII (February 7, 1923), 262–265.

Law. For the purposes of this article I shall divide the subject into two parts: First, Is prohibition a fad, suddenly sprung upon the Nation and adopted without due consideration, or can it be regarded as a permanent policy, deliberately established and here to stay? Second, What weight should be given to the protests of an opposing minority in this country and to hostile criticism from abroad?

As to the matter of securing prohibition and the methods employed, it would be unnecessary to refer to the time required and the methods employed to secure prohibition but for the constant and willful misrepresentation of the facts. If a foreigner, coming into this country, should chance to read the editorials in wet newspapers, he would be led to the conclusion that prohibition was suddenly sprung upon the country by a few fanatics and adopted without discussion. Why this attempt to falsify history? What reform has ever had a longer and harder fight or ever won a more conclusive victory? It is now nearly fifty years since the Woman's Christian Temperance Union was organized. Prohibition of the liquor traffic was one of its cardinal principles and for more than a quarter of a century the only subject to which it gave any considerable amount of attention. It was also advocating woman suffrage, but that reform did not occupy a large place in its programme until within the last decade. Suffrage has no place in the name of the organization, while temperance has. During the almost half–century of its existence it has grown and spread until now it is an active organization in all the States. It never lowered its flag; it never suggested compromise; it has always been the foe of the saloon; and it deserves a large part of the credit for the Eighteenth Amendment.

The Anti–Saloon League is nearly thirty years old. Its very name indicates its opposition to the liquor traffic. It began with a few men who, in prayer, consecrated themselves to the work. It also grew and spread until it has superintendents in every State and assistant superintendents in the larger States.

As the long–drawn–out fight drew to a close, as much as two million dollars a year were intrusted to this organization for the carrying on of its part of the propaganda.

One after another of the churches entered the fight, some of them more than a quarter of a century ago. These church boards have taken an active part and exerted an increasing influence. So, too, with the National Prohibition party and with other organizations; some singly and some, like the National Dry Federation, a collection of organizations, have espoused the cause of prohibition. The work was not done in a corner. The methods employed have been open and aboveboard. Platforms have boldly assailed the liquor traffic and called for its extermination. Literature has been circulated, meetings have been held, and instruction as to the effect of alcohol on the system was finally introduced into the schools.

State after State went dry by separate act and independently of its sister States until thirty–three States—more than two–thirds of the forty–eight—banished the saloon. Then came the demand for National prohibition, intensified by the fact that those engaged in the liquor traffic combined against the enforcement of State laws in dry States. They would use as a base of operations the nearest city in a wet State and make law enforcement as difficult as possible, at the same time using the wet newspapers to create the impression that prohibition did not prohibit, in order to keep other States from adopting it.

If the wet towns in a State had been content to establish saloons for the supplying of liquor only to those who licensed the saloon, at the same time restraining them from selling in dry territory, prohibition would not have spread so rapidly from town to town. And so, if the liquor interests in the wet States had been content to sell in the wet States, instead of invading the dry States around them, prohibition would not have spread so rapidly from the State to the Nation.

With the enforcement of the Webb–Kenyon Law (vetoed

on the ground that it was unconstitutional, and held Constitutional by the Supreme Court) the power of the State over
the liquor traffic was greatly increased, and, with this increase
of power, prohibition became more effective, and, becoming
more effective, proved its value.

Finally, the National Prohibition Amendment was submitted
by the necessary two–thirds vote in both houses. This ought to
be a sufficient answer to the charge that an active minority
forced prohibition upon a passive majority. If the wets could
have controlled one more than one–third of either branch of
Congress, the submission of the National Amendment could
have been prevented. But more than two–thirds of the Senators and more than two–thirds of the members of the House
went on record in favor of submission of National prohibition.
And this Congress, it must be remembered, was elected in
1916, before our Nation entered the war. As the members of
the National House of Representatives represent districts of
approximately the same size, the two–thirds vote for submission represented two–thirds of the population.

Then came a more rigid test of the strength of prohibition.
It was handicap enough to have to control two–thirds of both
houses when the wets would have been successful had they
been able to control one more than one–third of one house;
but *ratification required three–fourths of the States.* The wets
had even a greater advantage. They needed only one branch
of the Legislature in thirteen States, while the drys were compelled to secure both branches of the Legislature in thirty–six
States, or seventy–two branches of the Legislatures in thirty–six
States as against thirteen branches in thirteen States. And yet,
when the fight was over, the drys had secured ninety–three
branches of the Legislatures out of ninety–six and the wets
were able to hold only three branches of the Legislatures in
two States—two in Rhode Island and one in Connecticut.
When it is remembered that all of the large States ratified—
leaving the two small States, Connecticut and Rhode Island,

the only ones that did not ratify—the absurdity of the wet charge that they did not have a fair chance becomes apparent.

Another indictment made against the Amendment was that it was ratified by the States instead of by popular vote. Nineteen amendments have been adopted, and all of them have been ratified by the States instead of by popular vote. Why should the Eighteenth Amendment be the only one the validity of which is questioned on this account? And since when did the wets become so much interested in the popular vote? They have opposed a direct vote on the liquor question wherever the question came up. In the States which they controlled no unit, large or small, was allowed to vote upon the question. It was comparatively recently that the cities of New York and New Jersey secured the right to vote directly upon the licensing of the saloon.

But why distrust the State Legislatures? They are responsible for legislation on all the subjects that affect human welfare. They enact laws for the punishment of criminals, including the death penalty; they pass laws for the acquiring, conveying, and devising of property; they provide for marriage and divorce and for the care of children—are these not important subjects? Why should the saloon only be regarded as too sacred for Legislatures to act upon?

As a matter of fact, the people have voted directly upon the saloon question in nearly all the States that adopted prohibition, and have voted directly for Representatives who voted on the subject. Both Senators and members of Congress are elected by direct vote, and they have often been elected on the prohibition issue. Members of the State Legislatures are elected by direct vote, and they have been elected on the prohibition issue. Prohibition was an issue in both Pennsylvania and New York when Legislatures were elected which acted on prohibition. In both Pennsylvania and New York Governors were elected pledged to the enforcement of prohibition.

Governor Pinchot, of Pennsylvania, elected in 1922, declared strongly for prohibition both in his canvass for nomination and in his campaign after his nomination, and his Democratic opponent was likewise pledged to prohibition. In the State of Ohio the people have voted directly on prohibition seven times, beginning in 1914. In 1914, 1915, and 1917 the wets won by majorities decreasing from 84,000 to 2,000. In 1918, 1919, 1920, and 1922 the drys won by increasing majorities running from 25,000 to nearly 200,000.

The facts above given leave no doubt as to the length of the controversy, the constancy of the progress, and the conclusiveness of the victory. These facts also prove the permanancy of the triumph. Five dry Congresses have been elected in succession. The first made the District of Columbia dry; the second submitted the Eighteenth Amendment; the third passed the Volstead Law; the fourth passed the Anti–Beer Bill; and a fifth was elected last November. For ten years the drys have controlled both houses of the Federal Government. In three of these Congresses—the second, third, and fourth referred to—the recorded vote for prohibition was more than two to one. No test has been made of the Congress recently elected, but there is no doubt that the drys have gained in the Senate. The vote on the Anti–Beer Bill in the Senate stood 56 for to 22 against. The percentage will be larger when the new Congress convenes.

The House is also overwhelmingly dry, probably by a two-thirds vote. If the wets have made any gain at all, the gain is slight and due, not to an increase in wet sentiment, but to the fact that Democratic gains were uniform throughout the country. The reaction against the Republican party was so great in many districts that the Democratic candidate was elected regardless of his position on the liquor question. No Democratic Congressman who voted for or against prohibition was defeated. There is not the slightest indication that any of the thirty–three dry States will return to the license system. Some of the States that were wet are still wet, but no person who will examine the figures without bias can doubt the permanency of the prohibition victory.

When the liquor forces found that the existence of the saloon was threatened, they tried to save the business by separating wine and beer from whisky, but the votes do not indicate that a wine and beer saloon is any more popular than the old–fashioned saloon which sold all kinds of liquor. Beer was defeated in Colorado after the State went dry. Wine and beer were defeated in Michigan by over two hundred thousand two years after the State went dry. Wine and beer were defeated in Ohio this year by nearly two hundred thousand, and law enforcement won out in California—a wine State—this year by a referendum vote, after being defeated two years ago.

Now for the second question: What weight should be given to the protests of an opposing minority in this country and to hostile criticisms from abroad? No concession can be made to the minority in this country without a surrender of the fundamental principle of popular government. The people have a right to have what they want, and they want prohibition. They adopted prohibition before woman suffrage became a National policy. Only a few of the States went dry with the aid of the women's vote. A majority of the men favor prohibition, and a still larger majority of women favor it. How can a backward step be asked or expected? The Amendment is in the Constitution, and the wets are powerless to repeal it—shall the drys repeal it for them? The wets are powerless to prevent law enforcement—shall the drys consent to lawlessness just to please a rebellious minority?

In the enforcement of the law we have two classes to deal with, viz., those who deliberately violate the law for the money that they make out of it and those who patronize the bootlegger. Why should any more consideration be shown to men who try to make money by violating the Prohibition Law than to men who try to make money by larceny or burglary? And what consideration should be shown to those who patronize the bootlegger? By what logic can they claim to be superior to those who knowingly purchase stolen goods? Does appetite furnish a more legitimate excuse than love of money?

We have a few officers who refuse to enforce the law; do they commend themselves to right-thinking people by their willingness to violate their oath of office? The thing most needed now is a resumption of the educational work which created the prohibition sentiment, but which has to some extent been suspended because attention has been directed to legislative prohibition rather than to the moral suasion that preceded prohibition. While the prohibition sentiment is sufficiently strong to make sure of no return to the saloon at present, it is necessary to instruct each new generation in the effect of alcohol. In other words, the only way to make prohibition secure is to keep the temperance sentiment at full tide. Now that prohibition has the law upon its side and can insist that all law-abiding citizens shall respect the law and help enforce it, the enemies of the drink habit should enroll all of the opponents of the saloon on the side of total abstinence. The bootlegger will cease to trouble us when people cease to patronize him; the total abstainer is therefore the best guaranty of prohibition. Every church should be a rallying point for total abstinence and every pastor should lead in the effort to build up a total abstinence sentiment back of prohibition.

And why should not our schools, colleges, and universities be brought up to the support of the Eighteenth Amendment? What would be more effective in the creation of public opinion and the crystallization of sentiment in favor of the enforcement of the law than a total abstinence pledge signed by the teachers in our universities, from the president down, and then by the students? So far as America is concerned there is no doubt as to the obligation resting upon all friends of law and order to support the Prohibition Law the same as every other law.

Enforcement has its problems, but they can and will be solved. When the Volstead Law went into effect, whisky was stored in more than three hundred places scattered through the United States. These have been consolidated into something like one–tenth of that number. This is a step in the right direction, but a better remedy would be for the Government to take over all liquor on hand and distribute it to those who can lawfully use it. After that, all distilling should be done by the Government. Private interest must be eliminated if the law is to be made effective.

One defect in enforcement has been the appointment of wet officials to enforce dry laws. Of course fidelity could not be expected in such cases, and was not expected by the influences that secured the appointments. The officials intrusted to the enforcement of the law should be selected because of their special fitness, and one necessary quality in an enforcement officer is total abstinence. How can a wet official be trusted to enforce a dry law when by doing so he cuts off his own supply?

We have also to consider foreign opposition, which may be divided into two classes. First, we have the influence exerted by people interested in the liquor traffic, who, for pecuniary reasons, want to destroy prohibition and who are using the same methods employed by the liquor interests in this country when they misrepresented prohibition in the dry States. All sorts of false reports are being circulated. These deliberate and widespread misrepresentations contributed to the success of the wets in Sweden, where recently prohibition was, through the vote of the cities, defeated by a small majority.

The opposition organized in Europe to overthrow prohibition in the United States is strong enough to exert an influence on the policy of European governments. How else can their protection of bootleggers be explained? There is an international agreement against piracy, and no nation would permit its flag to be used by a pirate craft while preying upon the commerce of another nation. Why should any nation permit the use of its flag by a bootlegging craft engaged in a conspiracy against the laws of a friendly nation? The three–mile limit was not intended for the protection of outlaws and it cannot long be used for that purpose when our Nation takes the matter up in earnest.

I have reserved for the last point reference to the comments made by some of our visitors. Mr. G. K. Chesterton may be taken as a fair sample of the unfairness with which uninformed foreigners regard American prohibition. He wrote a book on what he "saw in America." He tells what "well-to-do Americans" said when they discussed prohibition "over their nuts and wine." He reports those Americans as declaring that prohibition does not exist. He concedes that it may be enforced to "some extent among the poor," but he doubts whether it was ever intended to be enforced among the rich. It takes a very presumptuous visitor to generalize so freely after meeting so few out of the hundreds of thousands of well–to–do people in the United States. We have forty–seven hundred who pay taxes on incomes above $50,000; how many of these homes did he visit?

Mr. Chesterton, instead of putting his opposition to prohibition on personal grounds, which evidently is the real basis of his dislike for it, says that his primary objection is that it puts the workingman under a form of slavery and "enables him to work harder, and therefore the employers get richer." He says: "The real power back of prohibition is simply the plutocratic power of pushing employers who wish to get the last inch of work out of their workmen."

If Mr. Chesterton were not entirely ignorant of the subject, such a statement would subject him to the charge of deliberate falsehood. Of course every American knows that prohibition did not originate with the plutocrats. It not only originated in the agricultural district, but won its way by the aid of the masses and against the opposition of the very influences which Mr. Chesterton credits with supporting it. Our plutocratic influences are in the cities, not in the country, and the cities were not only the last to be captured by prohibition, but *have not yet been captured.* The opposition to prohibition to-day is in the cities, just where these plutocrats exert the largest influence in politics.

But to relieve Mr. Chesterton's fears that the rich will continue to be exempt from the rigors of the law, I venture to suggest to him that the inequality will be remedied by taking the liquor from the rich instead of by restoring it to the poor. The advocates of prohibition have no desire to favor the rich above the poor; as a matter of fact, the law makes no discrimination whatever. The rich were better able to take advantage of the law, but that is not the fault of the friends of prohibition. They went as far as they felt it safe to go at the time. They allowed individuals having liquor on hand, whether they were rich or poor, whether they had much or little, to use it up. The law, while its language bore equally upon all, gave a privilege which was valuable in proportion as individuals could take advantage of it, and the rich took advantage of it to a greater extent than the poor. There is no reason, however, why this law should be allowed to stand, if in practice it has worked injustice, especially if it has given to such visitors as Mr. Chesterton a misconception of the purpose and operation of prohibition.

Why not compel every one who has liquor on hand to file an inventory accessible to the public? If liquor is kept as a *right,* why should the right be exercised *secretly?* And why not a progressive tax on the liquor held for private use? We have a progressive tax on incomes, however honestly acquired. Why should liquor, kept for private consumption, be exempt from the burdens of a progressive tax? The result of a law requiring the filing of an inventory and taxing the quantity on hand would soon dry up the private cellars and save the rich from the aspersions cast upon them by the distinguished visitor whose words have been quoted.

To sum up the subject: After a long–drawn–out contest, prohibition came as the triumph of the conscience of the Nation. The reform progressed slowly but surely, and there is no turning back. It is the greatest moral victory ever won at the polls, and gives to our Nation an enviable leadership among the nations. That intoxicating liquor as a beverage is destined to disappear throughout the civilized world is as sure as the rising of the morning sun.

Enforcement in this country is the only problem we have to deal with, and it will be dealt with successfully. The pecuniary interest of individuals must be eliminated; trustworthy officers must be employed in enforcement and new remedies must be applied wherever experience discloses a defect that needs attention.

Our Government is in the hands of the people, and the people will use the Government for the protection of their rights and for the advancement of their welfare. Alcohol as a beverage has been indicted as a criminal, brought to the bar of judgment, condemned, and executed. Our Nation will be saloonless for evermore and will lead the world in the great crusade which will drive intoxicating liquor from the globe.

I appreciate the opportunity which The Outlook has given me of presenting so important a subject to its large and intelligent constituency.

30. Freedom of Religion and the Ku Klux Klan

The attachments of William Jennings Bryan were always strong not only to the plains states but also to the South. His eulogy of popular sovereignty had an especially seamy manifestation in his views on Negroes (see Document 8). He argued in effect that if most white Americans wanted to be white supremacists, they had a right to their prejudices. In urging the establishment of municipally sponsored men's clubs in the nation's capital in 1914 as competitors to the saloons, he wanted to start "with three rooms, two for whites and one for colored." After Bryan left the Department of State he set up a home in Florida, and in 1921 he transferred his legal residence there. The next year he declared that passage by Congress of a Federal antilynching bill would be a grave mistake. This line of policy came to its climaxes in the last year of his life, once in New York City, and once in Dayton, Tennessee. When the Democratic national convention met in Madison Square Garden in June 1924, Bryan was chairman of the resolutions committee. A plank was offered affirming the ancient rights of free speech, free press, free assembly, and freedom of religion. A minority wanted to include a specific denunciation of the Ku Klux Klan. Bryan, aware that the Klan had its strength in the very areas that were supporting his campaigns for prohibition and against Darwinism, gave the following speech on the convention floor in opposition to the minority report from his committee. The amendment lost—by a single vote.

Mr. William Jennings Bryan (of Florida): Mr. Chairman, ladies and gentlemen, members of the Convention: It is now

Official Report of the Proceedings of the Democratic National Convention, 1924 (Indianapolis: Bookwalter–Ball–Greathouse Printing Co., 1924), pp. 303–309.

twenty–eight years since Democratic Conventions became gra-
cious enough to invite me and patient enough to listen to me,
and I have not words in which to express my gratitude for the
love and loyalty of millions of Democrats who have been my
co–laborers for more than a quarter of a century. (Applause.)
I have spoken to you on many theses, never on themes more
important that this today, and since they take applause out of
my time, and since I am speaking to your hearts and heads and
not to your hands, keep still and let me speak to you.

(Cries of "We'll do it.")

MR. WILLIAM JENNINGS BRYAN (of Florida—continuing):
I have only a short time in which to lay before you the arguments that seem to me pertinent to this occasion, when we
are about to decide not only the line of our campaign this Fall,
but questions which may affect larger things than parties.

Let's understand each other. Let's eliminate the things that
are not in this issue and come down to the three words that
these, our good friends, as honest, as patriotic and as anxious
for the welfare of the party as we are, take out of the language and exalt above any other three words that will be
used in this campaign. Note, my friends, that they take our
report, every word of it, and note also that we offered to take
every word of their report but three. We said, "Strike out three
words and there will be no objection." But three words were
more to them than the welfare of a party in a great campaign.
(Applause.)

You have listened to the applause when we have had read to
you the best Democratic platform that was ever written, the
noblest principles that have been written into a platform. We
have there pleas pathetic for people in distress, but none of
our principles, none of our pleas stirred the hearts of these
men like the words, "Ku Klux Klan." (Long and continued
hisses, boos and jeers.)

(The Chairman rapped for order.)

THE PERMANENT CHAIRMAN: The delegates of the Convention will preserve order. I shall have to recall Mr. Bryan when the time has expired unless you permit him to proceed.

MR. WILLIAM JENNINGS BRYAN (of Florida—continuing): I call you to witness that these men never took the standards of their States and marched when we appealed on grand principles; it was only when they said "Ku Klux Klan," that's the only thing—(Hisses, boos and jeers.)

THE PERMANENT CHAIRMAN: The officers will preserve order—

A VOICE: Clear the galleries of the hoodlums.

THE PERMANENT CHAIRMAN: (continuing):—or these proceedings will cease. Please let us have order here.

MR. WILLIAM JENNINGS BRYAN (of Florida—continuing): Citizens of New York, you show your appreciation of the honor we did you in holding our Convention here. (A confusion of cries from the floor, with the Chairman rapping for order.)

THE PERMANENT CHAIRMAN: If the speaker is again interrupted by the galleries, they will be cleared. (Applause and some hisses.) I shall order this in the name of the delegates of this Convention, for whom I speak. I warn the delegates that this speaker is to continue, and without interruption from them.

MR. WILLIAM JENNINGS BRYAN (of Florida—continuing): Let me place before you the five reasons which I submit to your judgments and your consciences. First, this plank, these three words, are not necessary.

A VOICE: Yes, they are.

OTHER VOICES: Put him out; put him out.

MR. WILLIAM JENNINGS BRYAN (of Florida—continuing): There is not a State in the Union where anybody whose rights are denied cannot go and find redress, (applause) not a State in the Union; and the Democratic Party in its platform, the part of it on which we all agree, in words as strong as can be written, with emphasis as great as can be employed, puts all the strength of a great party back of every right, and especially back of the right of religious liberty for which we stand, (applause) as well as those who call us cowards because we do not take three words with which they seek to conjure. It is not necessary, I repeat, first, because the laws protect everyone.

Second, it is not necessary to protect any Church. I, my friends, have such confidence in the Catholic Church, which was for over a thousand years my mother church as well as yours—(Applause.)

A Voice: That is your faith.

Mr. William Jennings Bryan (of Florida—continuing): It was the Catholic Church that took religion from its founder and preserved it, the only custodian, for over a thousand years. And when they did it for the Catholic, they did it for me and for every Protestant.

The Catholic Church, with its legacy of martyred blood and with all the testimony of its missionaries who went into every land, does not need a great party to protect it from a million men. (Cheers and applause.) The Jews do not need this resolution. They have Moses. They have Elijah. They have Elisha, who was able to draw back the curtain and show upon the mountain tops an invisible host greater than a thousand Ku Klux Klans. (Cheers and applause.) And both the Catholic Church and the Jewish Faith have their great characters today who plead for respect for them, and whose pleading is not in vain. It is not necessary, and, my friends, the Ku Klux Klan does not deserve the advertisement that you give them. (Cheers and applause.)

The minority, the fourteen members of our Committee who could not join with us in a report that would leave out those three magic and mystic words, have raised the Ku Klux Klan to a higher altitude than the Ku Klux themselves ever raised their fiery cross. (Cheers and applause.) Mr. Colby tells you that this is a transient organization; that it will soon die. If that be true, then really, my friends, the motto of the minority ought to be, "Hurry up if you would see George; he is nearly gone." (Laughter.)

My friends, one objection that I have to making this issue the paramount issue of this campaign is that I am not willing to lift up the dying embers and start a prairie fire and carry this Klan into every Congressional District of the United States. (Cheers and applause.)

My third objection is that we have no moral right to let them divert us from as great a mission as our party ever had. (Applause.)

They say we are cowards. My friends, it requires more courage to fight the Republican Party than it does to fight the Ku Klux Klan. Here we have farmers driven into bankruptcy, a million driven from the farms in a single year. We find monopoly spreading. We find nearly every great line of industry in the control of gigantic combinations of capital. And while we have distress in this Country that cries aloud for relief, and while we have a warworn world across the Atlantic that needs our help and needs our guidance, these minority men say that we lack courage if we do a big work instead of starting out on a little hunt for something which is nearly dead and which will soon pass away. (Applause.)

You may call me a coward if you will, but there is nothing in my life to justify the charge that I am a coward. (Applause.) But, my friends, I would rather have the anathemas of these misguided Democrats than have to answer on Judgment Day for a duty disregarded and a trust deserted. Anybody can fight the Ku Klux Klan, but only the Democratic Party can stand between the common people and their oppressors in this land. (Applause.)

Then, I am not willing to bring discord into my party. The Democratic Party is united on all the economic issues. We have never been so united since I have known politics, and nobody has had more reason than I to regret discord. (Laughter and applause.) Now, when we are all united and all stand with a dauntless courage and enthusiasm never excelled, these people tell us that we must turn aside from these things and divide our party with a religious issue and cease to be a great political party. Why, they tell us that if we do not do so and so, the Democratic Party is going to lose a large number.

My friends, if the Democratic Party will lose a considerable number because it insists on being what it has been, how many will it lose if it tries to be what it has never been? The Democratic Party has never been a religious organization. The Democratic Party has never taken the side of one church against the other. The Democratic Party must remain true. It cannot surrender its right to exist and the mission that was given it in the days of Jefferson, that it remained true to in the days of Jackson, and to which it was still loyal in the days of Woodrow Wilson.

But, my friends, I have left for the last what I regard as the greatest argument. If the Democratic Party is diverted from its duty, some other party will take up its task. (Cries of "No"; boos.)

But no party that takes up a noble task will find its leaders in the gallery today. (Laughter and prolonged applause.)

I repeat that if our party is turned aside from its transcendent duty as champion of the rights of the masses, another party can take our place. Even if our party were destroyed, another party would grow up to do its work.

And now I want to tell you my last and strongest objection, and let the galleries scoff if they dare: I say I am not willing to divide the Christian Church when we ought to stand together to fight the battles of religion in this land. (Cheers and applause.)

My friends, I am not responsible for your opinions. I am for mine. I have tried to defend the Democratic Party because of all I owe to it. It took me up when I was ten years younger than any other man had been when he was nominated by a great party, and it found me in a Western State, farther West than it had ever gone before, and it gave me a million more votes than it had ever given any Democrat before, (applause) and it nominated me twice afterward, and I never had to use any money, and I had no organization. (Applause.) The Democratic Party has done more for me than for any other living man, and, my friends, I am grateful. I cannot express my gratitude. I can paraphrase the words that are familiar when I express my sentiments:

"Partisans, spare that party, touch not a single bough;
    In youth it sheltered me, and I will protect it now."

(Loud cheers and applause.)

But, my friends, much as I owe to my party, I owe more to the Christian Religion. If my party has given me the foundations of my political faith, my Bible has given me the foundations of a faith that has enabled me to stand for the right without stopping to count how many stood to take their share with me. (Applause and cheers.)

My father taught me that I could afford to be in a minority, but that I could not afford to be wrong on any subject. He believed in the Bible and in God, and he believed that that God stood back of every righteous cause with an arm strong enough to bring victory to his side. And that has been my faith. And my friends, I believe religion is of more importance than politics, and I believe the world needs now not so much to get into a fight between denominations as it does to get back to God and a sense of responsibility to God. (Applause.)

Burglars stole sixty–five millions in a year and pickpockets stole nearly as much, and bank robbers and bandits took large sums; but the swindlers took two billions, ten times as much as all the people in the penitentiary took. Isn't it worth while, my friends, to unite the Christian Church in behalf of the Ten Commandments and the Sermon on the Mount, instead of dividing them into warring factions? (Applause.)

The world is coming out of the war, the bloodiest ever known. Thirty millions of human lives were lost, three hundred billions of property was destroyed, and the debts of the world are more than six times as great as they were when the first gun was fired.

My friends, how are you going to stop war? Oh, they say,

commerce will do it. But commerce did not do it, and commerce reached its highest point just before the war began. They said education will do it. But education did not do it. Education reached its highest point just before the war began. Some say science will do it. But science did not do it, for science had reached the highest point just before the war began. Yes, my friends, science instead of preventing war, mixed the poisonous gas and made the liquid fire. It was science that made war so hellish that civilization was about to commit suicide. Science cannot do it. There is only one thing that can bring peace to the world, and that is the Prince of Peace. (Applause.) That is, my friends, the One who, when He came upon the earth, the angels sang, "On earth peace, good will toward men."

My friends, Jew and Gentile, Catholic and Protestant, stand for God, on whom all religion rests, and Protestant and Catholic stand for the Prince of Peace. Is it possible that now, when Jesus is more needed, I say the hope of the world—is it possible that at this time, in this great land, we are to have a religious discussion and a religious warfare? Are you going, my friends, to start a blaze that may cause you innumerable lives, sacrificed on the altar of religious liberty? I cannot believe it. I call you back in the name of our God; I call you back in the name of our party; I call you back in the name of the Son of God and Savior of the world. Christians, stop fighting, and let us get together and save the world from the materialism that robs life of its spiritual values. (Applause.)

It was Christ on the Cross who said, "Father, forgive them, for they know not what they do." And, my friends, we can exterminate Ku Kluxism better by recognizing their honesty and teaching them that they are wrong. (Boos and hisses, followed by applause.)

31. "Aristocracy of Brains"

Mrs. William Jennings Bryan in the Memoirs compared the educational attainments of her late husband and his onetime chief, Woodrow Wilson: "Being fair, I must record that Mr. Bryan was the better student of the two. President Wilson in a class of 122, ranked forty-first, while Mr. Bryan was first in his class and delivered the valedictory oration with degree of Bachelor of Arts. President Wilson received his degree of Doctor of Philosophy at the hands of Johns Hopkins in June, 1886, and his thesis was 'Congressional Government.' Mr. Bryan, after two years' work in Union College of Law in Chicago, received his degree of Master of Arts at the hands of his Alma Mater in 1883, and the subject of his thesis was 'American Citizenship.'" It is significant, of course, that Wilson graduated from the College of New Jersey, soon to become Princeton University, while Bryan went to Illinois College where he graduated in a class that totaled eleven. But he would never have admitted that he was badly educated. Even if he had, he would not have regarded the defect as a major one. "The sin of this generation," he declared in 1921, "is mind worship . . ." The crucial quality in a person was morality; morality rested upon faith in the Bible, and faith resided not in the intellect but in the heart and soul. Here (item "A") is his message to high-school students at a Boston meeting of the evangelist Billy Sunday (see Document 15). Item "B" shows how his sense of egalitarianism was outraged at a suggestion that some men were better equipped than others to benefit from college. Item "C" suggests how Bryan would have reconciled his actions in the Scopes trial with his view that the "attempt to unite church and state has never been helpful to either . . ." (see Document 10). At Dayton, he might have said, he was simply in-

225

*sisting that the public schools should be truly neutral about religion
and that they should not be used to slur the Bible.*

A. GO BUY "THE BOOK"

This audience recalls a day in my life forty-two years ago
and more when I was a high school boy, for I was only fourteen when I became a member of a Christian church by conversion. I look back to that day as the most important day of
my life. It has had far more to do with my life than any other
day, and the Book to which I swore allegiance on that day
has been far more to me than any party platform.

I share in the joy you give to the older generation in coming
tonight to put your hearts under the influence of a great appeal.
Students, if you will count the books which you will have to
study before you complete the prescribed course you will find
that it takes a multitude of books to train the human mind;
and when you have studied them all, that mind is but the
agent of something greater than the mind itself. The mind is
but the instrument used by the heart, and it takes only one
Book to train the heart that ought to be the master of the mind.
All your books will not save your life from failure if your heart
goes wrong; if your heart goes right it can take a head, however dull, and make it useful to society.

You come, therefore, to hear something more important than
they teach in the school. You come to learn a truth that ought
to enter into the mind and sink into the heart of every student,
namely, that there is no reason why any boy or girl should
ever make a failure of life.

All your learning will not keep you from failing. Learning
has no power to save a human being from sin. You come
tonight to consider the claims of a Book that can save you,
that can add to every joy that comes through the body or the

mind, that can refine every pleasure known to the physical man or to the mental man. You have come tonight to learn of that larger life into which the great evangelist will invite you as he presents you to the only Book that is good always and everywhere—the Book that will guide your footsteps when you are young and throw light upon your path during mature years, and the only Book one cares to have beside him as the evening of life approaches. I am here to join with you in drawing inspiration from the address to which we are now ready to listen.

B. EQUALITY OF BRAINS

We see frequent manifestations of intellectual snobbery, but it has been left to President Hopkins, of Dartmouth, to make the most un-American proposition that has yet come from the mind worshippers. President Hopkins, in addressing the student body at the opening of the academic year, is quoted as saying,

"Too many men are going to college.

"The opportunities for securing an education by way of the college course are definitely a privilege and not at all a universal right. The funds available for application to the uses of institutions of higher learning are not limitless and cannot be made so whether their origin be sought in the resources of public taxation or in the securable benefactions for the enhancing of private endowments.

"It consequently becomes essential that a working theory be sought that will cooperate with some degree of accuracy to define the individuals who shall make up the group to whom, in justice to the public good, the privilege should be held.

"This is a two fold necessity—on the one hand that men incapable of profiting by the advantages which the college offers or

The Commoner, XXII (November 1922), 3.

indisposed, shall not be withdrawn from useful work to spend their time profitlessly in idleness acquiring false standards of living; and on the other hand that the contribution which the college is capable of making to the lives of competent men and through them to society shall not be too largely lessened by the slackening of pace due to the presence of men indifferent or wanting in capacity.

"Too often men reputed to be seeking an education are only seeking membership in a social organization which has reputation for affording an education.

"It would be incompatible with all of the conceptions of democracy," he continued, "to assume that the privilege of higher education should be restricted to any class defined by the accident of birth or by the fortuitous circumstances of possession of wealth, but there is such a thing as an aristocracy of brains, made up of men intellectually alert and intellectually eager to whom increasingly the opportunities of higher education ought to be restricted if democracy is to become a quality product rather than simply a quantity one, and if excellence and effectiveness are to displace mediocrity toward which democracy has such a tendency to skid."

President Hopkins said he would carefully safeguard these statements by reiterating that "it behooves all of us to avoid confusing the symbols and the facts of intellectuality."

"I should hope," he added, "that under any circumstances we might avoid confusing mental gymnastics and facility in appropriating the ideas of others with genuine thinking."

Could anything be more absurd? President Hopkins would not have the favored ones selected according to birth or according to wealth but according to alertness and eagerness. A board is to separate the smart sheep from the dull goats and close the universities to the latter. And this in America! The effect that higher education has had on President Hopkins is a conclusive argument against such an aristocracy of brains.

What this country needs is not more brains but more heart—not more intellect but more conscience. Wendell Phillips said, "The people MAKE history; the scholars write it—part truly and part as colored by their prejudices." Ex-president Roosevelt, speaking to Harvard law students, said that there was scarcely a great conspiracy against the public welfare that did not have Harvard brains behind it.

President Wilson said that the influences that control our nation do not come from our institutions of learning but from the plain people.

The arrogant attitude of President Hopkins explains the failure of our big colleges to furnish leadership for the people. They teach a selfish philosophy, based on a SUPPOSED BRUTE ANCESTRY, which makes its followers cold, cruel and mercenary. The heart must be restored to the throne and made the source of authority. The mind is but a mental machine—the more powerful it is the more dangerous it is unless it is under the direction of an enlightened heart. Instead of having a committee of college presidents to decide who shall be educated we are more in need of a common sense commission to protect our colleges from presidents who are deficient in moral enthusiasm and patriotism.

C. "BACK TO GOD"

The supreme need of the day is to get back to God—to a love of God that fills the heart, the mind and the soul, and dominates every impulse and energy of the life.

Evolutionists are leading their followers away from the Creator, away from the Word of God, and away from the Son of God. They teach that man is the lineal descendant of the lower animals—that he has in him, not the breath of the Almighty but the blood of the brute. They tear out of the Old

The Commoner, XXI (August 1921), 2.

Testament the first chapter of Genesis, and then, having discarded the miracle, they tear out the first chapter of Matthew and deny the Virgin birth of the Saviour. They would, in effect, dethrone Jehovah, strip the Bible of its claim to inspiration and libel the Master, by branding him as the illegitimate son of an immoral woman. Their creed denudes life of its spiritual elements and make man a brother of the beast.

Materialism has so paralyzed the mental machinery of the evolutionists that they cannot comprehend spiritual things. They can understand how gravity, though an invisible force, can draw all matter downward to the earth, but they cannot understand how an invisible God, all-powerful, all-wise, and all-loving, can draw the souls of men upward toward his throne. Their minds are open to the most absurd hypotheses advanced in the name of science, but their hearts are closed to the plainest spiritual truths.

These exponents of a brutish philosophy have entered our universities with boldness; they have crept into some of our Christian colleges by stealth; they have even wormed their way into a few of our theological seminaries. They make agnostics and atheists of a multitude of trusting students; they turn many young men away from the ministry; they palsy the zeal of some who stand behind the pulpit.

It is time the Christians of the country should understand the ravages that the groundless hypothesis of Darwin is making. It is depriving the church of the support of young men and young men who ought to be its leaders; it furnished Neitzsche [sic] with a basis for his Godless philosophy—a philosophy which led the world into its bloodiest war—and it is bringing chaos into the industrial world, What can be done to combat it and to save church and civilization from its benumbing influence?

First, those who preach and teach should be called upon to announce their views so that their positions may be clearly understood. Every citizen has a right to think as he pleases—

to worship God according to the dictates of his conscience, or to refuse to worship him. That is an inalienable right that should not under any circumstances be interfered with, but those who employ a minister for themselves or an instructor for their children have a right to know what the preacher is to preach and what the teachers are to teach.

Second, only Christians should be permitted to teach in CHRISTIAN schools and colleges. If denominational schools cannot find Christian instructors to teach every branch of learning that needs to be taught they have no reason for existence.

Third, Christian taxpayers should insist upon a REAL neutrality in religion wherever neutrality is necessary. The Bible should not be attacked where it cannot be defended. Professors, paid by the public, should not be permitted to undermind the religious faith of students. No amount of education can compensate for the destruction of faith. Out of the hearts, not out of the head, are the issues of life; as a man thinketh in his heart, not as he thinketh in his head, so is he.

The sin of this generation is mind worship—a worship as destructive as any other form of idolatry. To your tents, O, Israel.

32. Darwinism and the Schools

At the beginning of 1925 the Tennessee legislature passed the Butler Act banning from public schools all efforts to teach "any theory that denies the story of the Divine Creation of man as taught in the Bible, and to teach instead that man has descended from a lower order of animals." In a deliberately contrived test case, a young high-school teacher named John Thomas Scopes was indicted under the statute. After Bryan agreed to assist A. T. Stewart and the other prosecutors in the case, Clarence Darrow joined Arthur Garfield Hays of the American Civil Liberties Union on the defense staff. The trial opened July 10, 1925, in the little town of Dayton. Darrow and his colleagues had no intention of denying that Scopes had taught the theory of evolution. They sought to prove that the evidence for the theory's validity was so overwhelming that any law banning its teaching was not a valid exercise of the state's police power, but the judge refused to admit the proffered testimony by scientists. Thus the defense was pushed to another line: that the meaning of Genesis was so obscure that the Butler Act was invalid because of its ambiguity in defining what would constitute an offense. It would bolster their argument that Scriptural passages about the Creation needed to be construed if they could win an admission to that effect from a prominent fundamentalist. So they summoned Bryan as a witness for the defense. The following is an extract from his direct examination conducted by Clarence Darrow. Many fundamentalists in the audience were offended by Bryan's statement that the six days of the Creation were not necessarily

---

The World's Most Famous Court Trial: Tennessee Evolution Case (Cincinnati: National Book Company, 1925), pp. 284–304.

*six periods of twenty-four hours each. Five days after the trial
ended, on Sunday July 26, Bryan died.*

. . . Q—You have given considerable study to the Bible,
haven't you, Mr. Bryan?

A—Yes, sir, I have tried to.

Q—Well, we all know you have, we are not going to dispute that at all. But you have written and published articles
almost weekly, and sometimes have made interpretations of
various things.

A—I would not say interpretations, Mr. Darrow, but comments on the lesson.

Q—If you comment to any extent these comments have been
interpretations.

A—I presume that my discussion might be to some extent
interpretations, but they have not been primarily intended as
interpretations.

Q—But you have studied that question, of course?

A—Of what?

Q—Interpretation of the Bible.

A—On this particular question?

Q—Yes, sir.

A—Yes, sir.

Q—Then you have made a general study of it.

A—Yes, I have; I have studied the Bible for about fifty years,
or sometime more than that, but, of course, I have studied it
more as I have become older than when I was but a boy.

Q—Do you claim that everything in the Bible should be
literally interpreted?

A—I believe everything in the Bible should be accepted as
it is given there; some of the Bible is given illustratively. For
instance: "Ye are the salt of the earth." I would not insist that
man was actually salt, or that he had flesh of salt, but it is
used in the sense of salt as saving God's people . . .

The Witness—These gentlemen have not had much chance —they did not come here to try this case. They came here to try revealed religion. I am here to defend it, and they can ask me any question they please.

The Court—All right.

(Applause from the court yard.)

Mr. Darrow—Great applause from the bleachers.

The Witness—From those whom you call "yokels."

Mr. Darrow—I have never called them yokels.

The Witness—That is the ignorance of Tennessee, the bigotry.

Mr. Darrow—You mean who are applauding you?

The Witness—Those are the people whom you insult.

Mr. Darrow—You insult every man of science and learning in the world because he does not believe in your fool religion.

The Court—I will not stand for that.

Mr. Darrow—For what he is doing?

The Court—I am talking to both of you.

Gen. Stewart—This has gone beyond the pale of a lawsuit, your honor. I have a public duty to perform, under my oath and I ask the court to stop it.

Mr. Darrow is making an effort to insult the gentleman on the witness stand, and I ask that it be stopped, for it has gone beyond the pale of a lawsuit. . . .

Q—But when you read that Jonah swallowed the whale— or that the whale swallowed Jonah—excuse me please—how do you literally interpret that?

A—When I read that a big fish swallowed Jonah—it does not say whale.

Q—Doesn't it? Are you sure?

A—That is my recollection of it. A big fish, and I believe it, and I believe in a God who can make a whale and can make a man and make both do what He pleases.

Q—Mr. Bryan, doesn't the New Testament say whale?

A—I am not sure. My impression is that it says fish; but it

does not make so much difference; I merely called your attention to where it says fish—it does not say whale.

Q—But in the New Testament it says whale, doesn't it?

A—That may be true; I cannot remember in my own mind what I read about it.

Q—Now, you say, the big fish swallowed Jonah, and he there remained how long—three days—and then he spewed him upon the land. You believe that the big fish was made to swallow Jonah?

A—I am not prepared to say that; the Bible merely says it was done.

Q—You don't know whether it was the ordinary run of fish, or made for that purpose?

A—You may guess; you evolutionists guess.

Q—But when we do guess, we have a sense to guess right.

A—But do not do it often.

Q—You are not prepared to say whether that fish was made especially to swallow a man or not?

A—The Bible doesn't say, so I am not prepared to say.

Q—You don't know whether that was fixed up specially for the purpose.

A—No, the Bible doesn't say.

Q—But do you believe He made them—that He made such a fish and that it was big enough to swallow Jonah?

A—Yes, sir. Let me add: One miracle is just as easy to believe as another.

Q—It is for me.

A—It is for me.

Q—Just as hard?

A—It is hard to believe for you, but easy for me. A miracle is a thing performed beyond what man can perform. When you get beyond what man can do, you get within the realm of miracles; and it is just as easy to believe the miracle of Jonah as any other miracle in the Bible.

Q—Perfectly easy to believe that Jonah swallowed the whale?

A—If the Bible said so; the Bible doesn't make as extreme statements as evolutionists do.

Mr. Darrow—That may be a question, Mr. Bryan, about some of those you have known?

A—The only thing is, you have a definition of fact that includes imagination.

Q—And you have a definition that excludes everything but imagination, everything but imagination?

Gen. Stewart—I object to that as argumentative.

The Witness—You—

Mr. Darrow—The Witness must not argue with me, either.

Q—Do you consider the story of Jonah and the whale a miracle?

A—I think it is. . . .

Q—What do you think?

A—I do not think about things I don't think about.

Q—Do you think about things you do think about?

A—Well, sometimes.

(Laughter in the courtyard.)

The Policeman—Let us have order. . . .

Q—Do you think the earth was made in six days?

A—Not six days of twenty-four hours.

Q—Doesn't it say so?

Gen. Stewart—I want to interpose another objection. What is the purpose of this examination?

Mr. Bryan—The purpose is to cast ridicule on everybody who believes in the Bible, and I am perfectly willing that the world shall know that these gentlemen have no other purpose than ridiculing every Christian who believes in the Bible.

Mr. Darrow—We have the purpose of preventing bigots and ignoramuses from controlling the education of the United States and you know it, and that is all.

Mr. Bryan—I am glad to bring out that statement. I want the world to know that this evidence is not for the view Mr. Darrow and his associates have filed affidavits here stating, the purposes of which I understand it, is to show that the Bible story is not true.

Mr. Malone—Mr. Bryan seems anxious to get some evidence in the record that would tend to show that those affidavits are not true.

Mr. Bryan—I am not trying to get anything into the record. I am simply trying to protect the word of God against the greatest atheist or agnostic in the United States. (Prolonged applause.) I want the papers to know I am not afraid to get on the stand in front of him and let him do his worst. I want the world to know. (Prolonged applause.)

Mr. Darrow—I wish I could get a picture of these clackers.

Gen. Stewart—I am not afraid of Mr. Bryan being perfectly able to take care of himself, but this examination cannot be a legal examination and it cannot be worth a thing in the world, and, your honor, I respectfully except to it, and call on your honor, in the name of all that is legal, to stop this examination and stop it here.

Mr. Hays—I rather sympathize with the general, but Mr. Bryan is produced as a witness because he is a student of the Bible and he presumably understands what the Bible means. He is one of the foremost students in the United States, and we hope to show Mr. Bryan, who is a student of the Bible, what the Bible really means in connection with evolution. Mr. Bryan has already stated that the world is not merely 6,000 years old and that is very helpful to us, and where your evidence is coming from, this Bible, which goes to the jury, is that the world started in 4004 B. C.

Mr. Bryan—You think the Bible says that?

Mr. Hays—The one you have taken in evidence says that.

Mr. Bryan—I don't concede that it does.

Mr. Hays—You know that that chronology is made up by

adding together all of the ages of the people in the Bible, counting their ages; and now then, let us show the next stage from a Bible student, that these things are not to be taken literally, but that each man is entitled to his own interpretation.

Gen. Stewart—The court makes the interpretation.

Mr. Hays—But the court is entitled to information on what is the interpretation of an expert Bible student.

Gen. Stewart—This is resulting in a harangue and nothing else.

Mr. Darrow—I didn't do any of the haranging; Mr. Bryan has been doing that.

Gen. Stewart—You know absolutely you have done it.

Mr. Darrow—Oh, all right.

Mr. Malone—Mr. Bryan doesn't need any support.

Gen. Stewart—Certainly he doesn't need any support, but I am doing what I conceive my duty to be, and I don't need any advice, if you please, sir. (Applause.)

The Court—That would be irrelevant testimony if it was going to the jury. Of course, it is excluded from the jury on the point it is not competent testimony, on the same ground as the affidaviting.

Mr. Hicks—Your honor, let me say a word right there. It is in the discretion of the court how long you will allow them to question witnesses for the purpose of taking testimony to the supreme court. Now, we as taxpayers of this county, feel that this has gone beyond reason.

The Court—Well, now, that taxpayers doesn't appeal to me so much, when it is only fifteen or twenty minutes time.

Mr. Darrow—I would have been through in a half-hour if Mr. Bryan had answered my questions.

Gen. Stewart—They want to put in affidavits as to what other witnesses would swear, why not let them put in affidavits as to what Mr. Bryan would swear?

Mr. Bryan—God forbid.

Mr. Malone—I will just make this suggestion—

Gen. Stewart—It is not worth anything to them, if your honor please, even for the record in the supreme court.

Mr. Hays—Is not it worth anything to us if Mr. Bryan will accept the story of creation in detail, and if Mr. Bryan, as a Bible student, states you cannot take the Bible necessarily as literally true?

Mr. Stewart—The Bible speaks for itself.

Mr. Hays—You mean to say the Bible itself tells whether these are parables? Does it?

Gen. Stewart—We have left all annals of procedure behind. This is a harangue between Col. Darrow and his witness. He makes so many statements that he is forced to defend himself.

Mr. Darrow—I do not do that.

Gen. Stewart—I except to that as not pertinent to this lawsuit.

The Court—Of course, it is not pertinent, or it would be before the jury.

Gen. Stewart—It is not worth anything before a jury.

The Court—Are you about through, Mr. Darrow?

Mr. Darrow—I want to ask a few more questions about the creation.

The Court—I know. We are going to adjourn when Mr. Bryan comes off the stand for the day. Be very brief, Mr. Darrow. Of course, I believe I will make myself clearer. Of course, it is incompetent testimony before the jury. The only reason I am allowing this to go in at all is that they may have it in the appellate courts, as showing what the affidavit would be.

Mr. Bryan—The reason I am answering is not for the benefit of the superior court. It is to keep these gentlemen from saying I was afraid to meet them and let them question me, and I want the Christian world to know that any atheist, agnostic, unbeliever, can question me any time as to my belief in God, and I will answer him.

Mr. Darrow—I want to take an exception to this conduct of this witness. He may be very popular down here in the hills. I do not need to have his explanation for his answer.

The Court—Yes.

Mr. Bryan—If I had not, I would not have answered the question.

Mr. Hays—May I be heard? I do not want your honor to think we are asking questions of Mr. Bryan with the expectation that the higher court will not say that those questions are proper testimony. The reason I state that is this, your law speaks for the Bible. Your law does not say the literal interpretation of the Bible. If Mr. Bryan, who is a student of the Bible, will state that everything in the Bible need not be interpreted literally, that each man must judge for himself; if he will state that, of course, then your honor would charge the jury. We are not bound by a literal interpretation of the Bible. If I have made my argument clear enough for the attorney-general to understand, I will retire.

Gen. Stewart—I will admit you have frequently been difficult of comprehension, and I think you are as much to blame as I am.

Mr. Hays—I know I am. . . .

Mr. Darrow:

Q—Mr. Bryan, do you believe that the first woman was Eve?

A—Yes.

Q—Do you believe she was literally made out of Adam's rib?

A—I do.

Q—Did you ever discover where Cain got his wife?

A—No sir; I leave the agnostics to hunt for her.

Q—You have never found out?

A—I have never tried to find.

Q—You have never tried to find?

A—No.

Q—The Bible says he got one, doesn't it? Were there other people on the earth at that time?

A—I cannot say.

Q—You cannot say. Did that ever enter your consideration?

A—Never bothered me.

Q—There were no others recorded, but Cain got a wife.

A—That is what the Bible says.

Q—Where she came from you do not know. All right. Does the statement, "The morning and the evening were the first day," and "The morning and the evening were the second day," mean anything to you?

A—I do not think it necessarily means a twenty–four–hour day.

Q—You do not?

A—No.

Q—What do you consider it to be?

A—I have not attempted to explain it. If you will take the second chapter—let me have the book. (Examining Bible.) The fourth verse of the second chapter says: "These are the generations of the heavens and of the earth, when they were created in the day that the Lord God made the earth and the heavens," the word "day" there in the very next chapter is used to describe a period. I do not see that there is any necessity for construing the words, "the evening and the morning," as meaning necessarily a twenty-four-hour day, "in the day when the Lord made the heaven and the earth."

Q—Then, when the Bible said, for instance, "and God called the firmament heaven. And the evening and the morning were the second day," that does not necessarily mean twenty–four hours?

A—I do not think it necessarily does.

Q—Do you think it does or does not?

A—I know a great many think so.

Q—What do you think?

A—I do not think it does.

Q—You think those were not literal days?

A—I do not think they were twenty–four–hour days.

Q—What do you think about it?

A—That is my opinion—I do not know that my opinion is better on that subject than those who think it does.

Q—You do not think that?

A—No. But I think it would be just as easy for the kind of God we believe in to make the earth in six days as in six years or in 6,000,000 years or in 600,000,000 years. I do not think it important whether we believe one or the other.

Q—Do you think those were literal days?

A—My impression is they were periods, but I would not attempt to argue as against anybody who wanted to believe in literal days.

Q—Have you any idea of the length of the periods?

A—No; I don't.

Q—Do you think the sun was made on the fourth day?

A—Yes.

Q—And they had evening and morning without the sun?

A—I am simply saying it is a period.

Q—They had evening and morning for four periods without the sun, do you think?

A—I believe in creation as there told, and if I am not able to explain it I will accept it. Then you can explain it to suit yourself.

Q—Mr. Bryan, what I want to know is, do you believe the sun was made on the fourth day?

A—I believe just as it says there.

Q—Do you believe the sun was made on the fourth day?

A—Read it.

Q—I am very sorry; you have read it so many times you would know, but I will read it again: "And God, said, let there be lights in the firmament of the heaven, to divide the day from the night; and let them be for signs, and for seasons, and for days, and years?

"And let them be for lights in the firmament of the heaven, to give light upon the earth; and it was so.

"And God made two great lights; the greater light to rule the day, and the lesser light to rule the night; He made the stars also.

"And God set them in the firmament of the heaven, to give light upon the earth, and to rule over the day and over the night, and to divide the light from the darkness; and God saw that it was good. And the evening and the morning were the fourth day."

Do you believe, whether it was a literal day or a period, the sun and the moon were not made until the fourth day?

A—I believe they were made in the order in which they were given there, and I think in dispute with Gladstone and Huxley on that point—

Q—Cannot you answer my question?

A— ——— I prefer to agree with Gladstone.

Q—I do not care about Gladstone.

A—Then prefer to agree with whoever you please.

Q—Can not you answer my question?

A—I have answered it. I believe that it was made on the fourth day, in the fourth day.

Q—And they had the evening and the morning before that time for three days or three periods. All right, that settles it. Now, if you call those periods, they may have been a very long time.

A—They might have been.

Q—The creation might have been going on for a very long time?

A—It might have continued for millions of years.

Q—Yes. All right. Do you believe the story of the temptation of Eve by the serpent?

A—I do.

Q—Do you believe that after Eve ate the apple, or gave it to Adam, whichever way it was, that God cursed Eve, and that time decreed that all womankind thenceforth and forever should suffer the pains of childbirth in the reproduction of the earth?

A—I believe what it says, and I believe the fact as fully——

Q—That is what it says, doesn't it?

A—Yes.

Q—And for that reason, every woman born of woman, who has to carry on the race, the reason they have childbirth pains is because Eve tempted Adam in the Garden of Eden.

A—I will believe just what the Bible says. I ask to put that in the language of the Bible, for I prefer that to your language. Read the Bible and I will answer.

Q—All right, I will do that: "And I will put enmity between thee and the woman"—that is referring to the serpent?

A—The serpent.

Q—(Reading) "and between thy seed and her seed; it shall bruise thy head, and thou shalt bruise his heel. Unto the woman he said, I will greatly multiply thy sorrow and thy conception; in sorrow thou shalt bring forth children; and thy desire shall be to thy husband, and he shall rule over thee." That is right, is it?

A—I accept it as it is.

Q—And you believe that came about because Eve tempted Adam to eat the fruit?

A—Just as it says.

Q—And you believe that is the reason God made the serpent to go on his belly after he tempted Eve?

A—I believe the Bible as it is, and I do not permit you to put your language in the place of the language of the Almighty. You read that Bible and ask me questions, and I will answer them. I will not answer your questions in your language.

Q—I will read it to you from the Bible: "And the Lord God said unto the serpent, because thou hast done this, thou art cursed above all cattle, and above every beast of the field; upon thy belly shalt thou go and dust shalt thou eat all the days of thy life." Do you think that is why the serpent is compelled to crawl upon its belly?

A—I believe that.

Q—Have you any idea how the snake went before that time?

A—No, sir.

Q—Do you know whether he walked on his tail or not?

A—No, sir. I have no way to know. (Laughter in audience).

Q—Now, you refer to the cloud that was put in the heaven after the flood, the rainbow. Do you believe in that?

A—Read it.

Q—All right, Mr. Bryan, I will read it for you.

Mr. Bryan—Your honor, I think I can shorten this testimony. The only purpose Mr. Darrow has is to slur at the Bible, but I will answer his question. I will answer it all at once, and I have no objection in the world, I want the world to know that this man, who does not believe in a God, is trying to use a court in Tennessee—

Mr. Darrow—I object to that.

Mr. Bryan—(Continuing) to slur at it, and while it will require time, I am willing to take it.

Mr. Darrow—I object to your statement. I am exempting you on your fool ideas that no intelligent Christian on earth believes.

The Court—Court is adjourned until 9 o'clock tomorrow morning.

Index

THE AMERICAN HERITAGE SERIES

THE MIDDLE PERIOD

THE LATE NINETEENTH CENTURY

THE TWENTIETH CENTURY

TOPICAL VOLUMES